UNBROKEN
CHAINS

Also by Melissa Hope Ditmore

Prostitution and Sex Work
(Historical Guides to Controversial Issues in America)

Sex Work Matters (co-editor)

Encyclopedia of Prostitution and Sex Work (editor)

UNBROKEN CHAINS

THE HIDDEN ROLE OF HUMAN TRAFFICKING IN THE AMERICAN ECONOMY

MELISSA HOPE DITMORE

Beacon Press
Boston

BEACON PRESS
Boston, Massachusetts
www.beacon.org

Beacon Press books
are published under the auspices of
the Unitarian Universalist Association of Congregations.

26 25 24 23   8 7 6 5 4 3 2 1

This book is printed on acid-free paper that meets the uncoated paper
ANSI/NISO specifications for permanence as revised in 1992.

Text design and composition by Kim Arney

Library of Congress Cataloging-in-Publication Data

Names: Ditmore, Melissa Hope, author.
Title: Unbroken chains : the hidden role of human trafficking
in the American economy / Melissa Hope Ditmore.
Description: Boston : Beacon Press, [2023] | Includes bibliographical
references and index. | Summary: "An urgent exposition of the pervasive
human trafficking that lies just beneath the surface of the US economy-from
the stories of its survivors"—Provided by publisher.
Identifiers: LCCN 2022053695 (print) | LCCN 2022053696 (ebook) |
ISBN 9780807006771 (cloth) | ISBN 9780807006795 (ebook)
Subjects: LCSH: Human trafficking—United States. | Human trafficking
victims—United States. | United States—Economic conditions—21st century.
Classification: LCC HQ125.U6 D58 2023 (print) |
LCC HQ125.U6 (ebook) |
DDC 306.740973—dc23/eng/20221104
LC record available at https://lccn.loc.gov/2022053695
LC ebook record available at https://lccn.loc.gov/2022053696

For Angus, with love

To the memory of
Petra Mayer and Dan Allman

CONTENTS

LIST OF ILLUSTRATIONS

TIME LINE

1619   First enslaved people arrive in the colony of Virginia.

1639   Maryland declares that Christian baptism does not confer freedom on enslaved people.

1662   Hereditary Slavery Law is enacted in Virginia.

1669   The colony of Virginia declares that it is not a crime to kill an enslaved person in the course of punishment.

1676–77   Bacon's Rebellion occurs in Virginia. Jamestown is looted and burned by an interracial mob composed of free people, indentured servants, and slaves, angry at the ruling class.

1692   Maryland stipulates the humane treatment of enslaved people in response to the mutilation of an individual by her owner.

1705   An Act Concerning Servants and Slaves (also known as the Virginia Slave Code) is passed in Virginia. In determining who is indentured for a fixed time and who is enslaved for life, it establishes that one must have been a Christian *before arriving* in the colonies, which means that conversion to Christianity is not a route to manumission.

1718   The British government passes the Transportation Act, authorizing the transport of convicts to the colonies to be sold into indenture.

1739   Stono Rebellion, a large rebellion of enslaved people, takes place near the Stono River, in North Carolina.

1740   First laws restricting the education of enslaved people are passed in colonial South Carolina.

1751   Slavery legally allowed in Georgia.

1774–1804 All northern US states outlaw slavery.

1780 Pennsylvania becomes the first state to initiate emancipation with the Gradual Abolition Act.

1793 Invention of the cotton gin.

1808 Importation of slaves ends.

1830 Indian Removal Act is passed, leading to the forcible removal of Native Americans from the US southeast to the Oklahoma Territory, including people enslaved by tribes, through 1850.

1831 Nat Turner's Rebellion, during which enslaved people under the leadership of Turner, an educated enslaved person, rebel violently, killing more than fifty whites, for which fifty-six enslaved people are executed.

1848 Gold discovered in California, leading to migration to California from the eastern US and East Asia.

1860 The last slave ship arrives—illegally—in the United States.

1862 Act to Prohibit the "Coolie Trade" is passed—but it is not enforced, owing to the difficulty of identifying people in servitude.

1863 Emancipation Proclamation is declared.

1865 Slavery ends in the United States.

1866 Enslaved people emancipated from Native American slavers.

1867 Peonage Abolition Act bans an employer from forcing a laborer to work to pay off a debt.

1868 Birthright citizenship is granted as part of the Fourteenth Amendment.

1875 Page Act is passed, restricting entry of Chinese women to the United States.

1882 Chinese Exclusion Act restricts entry of Chinese people to the United States.

1896 Wong Wing case ruling establishes that foreign nationals who enter the country illegally cannot be compelled to work without a jury trial.

1903, 1907 Immigration Acts are passed, restricting entry of "undesirable" immigrants, including prostitutes and the mentally ill.

1910 Mann Act prohibits interstate travel for "immoral purposes."

1917 *Caminetti v. United States*, a Mann Act case, rules that any type of immoral sex is included under the Mann Act.

1932   *Gebardi v. United States*, another Mann Act case, rules that only commercial sex is included under the Mann Act.

1935   National Labor Relations Act encourages employees and employers to engage in collective bargaining and establishes the right of employees to strike.

1938   Fair Labor Standards Act establishes wage and hour laws.

1942   Viola Cosley writes to Eleanor Roosevelt about her son being detained at a sugar plantation in Florida.

1975   Minnesota Supreme Court rules that traveling sales crews are employees rather than independent contractors.

1978   Mann Act revised to include transportation of minor boys for sexual purposes.

1986   Changes to Mann Act limit prosecution to acts that are a crime in the place where they are committed.

1987   Congress holds hearing about traveling sales crews.

1995   El Monte sweatshop case is heard.

1997   Deaf Mexican peddlers case is heard.

2000   Congress passes the Trafficking Victims Protection Act, which defines trafficking and makes available assistance for survivors, including conditional aid with immigration status issues.

2009   A Wisconsin law regulating working conditions for sales crews is passed.

2010   New York State passes first Domestic Worker Bill of Rights and vacatur law allowing survivors of trafficking to vacate prostitution convictions that have resulted from their having been trafficked.

2012–14 C&C Farms case is heard.

2013   California passes Domestic Worker Bill of Rights, assuring domestic and care workers wage and overtime pay protection.

2013   Domestic service workers are newly included under the Fair Labor Standards Act.

2014   Massachusetts passes Domestic Worker Bill of Rights, which assures domestic and care workers minimum wage, overtime pay, and time off.

2018   FOSTA-SESTA legislative package makes internet platforms responsible for user posts related to trafficking for sex.

2021   Survivors of Trafficking Attaining Relief Together (START) Act passes in New York State, making it easier for persons to clear their records of crimes committed while being trafficked.

2022   California's Garment Worker Protection Act combats wage theft in the garment industry.

DOWN THE RABBIT HOLE

I BECAME INVOLVED in the issue of human trafficking through my work as a social scientist focused on public health and gender. In 2001, I cofounded the Urban Justice Center Sex Workers Project (SWP) in New York City. SWP offers legal services to people in the sex trades and pioneered a research agenda focusing on violence against sex workers. With every piece I published about sex work, whether for a mainstream website or as an academic paper, I received many questions about trafficking. Everyone outside the sex industry asked me about human trafficking, including someone at the next table in a restaurant, social media contacts, my mother's colleagues, people in nearly every profession, and legislative aides—a true cross section of society.

My efforts to answer their questions altered my focus, which had been primarily on sex work, and I went on to publish reports, essays, and academic papers not only about sex work but also about human trafficking in the twenty-first century.[1] I saw how trafficking was a tidal wave that would undermine the already precarious human rights of sex workers in the US and elsewhere. For that reason, I have advocated for human rights protections in legislation and have interviewed victims about their experiences—people whose identification papers were held by others in order to control them, people whose movement was constrained, people who were under very high levels of surveillance by their employers, people who took a job only to find that the conditions were far worse than what they had been led to expect. My hope for this book is that it will help readers to understand the extent of labor abuses in the United States today, and to promote more effective help for survivors by listening to them.

Survivors taught me about the troubling scope of contemporary human trafficking in the United States. Looking at trafficking through the eyes of people who had actually lived through it was like falling down the proverbial rabbit hole. In this anti-Wonderland, I found reasons to question much of what I had taken for granted. I had imagined that people in trafficking situations had started without much agency or self-determination, but in their home communities they in fact had been the go-getters, the people who sought to improve their lives. Young men told me about leaving their family homes to pursue a better life at an age when I myself could scarcely reach the top lock on my family's front door. Some were fleeing violence; some were seeking work to help support their families. People of all genders in the United States and around the world told me about choosing to leave exploitative conditions in mainstream factory jobs for the unregulated business of prostitution, attracted to the greater income and autonomy it offered. Many people assume that trafficking is synonymous with prostitution, but among adults, prostitution and sex work are usually undertaken voluntarily. (As we will see, the popular tendency to conflate sex work and trafficking has a long history in this country, going back to the "white slavery" panics of the early twentieth century.)

I learned and heard horrific things. I was told stories of how newly hired workers faced exploitation—enduring slavery-like conditions while selling magazines door-to-door in the American South or having to steal food to survive while working in agriculture and food service. People told me stories of struggling to pay "debts" owed to their employer that only ever seemed to grow larger no matter how hard they worked.[2] They described being forced to steal things to be used by their captors in other income-generating schemes.[3] I learned that many of those in agriculture and factory work, especially in the clothing industry, were routinely underpaid or went entirely unpaid, both in the United States and abroad. Some companies would simply close and disappear rather than pay their employees. The problem of wage theft in the fashion industry is so prevalent that to combat it California passed the Garment Worker Protection Act, which went into effect on January 1, 2022.[4] I was forced to confront an unpleasant and astonishing reality: the price I pay for food and clothes may feel exorbitant, yet many of those who make it possible for me to eat are themselves working without pay; the people who make the clothes I wear may work in life-threatening conditions for less than even the paltry legal minimum wage supposedly in force in their countries.[5]

WHAT TRAFFICKING IS

Trafficking is an extreme form of labor exploitation that involves fraud, force, or coercion. The most prevalent image of trafficking involves people being kidnapped and forced to work (particularly in the sex industry). In reality, most trafficking victims are lured into starting what may seem like a normal job. It's only after they have started work that they begin to encounter increasingly abusive conditions, including threats, violence, forced labor, and debt bondage. Juhu Thukral, founder of the American social impact consulting firm Apsara Projects and my cofounder of the Sex Workers Project, is an attorney who has represented many survivors and successfully advocated for policy change; she explained that a climate of fear must be present for a situation to be considered trafficking: "Does the person understand some kind of harm will come to them or someone they care about if they do not acquiesce?"[6] Movement of persons is not necessary for a situation to be considered trafficking, but it can be a factor in certain cases, particularly those trafficking cases involving people who come to the United States from other countries. The end goal of all forms of forced labor is for the employer to get something for nothing, or nearly nothing. Various forms of trafficking have allowed American employers to obtain labor for below-market wages—or no wages—for hundreds of years.

Most people who have been trafficked are vulnerable in specific ways. All but one of the hundreds of victims I have met were economically deprived. All had been physically abused, and some were literally beaten into submission. Many were threatened with death and told that their family members would be harmed if they did not do as they were told. Many had little education, and few knew their rights under the law.

FEATURES OF EXPLOITATION

Force, fraud, and coercion are the hallmarks of contemporary human trafficking as defined by the Trafficking Victims Protection Act, which I describe in chapter 2. The phenomenon of compulsory labor has always

TABLE 1 *Exploitation Tactics, by Melissa Hope Ditmore*

Trafficking Situation	Sales crews	Domestic and care workers	Agriculture	Sex work	Prison labor	Enslavement	Indenture	Number of situations using this tactic—max 7
Trait of exploitation								
Retaining control of identity papers or travel passes		√		√		√		3
Control of money and contracts								
Manipulating accounts, controlling money	√	√	√	√	√		√	6
Arbitrary fines	√			√				2
Abuse of contracts	√	√		√	√		√	5
Threats and abuse								
Verbal abuse	√	√	√	√		√	√	6
Threats to the worker	√	√	√	√	√	√	√	7
Physical abuse	√	√	√	√		√	√	6
Sexual assault	√	√	√	√	√	√	√	7
Threats to others			√	√				2
Children used to exploit parents				√		√		2
Fears of law enforcement								
Told to avoid the police and/or border patrol, or that police won't help them	√	√	√	√		NA—*police modeled on slave patrols*		4
Forcing criminal acts	√		√	√				3

TABLE 1 *Exploitation Tactics, by Melissa Hope Ditmore, continued*

Trafficking Situation	Sales crews	Domestic and care workers	Agriculture	Sex work	Prison labor	Enslavement	Indenture	Number of situations using this tactic—max 7
Isolation								
Physical isolation	√	√	√	√	√			5
Overwork/no leisure	√	√	√					3
No time apart	√	√	√		√			4
Control of communication	√	√	√		√			4
Language barrier used for control		√	√	√				3
Control and sadism								
Strange tasks (ironing underwear, feeding the meter)		√						1
Restriction or control of food	√	√	√		√	√	√	6
Deprivation of education		√				√	√	3
No complaints or negative talk	√		√					2
Test of manipulability								
Forcing quick decisions	√							1
Number of traits (22 max):	16	16	15	14	8	8	8	

existed, although it was not always labeled as trafficking, and some compulsory labor—as that of enslaved people and prisoners during the antebellum era—has been enforced by law. The tactics used by traffickers differ across workplaces and forms of exploitation. Some tactics overlap, while others are particular to a specific field. I have identified twenty-one tactics used by traffickers to control people and their labor. The easiest tactics to understand are threats and abuse, including verbal, physical, and sexual abuse and assault; and threats to others, including children and other family members. Manipulating financial accounts and imposing arbitrary fines can be forms of abusing worker contracts. Retaining the identity papers or travel documents of a worker can be a way to keep that worker physically confined or prevent them from leaving the country. Traffickers often keep the passports of immigrant workers; historically, slavers prevented their enslaved people from traveling by withholding travel passes. Sometimes the law is used to maintain leverage over victims: workers who have been forced to commit crimes, who have been arrested, or whose immigration status is irregular may be rightly afraid of interactions with law enforcement, and their exploiters capitalize upon this fear.

Isolating workers from others who might help them is another tactic, and it takes many forms. Exploiters may fill up all their victims' time with unnecessary tasks so they have no leisure time to spend with others. They may control forms of communication such as calls and messages or count on language barriers to keep their victims isolated. The most unfortunate victims may have no time apart from their exploiters or be isolated in the home of their exploiter.

Other trafficking tactics are more subtle. For example, managers of traveling sales crews typically tell potential recruits that they have only a few hours or overnight to decide whether to join the crew. Sometimes this is true, because these crews often move quickly from place to place. But forcing a quick decision can also be a way to determine how manipulable a candidate is, and thus whether they would be easy to exploit.

Not all forms of mistreatment serve a practical purpose. Some can only be explained as expressions of sadism: depriving workers of food or giving them tasks that serve no purpose except as exercises or tests of the exploiter's power, such as insisting that they iron socks, underwear, and towels, or that they hand-wash laundry when a machine is available. Depriving young people of education is another tactic that seems motivated as much by cruelty or spite as by a real fear of losing control. In some cases, it seems people wanted to deprive others of education simply because it was something that young people desired. These tactics have recurred throughout history.

HALLMARKS OF GOOD PRACTICES

The best organizations addressing human trafficking offer evidence-based and trauma-informed services to survivors using a rights-based approach. These service providers emphasize the survivor's self-determination, which is particularly important after a survivor has endured a trafficking situation in which they had little self-determination or control over their life. They offer all the information necessary to enable a survivor to make decisions about their future. This sounds simple, but it is not always easy. Survivors in the United States must be able to decide for themselves whether they want to leave the United States or remain and speak to law enforcement and cooperate with the prosecution. When these organizations advocate for policy changes, they do so by drawing from their experiences working with survivors and seeking to enhance survivors' lives. Without valorizing or glamorizing their role, they work directly for the well-being of survivors.

Flags that indicate that an organization is less effective in its mission include

- awareness-raising without an action agenda
- the use of salacious imagery, particularly in awareness raising or fundraising materials
- fundraising without the provision of direct services
- former military, intelligence, or law enforcement agents raising money to "rescue" children abroad

Rescue fantasies and a hero complex are inimical to trauma-informed services.

MISREPRESENTATIONS OF TRAFFICKING

Some organizations and politicians take a narrow view of how to fight trafficking, choosing to reduce the issue to prostitution. Some of these organizations, such as Exodus Cry, are faith-based, and prostitution is counter to their moral agenda. Influential conservative politicians such as the late senator Strom Thurmond (R-SC), for example, have trumpeted their opposition to prostitution but declined to support the labor rights that would help sex workers and workers of all kinds. Some politicians, such as former president Trump, are overt in their loyalty to business constituents who would not appreciate the enforcement of labor rights.

Other organizations, such as Shared Hope International and RESTORE, use sensational stories about abused girls and young women to raise funds, but do not deliver services to victims, instead engaging in vague "awareness raising," usually in the form of advertisements or public service announcements. Awareness-raising for its own sake, without a goal, is a red flag; merely talking about trafficking with one's friends and neighbors, only to say that it exists, is unlikely to lead to the detection of a trafficking situation.

In the late twentieth century, faith-based organizations like the Salvation Army faced criticism for their stance against reproductive rights such as access to abortion; to improve their image, these organizations sought a women's issue that they could champion. In the 1990s they began to advocate for the further criminalization of people involved in the sex trade, including sex workers, clients, and online platforms that sex workers use to advertise their services.

Some of the people behind faith-based anti-trafficking organizations have promoted hateful views against gay and transgender people. For example, International House of Prayer is an anti-gay church with ties to anti-trafficking organizations; Exodus Cry is a faith-based organization founded in 2007 and was listed on International House of Prayer's tax statements until 2017. Personnel of both organizations have made hateful statements against gay people. Benjamin Nolot, the CEO of Exodus Cry, has compared abortion to the Holocaust and described homosexuality as "an unspeakable offense to God."[7] Exodus Cry's home page says, "Fight for the freedom of all sex trafficking victims," but the organization takes a stance against "all forms of commercial sexual exploitation," which is how some anti-sex work campaigners refer to the sex trades.[8] In an online application form completed by potential chapter leaders, the organization asked about their sexual experiences and whether they "have struggled with homosexual thoughts, feelings or behaviors."[9] (The form has since been quietly removed from the site.)

Exodus Cry is the parent group of Traffickinghub, an organization and a hashtag under which demonstrators picketed the offices of the pornography website Pornhub in 2020 to demand the closure of the website and the removal of pornography from the internet.[10] Subsequently, Exodus Cry CEO Nolot published an opinion piece in the *New York Post* that uses (unattributed) conspiracy theorist QAnon talking points about the harms of pornography on children.[11] QAnon uses the problem of child sexual abuse and child pornography as an entrée into leading reasonable people to believe in a fictional Satanist cabal of Democrat politicians involved in child sexual abuse and trafficking; although child pornography exists, such a Democratic cabal is an imagined fiction. Neo-Nazi vigilante activity against pornography and trafficking using the #Traffickinghub hashtag has included death threats and the doxing of Pornhub executives, accompanied by messages such as "Heil Exodus Cry."[12] When asked about vigilantes using the #Traffickinghub hashtag, Laila Mickelwait, founder of Traffickinghub, suggested without evidence that Pornhub had fabricated these threats themselves "to promote a false narrative," thereby promoting another conspiracy theory worthy of QAnon.[13]

Nolot of Exodus Cry has produced sensationalist documentaries including *Liberated: The New Sexual Revolution*, which focuses on hookup culture and shames women for sexual activity, and a film about sex trafficking that was screened for members of Congress in 2013.[14] Nolot believes that extramarital sex is immoral, and the films benefit from prurient interest in sexuality while opposing non-reproductive sex outside patriarchal structures.

Faith-based organizations are not the only ones that grew out of concern about pornography. The Coalition Against Trafficking in Women (CATW) grew out of Women Against Pornography; it lobbies for the further criminalization of sex work. Sex work is counter to the values of some sex worker exclusionary radical feminists, or SWERFs, such as Donna Hughes, who holds the Eleanor M. and Oscar M. Carlson Endowed Chair in Women's Studies at the University of Rhode Island, and Janice Raymond, former co-director of CATW. Raymond and Hughes have lobbied for the conflation of trafficking with sex work in US and international law in the definition of trafficking in US law and international law. Their anti–sex work stance has led to some odd alliances with right-wing Christians. Hughes has worked with conservative Christian representative Chris Smith (R-NJ) on anti-sex-work, anti-trafficking legislation and described sex work as a human rights violation of the person offering sexual services for hire. Another organization, End Child Prostitution, Child Pornography and Trafficking of Children for Sexual Purposes (ECPAT), trains hospitality workers and airline employees to identify sex workers and report them to authorities, leading at times to harassment of mixed-race families when they fly.[15] These incidents highlight the willingness of SWERFs to leave behind some women, particularly marginalized or otherwise disadvantaged women such as transgender people, sex workers, and people of color—all groups that are economically oppressed.[16]

Our society's current tendency to conflate trafficking with sex work, along with anti-pornography and anti-sex-work views in general, is reminiscent of the "white slavery" panics of the early twentieth century. This period saw widespread and largely baseless anxieties about white girls and women leaving their home countries and being forced to work in brothels.[17] Such panics seem to be cyclical and continue to spur new legislation.[18] The authors of such legislation in these panics typically present it as protecting women and children, but actually it promotes control of women and children in patriarchal and authoritarian regimes; the narrative of danger to women and children is used to justify increasing control and autocracy rather than securing rights-based self-determination for individuals.

Trafficking into agriculture, industry, and domestic work, meanwhile, has always received scant attention compared with trafficking into sex work, despite its enormous scale and impact on the economy. Farming in the US contributed $1.37 billion to the US economy in 2020, and manufacturing contributed more than $2 billion.[19] Jean Bruggeman, executive director of Freedom Network USA, a national network of organizations offering services to trafficking survivors, clarified, "Research into some labor fields including agriculture and domestic work tells us that labor trafficking is pervasive in these fields, and knowing how many people are employed in these fields, we know that the prevalence of labor trafficking is enormously high, and yet the focus in the US continues to be on sex trafficking."[20]

Although the current view among American progressives is that sex work is a kind of labor, prostitution is not legally recognized as such and is not afforded labor protection. US data on trafficking therefore looks at sex trafficking separately from labor. Between October 1, 2019, and September 30, 2020 (US fiscal year 2020), the federal government recognized 508 adults from other countries as trafficking survivors, 70 percent of whom were victims of labor trafficking and an additional 11 percent were victims of both sex and labor trafficking. Among children from other countries recognized as survivors of trafficking, 69 percent were victims of labor trafficking and an additional 5 percent were victims of both sex and labor trafficking.[21]

Even as the extent of trafficking in other fields is recognized by service providers and philanthropists in the field, many unscrupulous organizations still fall back on the same old tropes about sex workers. For example, the McCain Institute, named for the late senator John McCain, is an important philanthropic player addressing trafficking. Yet Cindy McCain, wife of the late senator and the public face of the institute, still uses a debunked urban legend about prostitution and sporting events to raise funds, claiming every January that prostitution will increase around the location and timing of the Super Bowl.[22] Erin Albright, former director of the New Hampshire Human Trafficking Collaborative Task Force, a group of service providers and law enforcement representatives that share information to build better victim-centered services, explained, "The Super Bowl is a good example of our current major challenges in the anti-trafficking field. The hype is unfounded and based on assumptions, not evidence; it diverts resources for personnel and training away from evidence-based strategies and victim support."[23]

When organizations present human trafficking as being limited to sex work, they divorce it from the capitalist system that led the United States to become the world's largest economy. Capitalism in America is inextricably linked to the exploitation of forced or unpaid labor in every economic sector.

MY APPROACH IN THIS BOOK

Unbroken Chains focuses on the personal stories of people who experienced trafficking situations or similar abuses throughout the history of the United States, from colonial-era indentured servants to enslaved people in the American South, from prison laborers post-Reconstruction to people trafficked in the twenty-first century. Race and gender figure strongly in their ordeals; slavery was race-based, while the victims of sexual abuse in trafficking situations are predominantly women and gender-nonconforming people. Even in the forced labor system, women, people of color, and gender-nonconforming people are paid less than their white male peers.

The book is organized into five sections, each focusing on a separate economic sector. The first section, devoted to sales, describes the exploitative traveling sales crews that have been operating throughout the country for decades. Cases like those featured in this section prompted the passage of the landmark 2000 Trafficking Victims Protection Act.

The second section addresses trafficking in agricultural work and opens with the contemporary story of Marlyn Perez, a trafficked farmworker who was part of a successful prosecution against traffickers in Florida. This section also traces a continuous, historical pattern of forced agricultural labor in the US, from indentured servants and enslaved African Americans to the Asian contract laborers (pejoratively and offensively called "coolies") who were brought to the US after Emancipation had made chattel slavery illegal. We shall also see how vagrancy laws and prison labor were used in the postbellum era to continue extracting labor from Black Americans.

The third section addresses trafficking into domestic work and opens with the stories of contemporary victims Nena Ruiz, Judith Daluz, and Natalicia Tracy. This section situates their ordeals within the long-standing lack of labor protections afforded to domestic workers (as we shall see, they were deliberately excluded from the New Deal) and the historical precedent that, dating from the colonial era, it was enslaved people and indentured servants who did domestic work. The section also addresses specifically gendered labor such as childcare, and even reproduction, because while the importation of slaves was banned in 1808, slavery itself was not, giving slave owners an incentive to renew and expand their unpaid workforce by forcing enslaved women to bear children.

Industry and infrastructure are the focus of the fourth section, which opens with the story of Thai sweatshop workers who were held captive in Southern California in the 1990s. Precedents for their ordeal can be found in the history of the nineteenth-century Chinese contract laborers who built railway infrastructure across the country, and in the chain gangs who worked on the roads.

Sex work is the topic of the fifth section, which opens with the contemporary story of "Flor" who was forced into prostitution first in her home country of Mexico and later in the United States.[24] Flor's story in particular highlights the contradictions in anti-trafficking policy. As we shall see, most American anti-trafficking legislation has focused disproportionately on the sex trades. Immigration restrictions passed in the late nineteenth and early twentieth centuries sought to limit immigration on supposed "moral" grounds, attempting to prevent women suspected of promiscuous behavior from coming to the United States. The White-Slave Traffic Act of 1910, still in force today, was another prominent attempt to legislate sexual morality. A new twenty-first-century law, the 2018 FOSTA-SESTA package (the Fight Online Sex Trafficking Act, the House bill, and the Stop Enabling Sex Traffickers Act, the Senate bill) makes websites responsible for the publication of content that leads to any act of prostitution (such as classifieds listings) and has led to the closure of many sites where sex workers advertised. Donna Hughes and CATW lobbied for this law, which I look at as an example of the continued narrow focus on sex, and how it has had a chilling effect on certain types of content or online behavior without providing any meaningful assistance to trafficked persons.

I also explore the deep connections between the gendered and racialized compulsory labor of the past and the sensational descriptions of trafficking in contemporary fundraising. These descriptions are often based on racist stereotypes of men of color as pimps and inflammatory imagery of objectified young women; trafficking, once again, seems inseparable from race and gender.

Our lack of awareness of the history of unpaid and forced labor in a broad cross section of industries has real-world consequences for people in dire and dangerous situations today. To create laws or design programs to assist people in such situations, we need to understand not just current forms of forced labor but its history. Including the perspective of survivors is also critical, because their lived experiences should inform our responses to trafficking. Survivors have showed me how many of the interventions in place that purport to serve trafficking persons do not address their most pressing needs; assistance can be improved with their input. Without this fuller perspective, we risk recreating the errors of the past, where attempts to assist people in exploitative situations have occasionally been well thought out, but more often than not were unhelpful or even harmful. The book concludes with an analysis of what kinds of aid would most benefit current victims of trafficking.

I hope to share my knowledge with readers who may have similar preconceptions to the ones I once held, and I hope that the United States will move toward laws and policies about trafficking that address the real needs of victims of trafficking today.

PART I

TRAFFICKING INTO SALES

CHAPTER 1

YOUNG AMERICANS ON TRAVELING SALES CREWS

T HIS CHAPTER DESCRIBES the phenomenon of young people on traveling sales crews. They sell cleaning supplies, magazine subscriptions, or other items, and they work within an exploitative labor model. They frequently go unpaid or are not paid in line with fair practices, are often threatened or physically abused, and may be held in a kind of debt bondage in which they are unable to earn money no matter how much they work. Chapter 2 describes the Trafficking Victims Protection Act, passed in 2000 in the aftermath of notable cases involving traveling sales crews around the United States. This law focuses on the use of force, fraud, and coercion in all economic sectors, and includes assistance for survivors and criminal penalties for people convicted of trafficking.

When the US Congress passed the Trafficking Victims Protection Act in 2000, my friend Jo Weldon asked me how the law defined "trafficking." I explained that it involves the use of force, fraud, or coercion. Of the three, fraud is far more widespread than is commonly realized. Many individuals who meet the legal definition of "trafficked people" have been lured into their situation by traffickers who misrepresent the work conditions.

Jo's eyes grew wide. "That happened to me!" she exclaimed.

Jo told me that, in 1980, she had been part of a sales crew selling magazine subscriptions door-to-door in the American South. Such crews often hire young people for jobs as sales agents.[1] The minimum age for employment in the United States is fourteen, and there are restrictions until eighteen years of age. But the young people who join these crews—often recent high school graduates or dropouts—frequently find that their working conditions are quite different from what the recruiters promised. Moved continually from place to place, made to work in unfamiliar areas where they have no contacts or support network, they find themselves under intense pressure to make sales, with every aspect of their lives controlled by their handlers. To keep Jo and the other young members of the crew compliant, their handlers supplied them with large quantities of alcohol. The alcohol not only kept them content but also added to their sense of disorientation, making them easier to manipulate.

Jo was eighteen years old and believed that she had found a decent job, one that would enable her to get away from a difficult situation with her immediate family in her hometown and allow her to see the country. She thought she would have control of her own life and her evenings to herself after a day's work. Instead, she found her movements tightly controlled. The magazine crew was moved to a different neighborhood each day, and none of the neighborhoods were familiar to her.

Jo was able to escape from her sales crew after a few months. She understood at the time that she was a victim of deception and coercion, but it would never have occurred to her to describe herself as being trafficked. It was only many years later, in our conversation, that she recognized her own magazine crew experience for what it was, with many of the same elements found in other trafficking situations.

INDUSTRY STRUCTURE

The major source of revenue for magazines is not subscription fees but advertising. The prize in a subscription sale isn't the income from the subscription itself but rather its impact on circulation numbers. More subscriptions mean higher circulation numbers; higher circulation numbers mean that the magazine can charge advertisers more; higher ad rates mean more revenue for the magazine and its owners. This is the logic that drives the demand for magazine crews.

Magazine subscriptions are sold in a variety of different ways: online, via subscription cards in print magazines, or through "clearinghouses" that hire subcontractors to sell subscriptions. Magazine crews are typically employed, directly or indirectly, by these subcontractors. The young sales agents, the ones going door-to-door, are hired as independent contractors. These layers of subcontracting relationships provide plausible deniability and shield both the publisher and clearinghouse from any liability for anything that happens on the magazine crew.

Reputable clearinghouses, such as Priority One, review the backgrounds of their subcontractors through the Better Business Bureau. If a contracted company, known as a subagent, is found to engage in fraud, Priority One cancels the contract with the company and informs the magazine publisher that there were problems with that particular subagent.[2] Not all subagent companies are reputable, and many have poor ratings with the Better Business Bureau and/or multiple complaints about sales agents or subscription orders that were not fulfilled. One such complaint reads: "Had someone come to my door today and get super uncomfortable and pushy. . . . Leaves me to believe there was something sketchy going on, since the demeanor completely shifted when the word verify came up."[3] A fascinating 2015 *Atlantic* piece by Darlena Cunha documents the author's attempt to learn how a publisher handles the risk of being connected in any way to door-to-door magazine sales.[4] She concluded that publishers have no desire to work with magazine crews, and that publishers do not keep records of subscription vendors. In fact, they hire subagents to do that very task. However, even when there are known problems with a subagent, nothing prevents the people behind that company from simply changing the name and carrying on as before.

The *New York Times* reported in 2007 that "dozens of magazines are listed on order forms offered by crews, including Reader's Digest, Rolling Stone and Redbook," even as those publishers told the *New York Times* that they do not use subagents or when they do, "only sparingly." A representative of the Hearst Corporation explained to the *Times*, "We constantly fight unauthorized agents," adding, "It's an ongoing battle."[5] Magazine sales crew problems are so well known that a company specializes in documenting them: Periodical Watchguard is a company that publishers can hire to investigate such problems, and it has unsuccessfully been sued by magazine subscription scammers for its work.[6]

Traveling sales crews have existed for generations. The first news item I found about magazine crews was a *New York Times* article from 1948.[7] In

1984, the eastern Pennsylvania newspaper the *Morning Call* published a lengthy investigative piece focused on young people from that area who had been held against their will by traveling sales crews. They were not allowed to call their families, and experienced exhaustion and malnutrition.[8] In 1987, Congress held a hearing about sales crews selling both magazines and cleaning products in response to media coverage of abuses of young people in door-to-door sales.[9] Sales crew members from multiple companies testified, as did representatives from a magazine crew company and a cleaning products company.

RECRUITMENT

Traditionally, magazine crews recruit sales agents through small local papers. Advertisements promise good wages and describe a lifestyle in which agents can meet other young people on the job, socialize together after their workday is over, and get to travel the country. One young woman from North Dakota who became a magazine crew member with Subscriptions Plus in 1999 "was excited, telling her dad it paid $500 a week. She said she would get to see Florida and the ocean."[10] The form of the advertisements has changed over time to accommodate new media. Advertisements from the 1980s had titles like "Guys & Gals Travel $ Fun" and mentioned opportunities to earn sales commissions.[11] In 2007, a sales crew member described answering an ad that said "Fun, Travel, Adventure."[12] Advertisements for sales crew jobs now appear online, offering "high commission potential" and claiming, "As a Clean Display Ad Sales Rep, you will receive a base salary + uncapped commissions, so you determine your own income (potential of six figures +). The sky's the limit!"[13]

Recruiters use a variety of high-pressure tactics. Applicants interviewed in person are told that they must decide quickly—that the crew is leaving the area in just a few hours or the next morning, or that there is only one spot left. Once the applicant has signed up, they are often moved quickly to a different region or even a different state, the first part of a process of keeping them off balance and disoriented.

When applicants are interviewed by phone, they are then sent bus tickets to another part of the country to join up with a crew there. In 2014, there was a case in which two underaged sisters in North Dakota were hired by a sales company and traveled to North Carolina with bus tickets sent by the company, after being encouraged to run away to join a magazine crew without their parents' consent.[14]

Young people with limited skills have few work opportunities, especially in small towns. It's easy to see how they might be drawn by the promise of a job that seems to offer not just money but travel and excitement. Travel with other young people holds obvious appeal. And for those in marginal situations—an eighteen-year-old about to be made homeless by aging out of foster care, or someone in crisis who has no place to stay or is escaping an unstable or unsafe home situation—joining a magazine crew might look like a golden opportunity. Recruiters know all this, and they make a point of targeting young people who are vulnerable because of poverty, limited education or experience, or factors such as mental health or substance use issues.[15]

CONTROL

Once new members begin working with a crew, they typically remain in a place for a week or two at a time. They sell subscriptions during the day and spend their nights in motels. Crew members are kept in the dark about future travel plans and even their current location. Barbara McKnight, a former magazine crew member with a San Antonio, Texas–based company named TICOA, testified to Congress in 1987. She described being disoriented, because "we were not supposed to tell anyone what hotel we were staying in, and when we traveled, we never know where we were going until we got there."[16]

Drugs and alcohol are ubiquitous among the crews. Jo described being continuously intoxicated or hungover all the time, leaving her unable to make good judgments about her situation. Former magazine crew members described managers promoting daily drug and alcohol use among the sales agents, including those who were underage. Managers actively offered and supplied drugs to crew members. Former sales agent Jeffrey Medved, who worked for the Vincent Pitts Sales Organization collecting orders for Circulation Builders of America, testified to Congress that "there was a good deal of drug use as well. At times, these drugs were supplied by car handlers [dedicated drivers with administrative responsibilities]."[17] Barbara McKnight said, during the same hearing, "There was drug use on the crew. Some of it came from the outside, but some of it was supplied by a manager.

One of my car handlers once told me to check if customers had any drugs to sell."[18] Stephanie Dobbs, a crew member with Young People Working, said in 2015, "I've seen every drug you can imagine."[19]

Another way that crew managers maintain their control over their agents is by withholding pay. Crew members are usually given just a small amount of money daily for necessities. This is called the "draw"; it is presented as an advance on earnings to cover meals, laundry, and incidentals like toothpaste, and it is not always enough. Far from home, without any funds of their own, they are left wholly dependent on the crew.

While recruiters promise opportunities for leisure time and sightseeing, the reality is very different. Sales agents typically work six days a week. Sundays are spent in the car or van or doing laundry after a late afternoon check-in at a new motel. Employers charge sales agents for their lodgings. To reduce costs, accommodations are shared: crew members sleep doubled up in motel room beds, and some members may sleep on the floor, depending on the number of people sharing a room. Sales agents are never alone except when they are out selling.

SALES CREW STRUCTURE

Sales crews can be small, with only four or five people, or much larger, with twenty-five people or more. Above the street-level sales crew there is typically a junior manager and possibly a manager as well. There may be a dedicated driver, or "car handler," who may have administrative or management responsibilities, such as collecting money and keeping the ledger. Junior managers are a half-step above the sales crew: their main job is to manage the crew, but they may also make sales themselves. Real power lies with the managers, who are typically paid a commission on each sale. The managers process the subscription purchases and distribute the draw to the sales agents.

Draws are often too small even to cover basic daily expenses. Three former sales crew members from three different companies all testified to Congress that they'd experienced days when they did not receive their advance due to low sales, and that meant that "you had no money to eat." Former sales agent Rebecca Fox, who worked for the Ultra-Kleen Chemical Company, added, "I lost a lot of weight while I was with the crew as did other sales agents."[20] Barbara McKnight testified to Congress that she had so little money for necessities that she had "sold a magazine for cash, ripped up the receipt [subscription form], and used the money for shampoo and toothpaste. I know that other agents did this too, because they just didn't have enough money to eat and buy other things they needed."[21]

There is enormous pressure to sell, as crew members who do not make their sales quotas are abused verbally and physically. Barbara McKnight testified that crew members are expected to do anything to make a sale, saying, "One time, I told [magazine crew manager] Dora Cooper that I had not been able to sell a magazine to a cute boy, and she asked me why I hadn't slept with him."[22] Twenty years later, Isaac James, a former crew member (company not named) interviewed for a *New York Times* video segment in 2007, described stealing a wide variety of small, portable things from people's homes. He would sell the stolen goods and use the money to buy magazine subscriptions to bolster his own sales.[23]

RIGGED BOOKS

The *Times* video segment reported that sales agents' earnings are between 10 and 25 percent of their sales, against which their expenses are deducted.[24] Most of the crew members do not understand how the deductions will affect their earnings, and some become indebted to the company.[25] Former magazine crew members reported that, for the first few weeks, new recruits were typically treated well and well paid. After that, however, deductions for lodging and other expenses started to be withheld from their earnings, these deductions mounted, and they began to be treated increasingly poorly. The accounting books of the Ultra-Kleen Chemical Company, one of the companies investigated in the 1987 congressional hearing, showed that 413 out of 418 sales agents owed money to the company.[26] A former crew manager featured in the *Times* video said that they paid "slave wages."[27] Matt Ward, a former bookkeeper for subscription company American Community Services also interviewed in the video, explained that he'd left the company because "the sales agents remain almost always in the red while the managers, car handlers and everyone else is in the black almost from the start."[28]

Barbara McKnight testified to Congress that "I did make sales, and I was supposed to earn a commission. I have no idea how much I earned because I never saw my account. I asked the Coopers [crew managers] if I could see it, but I was always told 'later,' or they would change the subject. All I know is that when I left, they showed me a piece of paper that said I owed the company $400."[29] Former sales crew member Jeffrey Medved testified to Congress that he was shown the ledger for his account infrequently and was never given time to read it closely. He was told to sign the ledger, but he did not really understand the numbers.[30]

Lee Bradby, a former sales crew agent and car handler with the Ultra-Kleen Chemical Company, explained to Congress how the accounts and deductions were manipulated to prevent sales crew members from being paid:

> Most people owed [Ultra-Kleen Chemical Company owner and sales crew manager] Mr. [Horace] Robertson money, based on the account sheets. If a person was a very good salesman or a "car handler" he might be in the black. Not only were daily draws and hotel charges deducted from the 30% commission on sales, but Mr. Robertson deducted other amounts in what I thought was an arbitrary way.
>
> For instance, we were charged $2 per day for supplies. . . . We were charged various amounts for "fines," ranging from $5 for being late to meetings to $500 for "fraternization."
>
> There was money deducted if Mr. Robertson had to bail you out of jail for being stopped for soliciting without a permit. . . .
>
> Getting in the black on one's account, and staying there, was almost impossible, and being in debt to Mr. Robertson kept people on the crew longer than they might have stayed otherwise. Mr. Robertson promised when I was hired that he would provide a bus ticket back to Oklahoma whenever I wanted to leave. But I recall asking to leave one time and he told me to head out for the highway, and I recall several others getting the same treatment.[31]

These descriptions of employees trapped in debt to their employers are reminiscent of the "company store" model, where workers in remote areas—often in low-wage industries such as mining or logging—would, for lack of other options, buy their necessities from a store that had a relationship with or was sometimes run by the employer. The company store offered credit to employees, with purchases deducted from their future pay, but charged prices above the market rate. Between low wages and the high prices of goods, most employees never made enough to get out of debt to the company store. Such stores were part of a peonage system whose goal was to keep workers trapped in hard jobs in remote places. Over time, growing car ownership enabled people to travel further to shop, eliminating the company store model by the middle of the twentieth century. However, revamped versions of the model continue in managers' careful management of advances and the questionable bookkeeping practices they use to trap workers in sales crews.

VIOLENCE

Like other exploited workers, members of sales crews are often subject to violence. In his testimony to Congress, Medved said, "I twice saw one of the junior managers, Bob Cecil specifically, strike sales agents. One time, he punched a woman during a dispute between them, and she was very badly beaten."[32]

Michael Simpson, a former crew member (company unnamed) labeled an "enforcer" by the *New York Times* in its 2007 piece, described beating up crew members who were not selling enough, saying, "Managers will never directly tell you to assault someone, they will ask you to take care of it. There were times when we beat people 'til they could not move, there were times when we would beat people just enough so they got the point."[33]

Bradby testified to Congress, "I remember at least 3 occasions when Mr. Robertson hit me. I still have a chipped tooth from a punch by Joe Robertson, one of Mr. Robertson's brothers. And I am aware of other incidents involving sales agents who were struck by Mr. Robertson and others traveling with the crew."[34]

Members of sales crews may experience other forms of mistreatment. The National Human Trafficking Hotline states that in addition to violence, young people on crews are commonly subjected to sexual harassment, sexual abuse, and abandonment.[35]

CRIME

People on sales crews are not only victims of crime. They may also be coerced into committing crimes themselves. Crew managers demonstrate their disregard for sales agents' welfare by asking or forcing them to do things that are illegal. Door-to-door sales without a permit is a crime in many jurisdictions, and sellers are sometimes arrested. A former crew member testified to Congress that most of the time sellers were bailed out quickly by managers, with the cost of bail typically deducted from the sales agents' account. Some, however, were simply abandoned while in jail.[36]

Barbara McKnight testified to Congress that when she was hired by the sales crew and arrived for her first day, the managers who were supposed to meet her were not there because "they were at the police station bailing out half the crew who had been selling without permits."[37] Traveling sales crews typically move on before court dates, after which arrest warrants may be issued to sales agents for failing to appear in court. In this way, they can end up with arrest warrants in multiple states. Crew managers seldom take the time to explain to their employees the consequences of arrest and missing court. Some even boast about the number of arrests or warrants they have. Few of these managers have knowledge of workplace law or other relevant laws.

Because of these legal dangers, managers often tell crews to avoid the police. Barbara McKnight confirmed this in her testimony, saying, "We were told to stay away from the police and to try to get into a customer's house if we saw a police car. This attitude made me afraid of the police."[38]

Managers may encourage crew members to commit other illegal acts, such as petty theft or driving a motor vehicle without a license. In one case from 1999, a magazine crew van with Subscriptions Plus was involved in an accident in Janesville, Wisconsin, that killed seven members of the crew and seriously injured six more.[39] The van had been speeding and the driver, a member of the magazine crew, did not have a license and, in the frantic moments after hearing a police siren trying to pull him over, he crashed the van.

WHY PEOPLE STAY WITH THE CREWS

Magazine crew members who want to leave describe financial and logistical obstacles. Crew members have reported feeling unable to walk away from the crews because they lacked money. Their daily draw is typically spent on dinner and is never enough to cover lodging or a ticket back to their hometowns. Others are told by their managers that their contracts prevent them from leaving. When the two sisters from the 2014 North

Dakota case (mentioned earlier in the chapter) expressed their desire to go home, "they were told that they could not leave because they'd signed a contract."[40] Eventually, they were able to call their family and tell them where they were, and their family called the police in Fargo, who contacted law enforcement in North Carolina. As part of the investigation to find the two girls, the police in North Carolina went to every motel room rented by the company, and in so doing found two other teens in a similar situation as the girls. These young men, eighteen-year-old cousins from Tennessee, had also expressed wanting to leave North Carolina to return to Knoxville.[41] The girls' family sent them bus tickets to return home.

In other cases, crew members who complained about their conditions would be abandoned in unfamiliar locations without any money. Cut off from their home communities and support networks, some crew members have fallen back on resources for runaways and homeless youth. (The National Runaway Safeline, for instance, which is the national communications system designated by the federal government to serve youth in crisis, provides young people in need with free bus tickets to their hometowns.)[42]

Those who want to leave are subjected to other kinds of pressure. Rebecca Fox testified to Congress that she was detained:

> Mr. Robertson tried to talk me out of leaving. Then everybody in the room, like Mr. Robertson and his brothers, started yelling at Jeff [another crew member who wanted to leave with Fox] telling [him] that he could go but he couldn't take a good sales agent with him.
>
> Then Marie Martin, Ray's wife, took me up to Barbara Hilton's room. Marie was there and Barbara and three other women. They tried to talk me out of leaving. They said that we were not on the crew to meet guys, we were there to make sales. I was in tears by now.
>
> After about half an hour, another girl came into the room and said that Jeff had left and he said that I wasn't worth waiting for. I thought this was a lie, and it was, but I was in hysterics by now and all confused.
>
> I tried to get up and leave once, but they made me sit down and sign some papers. Then I got up to leave again, and they wouldn't let me. I broke free and ran down to the elevator but Marie Martin was holding the doors open so the elevator couldn't move. So I took off down the stairway, praying that nobody would be waiting for me on the first floor.

I could hear everybody else behind me, and when I got to the first floor, I went through a back door and into an alley, since I was afraid that Mr. Robertson or somebody with him would be around the front door. But they caught up to me outside and held me against the wall.

Then an ambulance drove up and two men got out of it and asked if I needed any help. I told them that these people were not letting me leave and the ambulance drivers threatened to call the police; they let me go.[43]

Fox's story is not unique; some who have stayed with crews describe being persuaded not to leave, or being talked into returning after they had left. Others have stayed because they "have no place to go."[44]

RELENTLESS INTIMIDATION

Former magazine crew member Barbara McKnight described feeling intimidated by her former crew and managers even after leaving the sales crew, saying,

When I see a white Suburban with a Texas license plate like the one my crew rode in, I still feel scared. Once, just before I was going to be on a television program to talk about my experience, I received a telephone call from one of the other crew managers, who was in Illinois at the time, where I am now living. He told me to come back and he would give me a car and my own crew. This was strange. . . . Although it could have been a coincidence, this call made me afraid, and I did not appear on the show.[45]

While traveling sales crews may sell a variety of products, the majority are involved in magazine subscription sales. The contracting companies that hire magazine crews are well insulated from any consequences. It's usually the sales agents themselves who are most vulnerable to legal repercussions. On the occasions when people above the street-level agents have been arrested, it has usually been the lower-level managers. For example, in the 2014 case of the two sisters from North Dakota, the people arrested were not the owners of the company but two junior managers who had sent bus tickets to the girls. The arrested managers—Justin Angermeier, twenty-eight, of Cameron, Missouri, and Jeremy Moots, nineteen, of Edmond, Oklahoma—were themselves both young, far from their own hometowns and apparently part of the magazine crew. Moots said that he worked for a company named Midwest Circulations LLC, registered in Missouri. The president (and sole listed contact) of Midwest Circulations is a woman named Bridgett Robbins. Before this case, Robbins and Midwest Circulations had been previously sued by the attorney general of Missouri for "misrepresenting the business to customers."[46] In 2022, eight years after the case, Midwest Circulations was apparently still in business, with Robbins still the only listed contact for the company. The Better Business Bureau website notes that the company is not BBB accredited and features a single one-star review.[47]

In a few cases, people higher up in the companies have faced consequences. The 1999 Janesville van crash that killed seven magazine crew members working for Subscriptions Plus led to lawsuits against the company brought by surviving victims of the crash seeking compensation for medical care and damages. The teenage driver was sentenced to prison; along with his manager, Choan Lane, he was held liable for $12 million in restitution. Wisconsin courts ruled that Karleen Hillery, the founder and owner of Subscriptions Plus, was also liable, but the ruling did not result in major changes. The restitution award went mostly toward the costs of caring for the two most debilitated victims, who will require specialized care for the rest of their lives.[48] While Subscriptions Plus was found liable, the judge ruled that the magazine publishers and the clearinghouse companies were not responsible.

DIFFICULTIES PROSECUTING

Members of traveling sales crews are well aware that there is something wrong with their situation, but they can generally do little to address these workplace issues because they are classified as independent contractors and are thus excluded from major workplace protections. The Fair Labor Standards Act of 1938, which set minimum wage and hour requirements, does not apply to people who work outdoors, including members of traveling sales crews. As we've seen, many of the managers are scarcely older or more experienced than the teenage workers they manage. The crews are instructed to avoid law enforcement, especially where they are supposed to have permits to work, and some crew members have committed crimes like theft or driving without a license and may be afraid of being arrested for these crimes. These circumstances can factor into the decision not to report their working conditions to police. Some who have tried to report crimes to police were told that as crew members were of age and could walk away at any time, or that because the crew members could not identify the people involved above the crew, the police were not going to investigate.[49] Few crew members are from families with the means to hire an attorney to pursue restitution. Only in the aftermath of high-profile tragedies like the Wisconsin traffic accident do attorneys offer to take the case for a percentage of a settlement.

Despite the abuses, sales crews persist to this day. Multiple lawsuits against companies that use sales crews have done little to change the business, in part because companies can close down and be quickly replaced by new ones. The few prosecutions that have occurred have focused on cases involving minors, who need parental permission to travel. Some such cases have led to convictions, but the person convicted has typically been a low-level manager rather than a company owner. Additionally, it is often unclear who has jurisdiction in these cases. Connie Knutti, a former manager of field enforcement for the Illinois Department of Labor, told the *New York Times*, "The local police can't keep up because the crews leave the state before they get alerted and the feds don't bother with them because they say it is a state's issue."[50]

Earlene Williams is the founder of Parent Watch, which tracks labor abuses of teens and young adults, particularly in sales crews. She told Congress in 1987 about the history and structure of sales crew subagents, including the names and backgrounds of the companies involved in the largest number of calls to Parent Watch.[51] In her testimony, Williams explained that the Federal Trade Commission had ruled in 1971 that publishers including Cowles Communications, the Hearst Corporation, and Time, Inc. used deceptive practices to get magazine subscriptions. Five subsidiaries of Cowles were charged with fifty counts in a criminal indictment; Cowles and the subsidiaries pleaded no contest, and each subsidiary was fined $10,000.[52] Williams cites this case as a turning point, because it halted the practice of self-regulation among clearinghouses, leaving the Federal Trade Commission to oversee practices. However, the FTC didn't conduct any oversight of sales agents and crews, thereby enabling publishers' subagents to continue exploiting young people.

Trafficking charges are also difficult to pursue, for different reasons. In 2015, Earlene Williams explained why:

> Yes, it could be considered labor trafficking. They work long hours, and if they don't make their quota, they might not be fed. They might be bullied and humiliated, and they're often made to believe they owe a debt and may spend months trying to work it off. But often when the law enforcement people try to apply the statute [Trafficking Victims Protection Act]—and they always want to prosecute on behalf of a group of victims, not an individual—the ambivalent behaviors or marginal status of crew members make it nearly impossible.[53]

In short, sales agents who wish to press charges are often discredited by their backgrounds (some are runaways) and by the criminal activities they have engaged in as part of the crew (underage drinking, drug use, and sometimes theft). Sales crew members have described being told to avoid the police, and many have been arrested. They do not see the police as a resource or trust them.

Given the difficulties around pressing trafficking charges, another way to help sales crew members would be by ensuring that their employers categorize their employment status accurately, making them either genuine independent contractors who were not forced to work in a crew structure in which their hours and conditions are set by the company or employees entitled to labor protections. However, this is not easy to enforce. In 1975, the Minnesota Supreme Court ruled that one door-to-door sales company, Mecca Enterprises, was in fact the employer of its crews and that the company had engaged in "fraudulent recruiting and sales practices." But little changed after the ruling. The company simply hired other companies with their own sales crews to make sales in Minnesota.[54]

Minnesota is not the only state to have responded to problems with sales crews. Wisconsin passed a law regulating sales crews in 2009 by requiring companies working or recruiting there to register with the state, for vehicles to be certified safe, and for crew members to be paid twice monthly.[55]

CHANGES IN THE INDUSTRY

The basic sales crew model has altered little over time, but some of the details have changed. Recruitment is often carried out online now, including on social media. Typical examples include Facebook pages with names like "Traveling Door-to-Door Super Cleaner Sales." Interestingly, this particular page stresses changes in business practices, claiming that their crews no longer stay in motels but instead stay in rented homes, where they can cook for themselves. Its advertisements also seem to target people with prior experience of sales crews. One advertisement posted to the page reads: "Would you like to sell clean & simple™ SUPER CLEANER for a living, but you're over the constant travel and crew drama? Well, we have good news for you! We have been experimenting with a new business model that is going great and we might want you to be a part of it!"[56]

OTHER SELLERS BROUGHT TO THE US

For door-to-door magazine sales, strong English language skills are essential. While trafficking operations in other industries tend to recruit recent immigrants, whose unfamiliarity with American culture makes them easier to exploit, sales crews target American-born young people. But there have also been cases involving people brought from outside the US and forced to work in similarly exploitative sales jobs. One example is the case of the deaf Mexican peddlers who in 1997 were discovered being forced to sell trinkets in New York City subways.[57] Adriana Paoletti Lemus, a Mexican woman married to the deaf son of a New York police officer, arranged to bring dozens of deaf Mexican people to New York to act as a specialized sales crew.[58] The vendors lived in Queens in very overcrowded conditions and were expected to bring back $100 every day by selling pens, cards with the sign language alphabet, and other small items in the subway.

Itinerant sales in the subway are not unheard of in New York, and typically consist of students selling candy on the train or women selling churro pastries on the subway platform, but the practice is much less established than in Mexico City, where selling items in the subway is a job much like any other. Subway riders there can expect to be offered a bewildering variety of products from artificial flowers to chocolate, from batteries to eyeglasses repair tools, shampoo to churro pastries, all during the course of a single subway ride.

In the New York subway system, however, the sudden influx of people selling small items was much more noticeable. The vendors' inability to communicate in either English or Spanish made them stand out even more. Subway riders who encountered the vendors understood that something was wrong but did not grasp the enormity of the situation. Eventually, some of the peddlers were able to deliver a note to the New York City police department.[59] This was perhaps New York's first truly visible modern trafficking case, too flagrant to be ignored, with vulnerable people forced to live in gross and unsanitary conditions and work under threat of violence.

Shutting down the trafficking ring was not entirely straightforward. When the police raided the house where the peddlers were being kept, it was necessary to find shelter for all the survivors. Locating shelter for so many people is difficult enough and was complicated by the fact that the group included men and women: city shelters for men were only for the homeless, and shelters for victims of domestic violence were exclusively for women. The women were able to go to domestic violence shelters, and the men involved were put up in hotels. Then there were communication difficulties. Because the victims spoke only Mexican Sign Language (MSL), the police had to find translators who could translate from MSL into spoken Spanish, and then into English.

There were other locations—California, the Midwest, and the South—with ties to the New York case, as different operations were coordinated across multiple locations.[60] The amount of money generated with this type of peddling seems almost too small, between about fifty and a hundred dollars per person each day, and the potential expenses involved too high to justify the effort. To house, feed, and supervise more than thirty people, to say nothing of forcing them to work using threats or actual violence, requires a certain amount of organization, which comes at a cost. The sheer paucity of the potential gains may explain why exploitative practices seem to be such a ubiquitous feature of sales crew operations: the margins are so slender for a company that there is simply no way to turn a profit without cutting corners and cheating its workforce. And this necessity of exploiting the workers explains why sales crew companies prefer to recruit only those who are least able to protect themselves: young people rendered vulnerable by inexperience and immaturity, or foreigners isolated by an inability to communicate and thrown into an environment where they have no allies. The real question is why sales crews persist at all.

Ultimately, some of the formerly trafficked peddlers returned to Mexico, while others remained in the US. The case itself was an important catalyst for the passage of the Trafficking Victims Protection Act in 2000.

JO

Following our discussion about sales crews and trafficking, my friend Jo began to pay close attention to media coverage of magazine crews and made a point of sharing links to articles and court decisions with me and others.

Like many others, her experience as a teenage member of a magazine crew was terrible. However, by the time I met her, she had recovered and was thriving. She had left the crew after a few months and subsequently worked in strip clubs in Atlanta. She created costumes for herself and many other dancers. Later, she learned fan dancing, which involves alternately concealing and revealing the body by twirling large feather fans in time to music. She explained to me that the solution to her problems was economic independence, something that had simply not been possible in the exploitative structure of the sales crews. For her, stripping was an enormous change for the better, enabling her to attend college and maintain distance from violent people in her life.

She eventually began to tour the country as a "feature dancer," a sought-after performer in strip clubs. She traveled in style and got to see America for herself—something that her magazine crew recruiters had always promised but never delivered. She has since spoken extensively about her experience of having been trafficked, contrasting it with her empowering experiences in the sex industry. She is quick to stress that while the sex industry can be exploitative, trafficking is not inherent to its business model. Despite the bad reputation of sex work, conditions that truly meet the definition of trafficking may often be found in other industries, such as sales, that are considered more socially respectable. Jo has since started teaching burlesque and has helped many people develop their own acts. Jo Weldon is the founder and headmistress of the New York School of Burlesque, and the author of *Fierce: The History of Leopard Print* (2018) and *The Burlesque Handbook* (2010).[61]

CHAPTER 2

SEX AND LABOR IN THE TRAFFICKING VICTIMS PROTECTION ACT

T HE CASE OF THE DEAF Mexican vendors described in the previous chapter was sandwiched between two other high-profile trafficking cases. The resulting media coverage helped garner the political will to pass a new law addressing modern human trafficking in the United States.

In the first case, in 1995, seventy-two Thai garment workers in El Monte, California, were discovered being held in peonage in a makeshift factory created within a fenced-in seven-unit apartment complex. There they had been forced by their employers, who were also Thai nationals, to sew clothing for such well-known brands as B.U.M. and Montgomery Ward.[1] They were freed after a letter from an escapee, complete with a map of the barbed-wire enclosed factory, reached the Division of Labor Standards Enforcement, part of the California Department of Industrial Relations.

The third case, reported on January 11, 1998, by the *New York Times*, involved women from the former Soviet republics who had been forced into prostitution in Israel. The paper's front-page story was accompanied by a picture of a victim, a blond woman in a brothel in Israel.[2] In 1997, the Global Survivor Network released a film about these unfortunate women, and the Israel Women's Network produced a report about them.[3] The *Times* piece described young, attractive blond women from former Soviet republics who had emigrated from impoverished economies and

35

were subsequently forced into prostitution not only in Israel but many countries around the world. Before the end of 1998, an international law on human trafficking had been proposed at the United Nations. The US Congress was also beginning to discuss an anti-trafficking law around this time. By 2000, a watershed year for anti-trafficking efforts, President Clinton had signed the new Trafficking Victims Protection Act (TVPA), and the United States had signed the UN Optional Protocol on Trafficking in Persons.[4]

The TVPA addresses force, fraud, and coercion in labor settings, and applies to everyone regardless of work status or citizenship. The types of force and coercion addressed in this law include physical violence, rape and sexual abuse, torture, starvation, imprisonment, psychological abuse, and threats to the victim and to others. The law also defines servitude and debt bondage as forms of human trafficking.

In addition to creating a new legal framework specifically for the prosecution of human trafficking crimes, the law also created services for victims and allocated up to five thousand visas annually to allow victims of international trafficking to remain in the US if they wished. The law also offers "continued presence" status to allow survivors to remain in the country while waiting for US Citizenship and Immigration Services to judge their applications. These visas, known as T visas, offer a path to permanent resident status (commonly known as holding a "green card") and then US citizenship. These visas do come with conditions, however. They require the applicant to cooperate with law enforcement in case there is a prosecution. A letter from a law enforcement officer stating that someone has cooperated can serve as an effective boost to an application, but people who offer legal and social services to trafficked persons say that such letters are very hard to get even for those who have cooperated extensively; generally speaking, officers do not prioritize helping the people who have cooperated.[5] Officers are often more occupied in dealing with the bureaucracy, paperwork, and other components that make up a large part of their daily work.[6]

Some of the problems with requiring victims to cooperate with law enforcement and prosecutions come from the lack of a standard procedure across the country. Law enforcement agencies are asked to support the applications for the T visa, but individual police officers can decline to write letters of support. Some police departments do not support T visa applications even when people have jeopardized their safety by cooperating with prosecutions. Supporting victims of crime after they have cooperated with a prosecution is low priority for a police department focused on arrests and convictions of criminals; supporting survivors is not seen as part of their job, and support for the applications is not guaranteed no matter the level of risk involved. Although cooperation is required, support letters for survivors should be standardized to make the process as easy as possible, and also should be mandated. A core reason why this process fails survivors is that human trafficking is addressed as a criminal justice issue rather than a human rights one. The criminal justice approach incentivizes law enforcement to prosecute criminals as opposed to helping victims of crime. A better solution would be to develop a support system that does not rely on law enforcement at all.

T visas also have other strings attached. People who hold them are expected not to travel outside the United States, and particularly not to their countries of origin. This is in part to ensure that they remain available to assist law enforcement and prosecutors, but also to protect them against dangers that they might face if they return home. Traffickers often have their roots in the same communities as their victims, so for a trafficking victim to go back to their hometown can be very dangerous.

The TVPA also made recognized trafficking victims eligible for the same assistance offered to refugees settling in the United States, including cash and medical assistance during their first eight months here, as well as English language classes. Case management—coordinating referrals to services—also became available.

Both the US law and the international law address trafficking for labor and for sex. Sex work, specifically prostitution, is recognized as labor in some countries but not others; for this reason, a footnote in the international law addressing trafficking signed at the United Nations in 2000 explained that each nation could address prostitution according to its national laws. As discussed in the introduction, prostitution in the United States is not recognized as labor and is not afforded labor protection. The US law therefore contains a separate paragraph in the definition of human trafficking that includes force, fraud, and coercion in the sex trades, and stipulates that any minors in the sex trades are defined as victims of sex trafficking. During the drafting process of both laws, human rights advocates worked hard to ensure the inclusion of trafficking for labor, which was part of the initial focus growing out of the cases involving peddlers but was not guaranteed to be retained in the US law, and every effort was made to reduce the likelihood of unintended consequences that would harm sex workers.

At the time, I was part of the Human Rights Caucus, a bloc of nongovernmental organizations advocating at the United Nations for the definition of human trafficking to include not just sex but also forced labor. The caucus included both international groups—such as the Asian Women's Human Rights Council, the Global Alliance Against Traffic in Women, Human Rights Watch, and the International Human Rights Law Group—and US-based groups, such as Break the Chains, the Coalition to Abolish Slavery and Trafficking, and Safe Horizon. As the most junior person in the caucus, I was assigned to reach out to US legislators who we knew would probably not be receptive to our message, Senators Strom Thurmond (R-SC) and Orrin Hatch (R-UT). I was told by one of Senator Thurmond's aides that the senator would not vote for any bill that promoted general labor rights. In contrast, they were eager to go on record opposing trafficking for sex.[7] At the time, conservative and religious groups were interested in reducing human trafficking to a women's issue related to sex. (In the end, both Hatch and Thurmond voted in favor of the bill, as did ninety-three other senators, in a level of bipartisan cooperation unfathomable today.)

This focus on the sex industry at the expense of other workers was also seen from SWERF organizations and faith-based charities—including the Coalition Against Trafficking in Women; End Child Prostitution, Child Pornography and Trafficking of Children for Sexual Purposes (ECPAT); Equality Now; and the Salvation Army—who wanted the international law and the US law to further criminalize prostitution and other forms of sex work.[8] These organizations have also supported newer laws making it difficult for sex workers to advertise; these laws will be discussed in chapter 14.

FUNDING SERVICES FOR TRAFFICKED PERSONS

When President George W. Bush, a conservative Christian, took office in 2001, he encouraged the funding from the newly passed TVPA to go to faith-based organizations, who would then coordinate the provision of services to survivors. A no-bid federal contract was awarded to the US Conference of Catholic Bishops (CCB) to manage all TVPA funding. For the first ten years after the passage of the law, the CCB forbade its grantees to discuss contraception and abortion with their clients. The American Civil Liberties Union (ACLU) sued the government over this issue in 2009 and won in 2011. While the CCB is now compelled to allow its grantees to address reproductive health care, it does not pay for this necessary care from the federal grants it manages.

The Office of Refugee Resettlement (ORR) ensures that foreign nationals who are victims of trafficking receive the same package of assistance and services as refugees; minors who are survivors of trafficking are placed in the Unaccompanied Refugee Minors program. Between 2017 and 2020, the director of ORR, Scott Lloyd, a Trump appointee, required all unaccompanied minors in the office's care to get his personal permission to access abortion care, and required providers to track the menstrual cycles of all female minors. If any were pregnant, they were to be taken to pregnancy centers, usually Christian organizations that encourage pregnant people to carry their pregnancies to term. ORR tried to force childbirth on the seventeen-year-old plaintiff in the case that overturned this policy.[9] Right-wing Christian anti-abortion politics have impeded the efficacy of the TVPA by inhibiting women's access to reproductive health care, even in cases of women whose histories included rape, forced abortion, and sexually transmitted infections.

A HUMAN RIGHTS FRAMEWORK OFFERS A BETTER RESPONSE

The fact that the US response to human trafficking is rooted in the criminal justice system affects outcomes for survivors. Survivors do not receive the care they deserve because the criminal justice system is punitive and intended to prosecute crimes. However, as we will see in the next chapters, while there are some high-profile cases, ultimately, few traffickers are prosecuted. Leanne McCallum, former coordinator for the Greater New Orleans Human Trafficking Task Force, said, "We are so focused on traffickers that we don't heal survivors, and we don't punish traffickers."[10] A human rights approach would emphasize survivors' recovery and self-determination. It would not require cooperation with prosecution and would review T visa applications in a way that didn't penalize those lacking letters of support from law enforcement. It would not include detaining survivors as material witnesses if they declined to cooperate with the prosecution. In the best-case scenario, a human rights approach would support trafficked workers' efforts to advocate for themselves, individually in some cases and collectively in others, similar to how unions representing a large workforce advocate for the workers' interests.

Despite the limitations of the TVPA, the law has made it possible for some of the people (whose stories I share in later chapters) to seek justice. As we shall see, the TVPA has enabled trafficked domestic workers such as Nena Ruiz and Judith Daluz (see chapter 6) to pursue restitution in the form of wages and damages, and to obtain a visa to remain and work in the United States. The TVPA is also the law that was used to prosecute the owners of C&C Farms in Clewiston, Florida, where Marlyn Perez (see chapter 3) and her coworkers were threatened, assaulted, and denied safe working conditions. And when the Mexican immigrant Flor (see chapter 10) participated in the prosecution of the family that had forced her into prostitution, that too took place under the auspices of the TVPA.

The TVPA and its subsequent reauthorization acts have benefited thousands of people in the past twenty years. Yet there have been many more missed opportunities to assist people in trafficking situations. For example, the young people on traveling sales crews have not been helped by the TVPA. Even though there have always been statutes that could be used to address the crimes committed in these situations—fraud, assault, and battery—young people in these situations had difficulty realizing their rights long before the TVPA was enacted, as demonstrated in the previous chapter. These problems thus are less about the existence of laws than their implementation. Law enforcement tends to focus on sex work situations rather than work situations, and sales crews move jurisdiction frequently, leaving one location for another in a different county or state, which hampers local investigations.

Law enforcement is not the only system that has overlooked young Americans in trafficking situations. The Children's Bureau of the Department of Health and Human Services and particularly its National Child Abuse and Neglect Data System (NCANDS), also lacks a focus on minors in these situations. Trafficking cases involving minors are reported to the NCANDS, but the focus of the system is on sexual abuse; labor trafficking falls under the category of "other."[11] The label "other" would indicate that the people who created this form did not anticipate that minors would be involved in trafficking for labor, and the variety of situations, like that of young people on traveling sales crews or in agriculture, predictable as they are, remain undifferentiated in NCANDS data. Furthermore, the TVPA was drafted with people from other countries in mind, and the services offered were tailored to their situations; this means that the assistance provided survivors is the same as refugees from other countries receive, which may not meet the needs of young US citizens like those on sales crews, who would not benefit from, for example, English language classes. Their needs are different.

A variety of factors contribute to these missed opportunities. One is a flawed identification process, in which the law enforcement arm of the federal government—instead of a human rights agency or related entity—determines who qualifies as an eligible trafficking victim entitled to remain in the country, usually on the basis of that person's willingness to cooperate with law enforcement, rather than basing the determination upon human rights. Some trafficked people are deported before being identified; unless an immigration raid on a workplace is coordinated with an anti-trafficking unit, it is unlikely that the authorities will screen to identify trafficked persons. Sometimes, people who have been deported are brought back to the United States in trafficking situations.[12] In such cases, because the authorities did not intervene, these individuals were made susceptible to being trafficked a second time.

Even when victims cooperate, not all cases culminate in prosecution. Moreover, the prosecution process can be another traumatic event for victims, who may be subjected to aggressive questioning by attorneys defending the alleged trafficker. Some victims choose to return to their native countries rather than cooperate with prosecutors, sometimes out of fear of retribution against their families. Even in the best cases, the process of cooperation can be profoundly stressful. Many victim-witnesses lead precarious lives with low-paying jobs, often in the same job sector they worked in during their trafficking ordeal. They may have to miss work to attend court, losing wages for those days or even losing their jobs altogether.

A rights-based approach would prioritize the recovery of the survivors, and success would be measured based on their well-being: Do survivors have secure housing? Do they have access to trauma-informed services?

Are they moving forward in their new lives? A victim-centered approach would not require cooperation with law enforcement to prosecute, but this does not necessarily mean that prosecution would be undermined. Survivors who feel supported may be better able to face the court process and offer better testimony.

PART II

TRAFFICKING IN AGRICULTURE

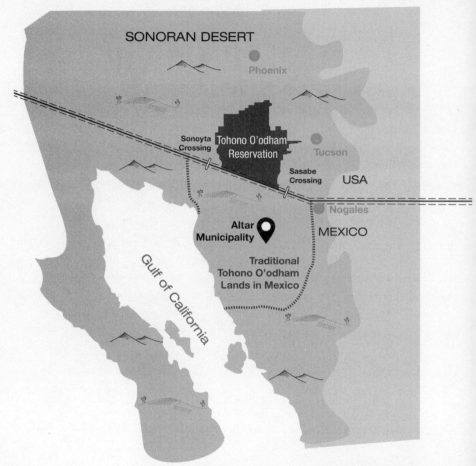

Marlyn crossed the border from Mexico into the United States in the Sonoran Desert. Map by Jack Taylor.

CHAPTER 3

IN THE DEVIL'S GARDEN

U S HISTORY INCLUDES multiple episodes of compulsory labor in agriculture, including indenture, enslavement, peonage, prison labor, and present-day human trafficking. This section opens with the story of Marlyn Perez, who survived a trafficking situation on a farm in Florida. Marlyn's case occurred in the twenty-first century, a recent episode in America's long history of forced labor in agriculture. This is followed by a chapter that traces the history of such exploitation back to the ages of indenture and enslavement. This section concludes with a chapter about the postbellum transition to agricultural prison labor and peonage.

Marlyn Perez grew up in La Libertad, a small farming town in Guatemala. The town has a population of only a few thousand, and when Marlyn was growing up many of the houses were made of earth with sheet metal roofs and had neither running water nor electricity. Marlyn's family grew and sold coffee beans, supplementing their farming income by weaving baskets to sell. Her father also worked as a bricklayer, but the family did not always have enough money to buy food and they often went hungry. When her father was away, her mother would travel for hours to find work to feed her family.

Marlyn attended school for only two years, then married when she was fourteen and had her first child at sixteen. This is not exceptional in small towns in Central America. She and her husband also farmed to support their three children. Because her husband drank too much and was violent, eventually Marlyn divorced him and moved to another town.

Marlyn's younger brother was stabbed in church when he was eighteen years old. The family has never learned the reason for the attack, which remains a mystery. Taken to the nearest hospital, the boy received medical treatment that saved his life, but the danger of further violence meant that he could not remain in La Libertad. He ended up moving to the same town that Marlyn had moved to after her divorce. There, however, the perpetrator of the assault continued to threaten him. This ongoing threat of violence is one of the reasons Marlyn listed in her eventual decision to leave Guatemala.

In 2011, when the oldest of her three children was ten years old, Marlyn headed north, alone, traveling first to Mexico and later to the United States. From Guatemala, she crossed the border into the state of Chiapas, Mexico. At the border, she asked where to get a bus to the next city. At each new city she would ask the same questions: where is the road to the next city, and where could she get a bus to the next destination? "Ya me iba asi asi," she said. "I was going like this and that."[1] From the border, she took a bus to Comitán and then a second to Tuxtla Gutiérrez, the state capital. From Tuxtla, she bought a bus ticket to Mexico City. From Mexico City, she took a final bus to Altar, a desert town of fewer than ten thousand people near the Arizona border. She was now more than two thousand miles from where she started.

Altar is almost two hours from the US border and is a known route for coyotes—paid guides who smuggle people across the border and into the United States. Marlyn spent ten days there, asking around to find the right person to help her cross the border. She searched for someone willing to accept payment *after* she reached the United States, because she knew that people who paid before departure were vulnerable to being abandoned en route, leaving them no option but to go back and try again to save the thousands of dollars needed to pay another coyote. On her last day in Altar, she finally met an elderly man who said that he knew someone who could help her.

There are two official border crossings in the region, one at the town of Sasabe, near the Buenos Aires Wildlife Refuge in Arizona, and a second at Sonoyta Valley, at the entrance to Organ Pipe Cactus National Monument, where a section of an anti-immigration wall was erected at the border.[2] The Tohono O'odhom Nation reservation straddles the border between these two official border crossings. Migrants heading north frequently cross into the United States through the reservation.

Conditions in the Sonoran Desert are extremely harsh and there is very little water. Hundreds of people have died trying to cross the border here.[3] Humanitarian groups set out jugs of water for people trying to cross the desert so that they won't die of thirst, but the water jugs are sometimes destroyed by officials or anti-immigrant groups.

Marlyn, the coyote, and another woman walked off the road into the desert and headed north. Nights were cold and days were hot. Like many other travelers before them, they lost their way. They wandered in the desert for ten days, during which the sun burned them in the day, and they lived in fear of scorpions and snakes when they slept at night. They ran out of water and food and nearly died. When they finally found a road, they were intercepted by the Border Patrol, which detained Marlyn for a month before deporting her back to Mexico.

Deportees are often simply deported to the closest town on the Mexican side of the border. When Marlyn set out again, she had to cross the same stretch of desert where she had nearly died before. This time, however, she evaded the Border Patrol and entered the United States successfully.

Marlyn came to the United States expecting to work hard but believing she would be able to find a decent job. Her employment options were limited because she was undocumented. She was able to find a job in agriculture, but found it was unrelated to the kind of farming that she'd known in Guatemala. She and her family had farmed small plots; in the United States, she found herself working on much larger farms that grew crops very different from the coffee she had grown at home.

The work paid little, but it paid, and Marlyn picked crops in several different locations in the southeastern United States. Then a friend and farm coworker suggested they go to a different farm that promised more money per hour and many hours of paid work.

Reyes Tapia-Ortiz was a farm labor contractor who recruited people to work in the fields on C&C Farms in Clewiston, Florida. He hired farmworkers to plant, pick, and pack crops that included tomatoes, squash, peppers, cucumbers, and other vegetables for distribution throughout the country. The farm was owned by Ernesto Ruben Cordero Jr. and Carlos Rodriguez, and workers were jointly employed by Tapia-Ortiz, Cordero, and Rodriguez.

Cordero also supervised workers in the fields. Between 2008 and 2012, Tapia-Ortiz recruited workers in Immokalee, Clewiston, and other towns, finding them in places where day laborers gathered. In the summer of 2011, it was through Tapia-Ortiz's recruitment that Marlyn ended up at C&C Farms. "I ended up in the job because another worker, Paulino, already had the number of the boss and said I should take the job with him," Marlyn says. "We called, and the boss came by to pick us up and then we were in the job."

Clewiston is a city of seven thousand near Lake Okeechobee, about ninety minutes west of Miami. Farmland extends from the city limits throughout the flat, fertile landscape of the Everglades, which was cultivated for sugar a century ago. C&C Farms was on the outskirts of Clewiston, about twenty minutes southwest of town.

Clewiston lies in a part of Florida known as the Devil's Garden. The region takes its name from a Seminole man known as Sam Jones, or Abiaki, who led a resistance against US soldiers during their campaign to relocate natives of the southeastern states to Oklahoma. Jones/Abiaki was also known as "the Devil" to his enemies for his apparent ability to be in many places at once.[4] He fought against the removal of Seminole people and is singularly credited with the Seminole Tribe of Florida not being moved to the Seminole Nation of Oklahoma, where other Seminole people were forcibly relocated starting in 1832.[5] A successful strategist, Jones ensured that Seminole people had enough to eat by growing crops in the area later called the Devil's Garden. Part of the area has since been returned to its natural state and is now named the Sam Jones/Abiaki Prairie.[6]

Marlyn found that the working conditions at C&C Farms were not as promised. There was no shade in the fields, no water, and no place to shelter during thunderstorms. There were no toilets nearby, and workers were punished for going to the bathroom or taking breaks from the sun. "From the beginning, the conditions were bad," Marlyn said. "I didn't know my rights in that time or the laws in this country; I had just gotten here from Guatemala."

In addition, people working on C&C Farms were exposed to pesticides that were sprayed on the fields several times each month. They were given no warning or opportunity to move to a place where they would not be exposed, nor offered equipment to shield them from the toxic spray. Instead, Tapia-Ortiz forced them to continue to work. The pesticides burned their eyes and skin, so they wore hats and covered their faces, arms, and

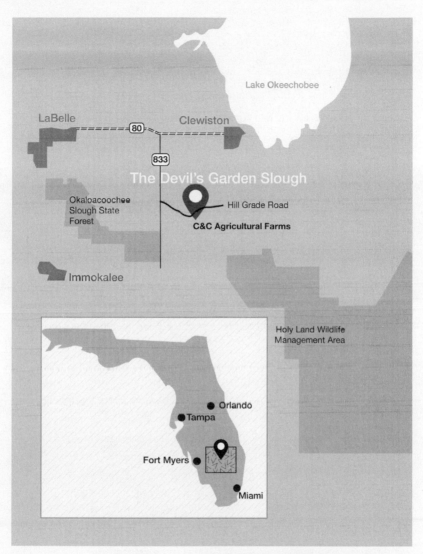

*Marlyn worked in the Devil's Garden area between
Clewiston and Immokalee. Map by Jack Taylor.*

hands as much as possible. Pesticide exposure caused headaches, burning eyes, skin rashes, and nausea. There was no way to wash off the pesticides while they were in the fields, as the only water available to rinse their eyes or skin after exposure to the irritating chemicals was the water that they carried with them.

Marlyn and the other farmworkers were charged seven dollars for lunch and five dollars for transportation to and from the fields every day, the equivalent of more than an entire hour of the wages they had been promised. Drinks, which were also charged, cost a dollar fifty for soda and two dollars and fifty cents for beer. Beer seems a surprising inclusion, but Tapia-Ortiz was well known for drinking beer in the fields. The photographs used to identify him during court proceedings included one of him holding a beer while driving.

Workdays ran from first daylight in the fields until long after dark in the packing house. The farmworkers typically worked ten to twelve hours in the fields, sometimes longer. After working outside all day, they were forced to pack the vegetables for an additional three or four hours or more, meaning a workday could run as long as seventeen hours. Tapia-Ortiz told them that they would not be paid for the day's work if they did not work at night too. Conditions inside the packing house, as in the fields, were bad; toilets were not always available and were too filthy to use when they were, so workers relieved themselves outside. That required sneaking out, as workers were reprimanded for leaving the packing house. For these long hours in dangerous and unsanitary conditions, women were paid an average of just $35 per day and men $45 per day, far below minimum wage, and far below the $7 per hour wage promised, by which workers would earn $56 for an eight-hour day, and more for the longer days they actually worked. Seven-day workweeks were routine. Workers also sometimes had to wait for hours after the end of their workday for transportation to the trailers where they lived, where they could finally wash and rest. Like many immigrants, Marlyn sent most of her wages home to her family.

Some of the workers might have been happy to work long hours if they had received the hourly wage they had been promised. However, even taking into account the deductions for transportation and food, the pay never matched the actual hours worked. While farm administrators were supposed to keep records of the hours each person worked, workers were never given access to ledgers or any kind of itemization of their hours and deductions as required by law.[7] Court documents allege that in fact no records were kept.

Marlyn understood that she was being taking advantage of. When she approached Ernesto Cordero, one of the farm owners, about not being paid correctly, he was unconcerned. He told her to take it up with Tapia-

Ortiz. "I just took the little money I was given, even though they didn't pay what we were owed," she says. "We worked many long hours. When I went to ask the farm owner about why we were being paid so little, when we'd been promised seven dollars an hour, he said that he didn't know anything because he paid our boss, Tapia, and from there Tapia was supposed to pay us."

Marlyn went on, "When we asked Tapia about the money, he said that we shouldn't be asking about such [a] thing, that we were illegal in this country, so we couldn't demand anything, and if we said anything else, he'd call the police." Tapia-Ortiz threatened Marlyn and others if they ever exposed him for not paying them what they had earned. When Marlyn confronted Tapia-Ortiz, he told her that she could not complain, because without a work visa she could be deported. He told her that troublesome workers could simply disappear. He also said that he would track her down and kill her if she ever left his crew.

These were not idle threats. Tapia-Ortiz kept a rifle in his truck and a handgun by his bed. In the fields, he carried both firearms. He was not the only armed person in the fields; Cordero also used weapons to intimidate the workers whenever they complained about wages or working conditions.

One of the supervisors warned workers that Cordero was dangerous. Cordero often yelled obscenities and threatened workers who were slow or had failed to pick every single vegetable. He said that he could "kill a worker and simply leave the body in a ditch," and told workers that their dead bodies would be eaten by alligators and no one would look for them. He also threatened workers individually, pointing his gun at them, and sometimes fired his gun in the air. When workers had to move tools from his truck, Cordero brandished his gun and said that he would hurt anyone who scratched the vehicle. He did the same thing when a worker leaned against the truck. Unsurprisingly, the workers were afraid of Cordero and talked among themselves about his threats. They agreed that if he did shoot someone they would use sticks and shovels—the only weapons they had—to defend themselves.

Workers had other things to worry about. They were routinely told to break the law, leading them to fear arrest and deportation for those crimes. For example, Marlyn's friend Paulino had no driver's license but was nevertheless tasked with driving the van to transport workers from their trailers to the fields. He knew that if he were pulled over for any reason, driving without a license would likely lead to his arrest and deportation. In addition to this, Paulino was not even paid for his driving time.

Tapia-Ortiz was also routinely violent toward women, including his own wife. One farmworker, known by the pseudonym "Jane," lived in the same trailer as Tapia-Ortiz and his wife. Jane later testified that she saw Tapia-Ortiz hit his wife with a gun, and she was afraid he would shoot her in the night with the pistol he kept under his pillow. Jane's boyfriend, who also lived in the trailer, often heard Tapia-Ortiz beating his wife and regularly saw her bruises. The woman told him that she feared for her life, because Tapia-Ortiz had threatened to kill her if she ever left him. She showed the farmworker that Tapia-Ortiz's handgun was loaded and asked him to help her get a cell phone so that she could call for help when Tapia-Ortiz was violent. She too was isolated and had no one to turn to for help except the farmworkers who were also victims of her husband.

Court documents record that Tapia-Ortiz abused women both physically and sexually. He repeatedly harassed Marlyn, both by phone and in person. He groped her on many occasions when she was in remote fields. When she threatened to go to the police, Tapia-Ortiz threatened her with deportation and showed her the gun in his waistband, telling her that if she left C&C Farms, he would track her down and kill her.

At C&C, Marlyn's experiences with sexual harassment and assault were far from unique or even unusual. Sexual assault in the fields was so common and so overt that one remote field where many assaults had happened was known as the "field of panties."[8]

In addition to harassing Marlyn, Tapia-Ortiz threatened to have Jane's boyfriend deported if Jane did not have sex with him. He required Jane and her boyfriend to live in his trailer and was violent toward them both. In December 2011, after receiving no wages for over two weeks, Jane and her boyfriend told Tapia-Ortiz that they wanted to quit, that they were leaving C&C Farms and moving to another job with a different farm and a different contractor. Tapia-Ortiz responded by saying that he would not pay their back wages unless they stayed on with C&C Farms and told them "they would be sorry" if they did not.

Jane and her boyfriend quit the next day. That night, before they had found another place to live, a man came to the trailer that they shared with Tapia-Ortiz. He wore a uniform and a badge and claimed that there was a warrant for Jane's boyfriend for unpaid court fees. The uniformed man chained Jane's boyfriend's arms and legs. He was delivered to the police in chains and ultimately deported, just as Tapia-Ortiz had threatened would happen.

Court documents make clear that this was not an actual arrest and thus was false imprisonment. The man was not a law enforcement officer but an unlicensed bondsman. When his identity was later discovered, he admitted that he did this at the behest of Tapia-Ortiz.

LEAVING C&C FARMS

After witnessing her boyfriend chained and taken away, Jane was too scared to remain in the trailer. More frightened of her trafficker than of Florida alligators, she spent the rest of the night hiding in the woods, where she was bitten by ants and mosquitos. Other animals crawled on her skin. Two days later, Tapia-Ortiz told her that if she ever told anyone about him arranging for her boyfriend to be seized and deported, he would "burn [her] in the trailer" and "shut her mouth forever."

Soon after, Marlyn also told Tapia-Ortiz that she wanted to quit. Tapia-Ortiz responded by pointing his pistol at her, his finger on the trigger.

Both Marlyn and Jane were convinced that Tapia-Ortiz was capable of carrying out his threats. Fortunately, before he could do so, they were able to make a call to the Fair Food Program's recently introduced hotline. The Fair Food Program (FFP) is a groundbreaking social responsibility program that enforces human rights protections for farmworkers. The FFP was founded in 2011 by the Coalition of Immokalee Workers (CIW), a farmworker-based human rights organization, and was awarded a Presidential Medal of Freedom by the Obama administration in 2015 for its unprecedented success in combatting human trafficking. The program was built on a foundation of legally binding Fair Food agreements with nearly a dozen of the largest food retailers in the world. Today, fourteen companies—including Walmart, McDonald's, Sodexo, and Whole Foods— have signed agreements with the CIW to pay a premium to participating growers, which is passed on to workers, and to preferentially purchase from growers determined to be in compliance with the human rights–based Fair Food Code of Conduct by the Fair Food Standards Council (the third-party monitor that enforces the CIW's agreements).

The CIW conducts worker-to-worker "Know Your Rights" education sessions on all FFP farms. Farmworkers on these farms are able to file complaints with the Fair Food Standards Council. Through its hotline, the CIW also fields complaints about farms not in the FFP, as was the case with C&C Farms. Marlyn explains,

> I got a [Fair Food Program education] booklet that they had made with a phone number I could call for help [when I was working at a different farm before C&C], and also information about all the rights we should have. I called, even though some of the other workers were afraid and said I shouldn't, that we couldn't tell anyone because Tapia would get mad, but I called anyway. Nely, Julia, and Laura from the Coalition [of Immokalee Workers] came to see us the same day that I called; they arrived at where we were staying to talk to us. They have supported us completely, taking on the case. I appreciate that they were there for the whole case.[9]

The CIW has addressed workplace abuses in agriculture since the early 1990s, investigating complaints received from farmworkers and partnering on multiple occasions with federal law enforcement officials in the prosecution of forced labor cases. Although its focus extends beyond human trafficking, heightened national awareness of human trafficking in the early 2000s brought attention to the work of the coalition and acclaim for its efforts. A grassroots worker organization that for the first several years was volunteer-run, the coalition has grown over time to include a small staff, the majority of whom are themselves farmworkers. CIW also retains a base of thousands of farmworkers from the Immokalee community. Those staff members provide the FFP's on-farm, popular education sessions to farmworkers about their rights under the FFP Code of Conduct. The FFP Code requires that participating farms comply with the law and specifies the consequences for various violations, including zero tolerance (in the form of suspension from the FFP) for human trafficking. Those consequences are backed up by the purchasing power of the retail food giants that make up the FFP's cadre of fourteen participating buyers: just as joining the FFP provides the farms access to those important customers, being suspended from the FFP cuts off that access, creating a system of market incentives that drives compliance and has achieved the gold standard in fighting human trafficking—namely, its prevention.

Marlyn and Jane had learned about CIW through one such education program. Before crossing paths again at C&C, they had worked together on an FFP farm where they had attended a "Know Your Rights" presentation by the CIW in 2011. For their part, CIW staff were aware of C&C Farms. They had received a complaint about the farm in 2010, but they had had no new information about conditions there until Jane and Marlyn called in 2012.[10]

Workers who attend CIW workshops are given a booklet that tells them about their rights and are shown a video. The booklet and video are available in English, Spanish, and Haitian Creole. Since the FFP's inception in 2011, CIW has delivered in-person, interactive sessions to over 69,297 workers, and over 298,800 have seen the video and received the booklet at the time they were hired.[11] The sessions take place on the FFP member farms, and workers are compensated for their time spent attending the workshop.

Among the staff members on its education team, CIW counts farm-workers who assisted in the first human trafficking cases prosecuted by the US government under the TVPA.[12] Marlyn's case and others like it revealed a long-standing and ongoing culture of exploitation in American food production. Since the prosecution of these early cases, CIW has pioneered responses to exploitation in agriculture, and the methods it developed have been adapted for use in other sectors of food production and in other industries.

Marlyn was fortunate to have encountered the CIW on an FFP farm and to have received the CIW's support in leaving C&C Farms and having her rights vindicated. Social workers and other service providers say that the best outcomes for survivors are seen in those who are able to leave trafficking situations without the involvement of law enforcement.[13] Trafficking is the only crime for which the victim is routinely arrested. Trafficking investigations conducted by local police or the FBI typically result in the arrests of everyone on-site, regardless of their role. Even when an investigation has been performed, law enforcement may not know who is who in the chaos of a raid. In addition, when Immigration and Customs Enforcement conducts workplace raids, deportation is a likely outcome for immigrants without legal status, including for trafficking victims working on farms and at food processing and meatpacking plants.

IN COURT

On April 10, 2014, a civil suit alleging forced labor and related charges was filed in federal court on behalf of Marlyn and six other C&C workers, including Jane. The charges included violation of the Migrant and Seasonal Agricultural Worker Protection Act, wage and hour violations, and violations of the Trafficking Victims Protection Act, as well as battery, false imprisonment, and sexual harassment. Marlyn and her six colleagues were represented by the Anti-Trafficking Project, an initiative of the International Human Rights Clinic at George Washington University Law School, which was supported by additional local counsel based in Miami.[14] Court cases can be very expensive—simply filing the initial suit incurred a fee of four hundred dollars—and the outcome is always uncertain. Fortunately, the entire case, including filing fees and travel expenses, was undertaken pro bono with resources shared by the GWU Clinic and the Miami law firm. Before the case went to court, there was a criminal investigation, though criminal charges were never ultimately filed.

Plaintiffs were able to testify at the hearing that determined the amount of damages to be awarded. This hearing was held remotely, in part because not all the plaintiffs were still in the United States, as some had already been deported. Even Jane's boyfriend, who had been deported after being unlawfully detained, was thus able to testify.

The case took three years to litigate. Marlyn expressed gratitude for the legal team and other support, saying, "[Our attorneys] and the CIW also helped us to negotiate a settlement with the farm. For all of my court dates and other things I needed to do, the CIW provided transportation, coming to get me and bring me to where I needed to go." Even with this support, Marlyn said that the court case had been particularly hard for her. She and the other plaintiffs still in the United States had had to appear in person at various points in the case.

On days when Marlyn met with attorneys or appeared in court, she missed work and lost wages. It is not clear how much work she missed related to the civil case, but regardless, it felt like an enormous sacrifice for someone living paycheck to paycheck while also supporting children and relatives in another country. I asked Marlyn what could have been done to make her situation easier after escaping this horrible experience. She said, "It would have been helpful to have more financial support." Losing wages worsened her already precarious financial situation, and the long case was difficult both emotionally and mentally. Moreover, while her T visa application was pending, her irregular immigration status left her at constant risk of deportation, and at one point, she was even in immigration detention (which is legally distinct from prison). She could have chosen to be sent to Guatemala, but she wanted to hold her traffickers accountable and see the lawsuit through. Finally, US Customs and Immigration Services approved Marlyn's application for a T visa. However, the travel restrictions associated with the T visa meant that Marlyn was unable to visit her family.

The court case brought by Marlyn and her colleagues was finally decided in their favor in 2017. C&C Farms itself was terminated as a company on June 2, 2015, its assets liquidated. Reyes Tapia-Ortiz was personally served with papers notifying him of the civil case in 2014, but because he never responded and failed to make an in-court appearance, the court entered a default judgment against him. On the basis of information shared during the damages hearing, the judge awarded the plaintiffs a total of over $3 million in damages.[15] Some, but not all, received back wages and unpaid wages through the settlement with C&C Farms, but they will probably never see the money awarded as damages. Tapia-Ortiz did not appear in court at any time during the proceedings and may have left the country. While the seven people who brought the suit are gratified that he is no longer part of their lives, real justice remains elusive.

Today, Marlyn Perez has a manufacturing job in another state. She likes the regular hours and paid holidays, and the wages are better. She has better housing. Her family is now in the United States with legal status. Marlyn has come far from the subsistence farming community where she grew up. To help people who find themselves in situations like that at C&C Farms, she has also provided peer education as a CIW trainer, visiting farms and telling the workers there about their rights. She has also spoken to non-farmworker audiences about her experience, so that they can better understand the realities faced by farmworkers and support efforts to transform those realities. "It feels good to me to talk about it," Marlyn says, "because I know that there may be others out there in my situation, and I hope that they can also get the help and support that I was able to get."

CHAPTER 4

INDENTURE, SLAVERY, AND CONTRACT LABOR IN AGRICULTURE

T HROUGHOUT THE SEVENTEENTH and eighteenth centuries, European colonists in North America worked to build shelter and cultivate food crops on land usurped from Indigenous tribes. These tasks required a great deal of labor, prompting these early settlers to seek out sources of cheap or unpaid workers.

Indenture was a large part of US immigration throughout the colonial era and into the nineteenth century. Many people entered into indenture, in which they guaranteed their future work to finance their passage, as a way to cover the high costs of traveling to the United States from Europe. Indentured servants recruited from the British underclass were estimated to comprise at least half of people arriving in the North American colonies.[1] After the Thirty Years' War (1618–1648), many indentured servants also came from continental Europe. Most were men and adolescent boys. Some indentured servants from Europe were free people of color; Black people who came to the American colonies from Europe were Christians and indentured, not enslaved. Ship owners and captains who were in the business of transporting these passengers to North America would first broker indenture contracts between the passengers and "masters" in North America who paid for the indentured servants' passage. In return, the masters were entitled to the servants' labor for a fixed period of time, usually between four and seven years. Under the terms of the contract, servants were entitled to receive room and board. For the young, indenture ideally included receiving an education and learning a trade. Some indentured servants were effectively apprentices learning trades. Indentured servants who already knew a trade, like carpentry, could command more advantageous terms, such as shorter periods of service. Although indenture worked out for people whose employers treated them well and helped them to develop useful skills, the system of indenture was also subject to abuse. Many indentured servants had their contracts forcibly extended, were made to work without pay, or were subjected to physical abuse.

Some indentured servants were people convicted of crimes in Great Britain and sentenced to expulsion to the country's penal colonies, including the future United States of America. In the beginning, convicts and voluntary indentured servants had similar contracts. Prior to 1718, some convicts volunteered to go to the colonies. In 1718, the British Parliament passed the Transportation Act, after which approximately fifty thousand convicts were transported between that year and 1775, when transportation was halted in the run-up to the Revolutionary War. More than 95 percent of these transported convicts were sent to the Chesapeake Bay area; approximately 80 percent were young men, most of whom had been convicted of petty theft. As the number of convicts sent from England increased after 1718, their treatment in the New World changed. Transported convicts were blamed for crime in Maryland and Virginia, and they were treated similarly to farm animals or enslaved people in that they were chained together and driven to be sold. Virginia passed a statute in 1748 denying them the right to give evidence in court.[2]

Travel to North America was not easy. Descriptions of travel conditions include high rates of malnourishment, disease, and mortality among indentured servants.[3] Many who survived the journey died during their first year in the New World from diseases like malaria and yellow fever that were not present in Northern Europe. Fewer than half lived out their servitude to enjoy freedom. While indenture was contractually time-bound, the duration was sometimes extended via additional travel expenses that masters tacked onto their servants' debt. People who were indentured were subject to strong constraints that left them with little recourse should they find themselves in an abusive situation. They were unable to leave their situations legally and could be punished for running away by having their term of indenture extended. When indenture worked out well for the servant, it was a sacrifice toward their future free life, but others suffered abuses akin to those found in today's human trafficking. Masters could sell the remaining time of their servants' indenture to another master.[4] In the colony of Virginia, if servants married, their period of servitude could be extended by a year.[5]

Those who did live through their indenture soon found that the supposedly limitless arable land to which they were entitled at the end of their servitude did not exist, as the best land had been claimed. Servants who attained freedom were pushed to the edges of their home colony, where the land was more difficult to farm and abutted land still controlled by Indigenous people. In these border areas, fighting was constant. Given these circumstances, the interests of indentured servants of all races, enslaved people, and free working-class people were aligned against the colonial elites who held people in servitude and had the best land and opportunities to prosper.

This inequality was the context when, in 1676, Nathaniel Bacon led an armed rebellion against the governor of Virginia with approximately four hundred armed people, including enslaved people and indentured servants, who burned the colonial capital. This event has been portrayed as a multiracial, class-oriented uprising, but the source of the conflict may in fact have been the governor's hesitance to kill the local native peoples, the Doeg, Occaneechi, Patawomeck, and Rappahannock. Bacon and other newcomers to the colony, including people who had completed their term of indenture, held land at the perimeter of the territory and wanted to kill and remove the Indigenous people living there, while the colonial governor was less bloodthirsty.[6] However, perhaps the greed and corruption of the governor and fellow elites were also key factors, because newer scholarship postulates that Bacon's Rebellion may have been rooted in the resentment of the governing class.[7]

Fearing a unified lower class in the aftermath of Bacon's uprising, Virginia's colonial elites now sought to set enslaved people, who were overwhelmingly Black, apart from indentured servants. Also, the landowning class of colonists increasingly preferred enslaving people over having indentured servants. Global factors worked in their favor: the slave trade grew, the numbers of enslaved people brought from Africa increased, and slavery expanded, along with the British empire. By 1700, the number of enslaved people in Virginia had grown, and many formerly low-status white people had become more established economically; on the basis of whiteness, the interests of white people in Virginia now aligned across class and counter to the interests of Indigenous and enslaved people.

Some indentured servants chose to break their contracts and run away. Ben Franklin wrote that upon his arrival in Philadelphia in 1723, "several sly questions were asked me, as it seemed to be suspected from my youth and appearance, that I might be some runaway."[8] Some who fled, as in the case of Victor, a Dutchman, and James Gregory, a Scot, both of whom were indentured to Hugh Gwyn, were punished by courts with thirty lashes and a year added to their term of indenture. In contrast, another man who'd run away with them, a "negro" named John Punch, was ordered to serve in bondage for the duration of his life. Indentured servants Christopher Miller and Peter Wilcocke were branded with the letter R after running away a second time and forced to wear shackles for a year.[9] Newspapers and periodicals carried advertisements for runaway indentured servants, similar to advertisements for runaway chattel slaves, with rewards offered for their return.[10]

The courts did not necessarily punish physical abuse of indentured servants. One illustrative case is that of Humut and Margaret Godfrey, an American-born couple who indentured themselves to a John Cook in Virginia in the 1740s. After Humut was injured and could not perform his duties, Cook cut the family's rations. When Margaret Godfrey had the temerity to complain about her husband's pain to Mrs. Cook, the overseer of Cook's tobacco farm whipped her, then tied her up to continue whipping her. Humut Godfrey went to Mrs. Cook, who did not intervene. He then tried to untie his wife, at which point the overseer beat him until blood came out of his ear. The Godfreys tried to take their employers to court, but the case was not accepted.[11] The Godfreys' case shows that not all indentured servants were immigrants; they also included impoverished American-born people, and their stories have a number of similarities to the abuses that occur in slavery or contemporary human trafficking: physical abuse, the refusal to accept any complaints, overwork to the point of injury, and deliberate deprivation of food.

By the start of the nineteenth century, it seems the number of indentured servants who were immigrants was waning. Falling travel costs may have been one factor, as people no longer needed indenture as a way of paying the costs of their passage to the New World. The availability of white indentured servants therefore declined.[12] Another factor was the increasing acceptance of chattel slavery, rooted in the ideology of white supremacy (which increased after Bacon's Rebellion), and the availability of enslaved African and African American people. Indentured servitude did continue into the nineteenth century, but after American independence from Great Britain it declined steadily until it was largely supplanted by chattel slavery.[13]

ENSLAVED PEOPLE IN AMERICA

Enslaved Africans and African Americans built the colonial and post-colonial American economy. Slavery was immensely profitable to enslavers: not only did they enjoy free labor; they could also hire out their enslaved people and collect the profit (enslaved people hired out in this way earned only half the rates of free workers). Enslaved workers toiled in agriculture, domestic work, building, and many other kinds of labor.

By the nineteenth century, even work requiring specific training and tools was being done by chattel slaves. This growing reliance on unpaid labor led to worsening working conditions and reduced wages for all workers, no matter their expertise, no matter whether they were enslaved, indentured, or free. The initial investment to purchase an enslaved person may have been high, but overall it was less costly than paying the wage a free person would demand for similar work over a comparable period of time.[14] A daily rate for wage labor cost approximately 44 percent more than the expense of using enslaved workers; according to other calculations based on an annual rate range, wage labor could cost between 67 percent and 219 percent more.[15] Slave labor was so much less expensive than free labor that Southern industries became internationally competitive; however, it may have impeded economic development in other ways as immigrants avoided the South because wages were so depressed by the use of enslaved labor.[16]

Given that one group was predominantly Black and the other group predominantly white, slavery and indenture had strong racial dimensions. Native American Indigenous people were also enslaved and were sold elsewhere out of the colonies in order to impede their ability to escape and to prevent against attacks by their ethnic compatriots.[17] Africans became the dominant enslaved population in part because the transatlantic slave trade did not include the risk of incurring war, as did capturing people from nearby native communities.

Advertisement for a sale of enslaved people, 1857. Courtesy
Alabama Department of Archives and History.

Enslaved people were brought to the New World primarily as agricultural workers. Their labor was used for extremely labor-intensive cash
crops like sugar, tobacco, and cotton, all grown in the southern colonies.
The slave labor camps on which they worked were known as plantations, a
general term that might cover anything from a modest tobacco patch to a
cotton farm covering thousands of acres. Farmers were known as planters.
Planting is hard work, and many British colonists were unfamiliar with
farming in warm climates such as the American South. People from Africa
enslaved in the colonies contributed more than just physical labor. They
brought African expertise and farming methods for crops such as rice to
the New World.

During the colonial period, each British colony was legally separate, and
the laws about work and slavery were enacted differently in each location;
no laws affirmed slavery, even as it was practiced in nearly all the colonies.
The exception was Georgia, which was founded as a colony settled by
convicts who would be reformed through labor; enslavement of Africans
was not permitted. This commitment to freedom did not last, however;
white Georgian residents saw the prosperity gained by slave owners in
neighboring colonies and wanted that for themselves.[18]

Three-quarters of white Southerners did not enslave others. Among
those who did, most owned fewer than ten enslaved people, while a tiny
minority owned many more, even hundreds. So much wealth was amassed
by these elite slaveholders that "output created by enslaved men, women,
and children in 1859 was of a comparable magnitude to the total value
of wages received by all manufacturing workers in the United States in

1859."[19] Simultaneously, inequality increased between slaveholders and non-slaveholders. Those who did not hold slaves fell into economic precarity, losing land and becoming tenant farmers; many left the South for the West in the decade before the Civil War.[20]

The cotton gin, invented in 1793, made it easier and faster to process cotton to be turned into thread and woven into fabric. Once it was possible to process as much cotton as could be grown, the demand for land on which to grow cotton increased enormously, leading to the renewed usurping of land from Indigenous people; this appropriated land was then sold to planters.[21] The increased acreage available for cotton cultivation increased the demand for enslaved field laborers to plant, grow, and pick the crop. Cotton provided over half of US export earnings. The wealth generated created new demands for consumer goods and for financial services.[22]

SLAVERY AND RELIGION IN THE COLONIES

For a time in the seventeenth and eighteenth centuries, slaves could sometimes gain their freedom by converting to Christianity. A 1705 declaration of the colony of Virginia stated,

- That all servants brought into this country without indenture, if the said servants be Christians and of Christian parentage, and above nineteen years of age, shall serve but five years; and if under nineteen years of age, 'till they shall become twenty-four years of age, and no longer.
- That all servants imported and brought into this country by sea or land, who were not Christians in their native country . . . shall be accounted and be slaves, and as such be here bought and sold notwithstanding a conversion to Christianity afterwards.[23]

State laws like this were not uncommon throughout slave states, and some slaves were able to sue for manumission by proving that they had been baptized. Maryland was the first of the original colonies to close this loophole in 1639, declaring that Christian baptism did not confer freedom.[24] Once conversion could no longer free enslaved people, race became a basis for chattel slavery. As the cost of indentured servants rose during the seventeenth century, demand for chattel slaves increased.

Chattel slavery is associated primarily with the American South, but Northern states also permitted slavery until 1804; New York City's slave market was located where Wall Street met the East River.[25] However, slave labor was not the foundational basis of the economy in most of the North.

TREATMENT OF ENSLAVED PEOPLE

Mistreatment of enslaved people was routine. They were punished physically at the whim of their owners and overseers. In a small number of cases, the courts forced slave owners to treat their enslaved people better and imposed penalties for abuse. One such case involved a mixed-race (then called mulatto) woman whose ears had been cut off by her owner in Maryland in 1692, and who was freed as a result of this mutilation; this led to the drafting of a clause stipulating the "humane treatment" of slaves.[26] In general, however, the laws did little to protect enslaved people, and gave owners license to do whatever they wanted to them. In 1669, the colony of Virginia declared that it was not a crime to kill an enslaved person in the course of punishment.[27] Another kind of death sentence for enslaved people was that of being sold and sent further south, to the Caribbean, where many slaves were worked to death in sugarcane fields. Tom, one of hundreds of enslaved people at Mount Vernon, the Virginia estate of George Washington, was punished for running away by being sold to slaveholders in the Caribbean. Washington gave specific instructions to the ship's crew to keep him in chains until they were at sea.[28]

In the early days of American slavery, work in the fields was not delegated by gender. Enslaved men and women did much the same work, clearing land, planting, weeding, harvesting, and processing crops. Field-work tasks also included butchering livestock, distributing dung to fertilize fields, hoeing, planting, plowing, and weaving baskets.[29] As slave labor became more widespread, slaves were assigned to other tasks; consequently, by the end of the eighteenth century, slaves were working in trades. Since men were more likely to be trained in a trade, by 1799 women outnumbered men as field workers.[30]

Trade workers who were enslaved included potters, carpenters, coopers, masons, blacksmiths, millers, and distillers. They were hired out and generated significant income for their owners. In some cases, they were able to sell their work and earn money for themselves, and in a very few cases, they earned enough to be able to purchase their own freedom. Leander Fairchild, for example, an enslaved man who lived in South Carolina during the colonial era, was hired out by his owners to Jacob Williman, a butcher. He negotiated with his slaveholders the amount of money he should bring them each day. He also negotiated with Williman to hold the extra money he earned, keeping a ledger of the amounts. Ultimately, Fairchild was able to purchase his freedom from the owners for nine hundred South Carolina pounds through Williman, who coordinated Fairchild's purchase and manumission in 1770.[31]

The existence of a pool of unpaid laborers led to worsened conditions for agricultural laborers and all people doing menial work, whether they were free people, convict indentured servants, or chattel slaves. A would-be worker from Georgia lamented that "the slaveholders could get the slave for almost nothing and the poor young men like myself, could not get a job" in the 1850s.[32] In places where enslaved people were given training for trades, conditions for other workers in those trades worsened as well. Slavery was economically detrimental for everyone who did not themselves own land or slaves.

INDIGENOUS SLAVEHOLDERS

During the eighteenth and nineteenth centuries, some Indigenous peoples also enslaved Africans and African Americans.[33] Some Choctaw and Chickasaw planters in the southeastern US had large farms that were worked by African American slaves. When, in 1830, the federal government forcibly moved these tribes from the southeast to reserved "Indian Territory" in what is now Oklahoma, they took their slaves with them. In this way, the brutal displacement of native tribes enabled the controversial westward expansion of slavery.

As white settlers moved west, they sought more land. By 1854, Indigenous residents of Indian Territory had feared white settlers would displace them once more and take over the Oklahoma lands on which they now lived. Chickasaw and Choctaw slaveholders sought to preserve their assets, both land and enslaved people. Indian Territory was transformed into farmland by enslaved people tasked with clearing land for cotton, corn, and livestock. Enslaved people also tended the crops and cattle. Enslaved women were not only expected to bear and care for their own children

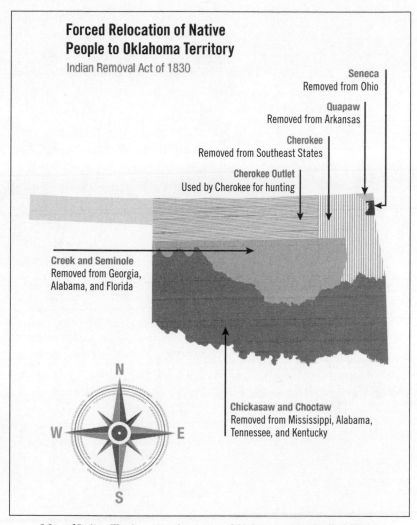

Map of Indian Territory in what is now Oklahoma, 1830. By Jack Taylor.

but, as in slave states, they also were ordered to wet-nurse and care for the children of slaveholders, which women resisted either by refusing to do or by minimizing their response when called for in a kind of work slowdown.[34] Punishment for "unruly" behavior included whipping, and eventually, by the 1850s, the territory's government enacted laws to control the behavior of enslaved people.[35] Some enslaved people rebelled violently, killing their slaveholders or overseers; those presumed to be involved were sometimes lynched.[36] Enslaved people who ran away from the Choctaw and Chickasaw were actively hunted, with advertisements and notices posted with details about their flight.[37] While enslaved people in Indian Territory ran to the west or to Texas en route to Mexico, those fleeing slave states ran to Indian Territory. Such instances raised questions about tribal sovereignty with respect to slavery.[38]

Enslaved people in Indian Territory were not emancipated until 1866—three years after the Emancipation Proclamation—because the question of sovereignty wasn't settled until a year after the end of the Civil War. In 1883, the Choctaw Nation granted African American residents tribal citizenship, with restrictions on marriage (they were only to marry other people of African descent); the Chickasaw never did so.[39] Freedpeople were allied with the native population in that neither group wanted their land to be vulnerable to white squatters, as had been the case in Mississippi and Alabama. Some of the freedpeople in Indian Territory were given the forty acres that General William Tecumseh Sherman had promised to formerly enslaved people in Special Field Orders, No. 15, issued in 1865. The forty-acre promise was rescinded in the eastern states, a move with long-lasting ramifications as it contributes still to today's racial wealth gap.[40] As of 1900, freedpeople who benefited from this land transfer on Cherokee land in Oklahoma had higher incomes, greater literacy, and better school attendance than freedpeople in the former Confederacy.[41]

POSTBELLUM CONTRACT LABORERS IN AGRICULTURE

In the years after the Civil War, Southern plantation owners and lawmakers believed that freed Blacks would demand "excessive" wages for agricultural labor. Planters and other former slaveholders claimed that Emancipation had led to a labor shortage. The truth was that workers were available, but no one was willing to work like slaves had to work. Thirty Swedes who had been imported by one planter in 1866 walked off the job after being housed in slave cabins and fed slave rations.[42] This led to rising numbers of imported Chinese laborers contracted to do the agricultural labor in the American South.

Importation of Chinese laborers had started in the American West before the Civil War, with most arriving in California. Postbellum, some of these workers were brought to do work on the Southern plantations. The status of these laborers was reminiscent of that of European indentured servants in eastern states. Their contracts differed from those of European and American indentured servants in that there was a provision in the Chinese laborer contract for return passage to their country of origin after a fixed number of years. On this matter, the Chinese workers' desire to be buried near their families aligned with American efforts to maintain a white society.

Some Chinese contract workers produced food crops in California's Central Valley. Others picked cotton and cut sugarcane in Louisiana and elsewhere. Like other exploited groups, the Chinese resisted the terrible working conditions. Some left plantations to work independently, making trinkets and toys that they could sell for more than they would earn in the fields.[43]

COMMON TACTICS OF EXPLOITATION IN AGRICULTURAL LABOR

Regardless of the particular form of labor—slavery, indenture, or contract labor—there were many exploitative methods available to compel the labor of others, ranging from verbal abuse to physical abuse and sexual assault. Deprivation of food was also used to control indentured servants and slaves.

Deprivation of education was another means of exerting control.[44] While education was sometimes included in the contracts of indentured servants, slaves were actively deprived of education. The first laws restricting the education of enslaved people were passed in colonial South Carolina in 1740, after the 1739 Stono Rebellion, the largest slave revolt in the southern colonies. The 1740 restrictions specifically banned teaching slaves to write. Post-independence, an American-born enslaved man known as Nat Turner led a rebellion in Virginia that lasted from August 21 through 23, 1831, culminating in the deaths of more than fifty-five whites and prompting the state to impose additional restrictions on both enslaved people and free Blacks. Black people were prohibited from gathering or meeting in groups and teaching Black people (whether free or enslaved) was also outlawed. Most other slave states enacted similar laws, reasoning that illiterate people were better suited to menial labor and that, kept from becoming literate, they were unable to read abolitionist pamphlets and other materials that could lead to their empowerment.

Each of the methods used to exploit slaves and indentured servants—violence, denial of education, control of food—is a common tactic found across exploitative situations of all kinds, including those that meet current definitions of trafficking. A key difference between contemporary forms of trafficking and historical slavery and indenture, however, is that slavery and indenture were backed by the law. They were not merely legal, but actively enforced by the existing authorities. As we will see in the following chapter, once abolition became the law of the land, former slaveholders sought new labor pools to exploit.

CHAPTER 5

FROM SLAVERY TO PRISON AND PEONAGE

I N OCTOBER OF 1942, Viola Cosley of Birmingham, Alabama, wrote a letter to First Lady Eleanor Roosevelt:

> I am a colored mother and I need your help.
>
> My boy answered an advertisement in our Post paper for a job as he was out of work and had myself and two younger boys depending on him. As it turned out they were sent to Clewiston, Fl[orid]a a month ago and he can't get away or write. I am worried about him as I've talked to some white people and told them just how they are being treated, guarded at night by armed guards and not allowed to write home.
>
> Won't you please help me get my boy home?[1]

How was it possible that Viola Cosley's son was forced to work without payment in the twentieth century? The letter describes working conditions that could well have met the definition of trafficking. And yet, while it is shocking, there were tens of thousands of others in very similar conditions. In fact, there were many such cases in the period between the 1860s until World War II. Most cases involved African Americans. This chapter addresses the American economy's transition from chattel slavery to prison labor and peonage, another form of forced labor akin to debt bondage.

EXPLOITATION OF CHILDREN AND YOUTH UNDER THE "APPRENTICESHIP" SYSTEM

During the Civil War, "apprenticeship" laws were passed in Southern states in order to forcibly separate freed Black children and youth from their families and force them to work under white masters, usually their former owners, for little or no payment. A federal provost marshal said in 1864 that "many . . . citizens are endeavoring to intimidate colored people and compel them to bind their children to them under the old apprenticeship law."[2] The justification for enforced apprenticeship of freedchildren was that their parents, newly freed under the Emancipation Proclamation in 1863, could not afford to keep them. Belying that assertion of charity is the documented fact that the nearly ten thousand children apprenticed this way tended to be male adolescents or on the cusp of adolescence—able to engage in hard labor, particularly work previously done by enslaved people on farms and in manufacturing. As apprentices they would do so until they reached eighteen years old, or twenty-one in Mississippi. Apprenticeship ended at the age of fifteen for girls.[3] At least one teenager who was supporting his own wife and child was forced to apprentice.[4] The forced apprenticeship of a son or husband resulted in the loss of a crucial source of income for families, along with the emotional stress of their absence.

Former slaveholders doubtless found their circumstances greatly changed by Emancipation. The economy of the South had been devastated by the war, and the money they had invested in enslaved people suddenly no longer figured in their asset balance. Feelings of vindictiveness, in addition to strong beliefs in white supremacy, fueled their desire to keep freedchildren in apprenticeship. In one instance, Sewell Hepburn of Kent County Maryland, justified his apprenticeship of twelve freedchildren as "an act of humanity," saying that their family could not care for them. This statement was proven to be justification for a different motive entirely. He wrote in a letter, "I am left with no body to black my boots or catch a horse. . . . I am now an old man, and in my younger days labored to raise these blacks."[5]

Victims of apprenticeship had little recourse. There was the Freedmen's Bureau, officially called the Bureau of Refugees, Freedmen, and Abandoned Lands, which Congress had set up in 1865 to assist newly emancipated people through forms of aid such as clothing and food, and fielding requests from parents seeking to free their children from apprenticeship. The bureau operated until 1872. During its seven-year tenure, the bureau was understaffed to meet the needs of the nation's nearly four million newly emancipated people, let alone confront new forms of exploitation devised to retain their labor at the lowest possible cost.

BLACK CODES

Beginning in 1865, all former slave states passed "Black Codes" to maintain their control over the movement and labor of freedpeople.[6] The Black Codes of Mississippi and South Carolina explicitly addressed only Black people. Other states did not specify race in their laws but enforced them along racial lines. In some locations, Black Codes restricted employment of Blacks to agriculture. The codes were enforceable by militias that were reminiscent of old slave patrols. In this way, they replicated the powers that enforced slavery and prevented formerly enslaved people from realizing their emancipation. The codes were on the books for only a short time and were largely repealed by 1867, the year the Reconstruction Act was passed, but enforcement and implementation were slower to change, and Southern judges persisted in the enforcement of vagrancy laws, labor contracts that favored whites over formerly enslaved people, and apprenticeship.[7] In its statutes prohibiting integration in schools and public settings, Black Codes foreshadowed Jim Crow. In addition to regulating work and mobility, the Black Codes classified acts such as "insulting gestures" and "mischief" as crimes.

VAGRANCY

The Black Codes typically required that freedpeople have an employment contract, which was often with their former owner. Those without labor contracts were deemed vagrants, and nine Southern states also criminalized vagrancy, meaning that those without labor contracts had criminal status. Vagrancy statutes were applied to anyone without a yearly labor contract, including traveling circuses and actors, although vagrancy's primary use was to limit the mobility of former slaves.[8] Vagrants could be imprisoned and their children "apprenticed," and a vagrancy conviction could lead to prison time and forced labor (discussed in more detail below). These statutes essentially trapped freedpeople in a new form of compelled labor in state custody, via a sentence at a penal farm, a convict labor camp, or in a prison.

Labor contract for eight African American freedpeople.
Courtesy Alabama Department of Archives and History.

LABOR CONTRACTS

These labor contracts with emancipated people were initially oral agreements (written contracts were required by the Freedmen's Bureau after 1865), and they were typically very unfavorable and exploitative. Offering only starvation and subsistence wages, these contracts were the roots of the sharecropping system, in which formerly enslaved people were offered a small amount of money and/or a share of the crops they harvested in exchange for working in the fields.[9] Wages for freed slaves in Virginia were set at five dollars per month for men and three dollars for women and boys.[10] White workers had complained about five dollars per month being too low in the late 1850s.[11] The commissioner of the Freedmen's Bureau wrote in an 1865 report that the low wages paid to freedmen were responsible for the resistance to such employment.[12]

Labor contracts in some states followed a calendar year and bound a freedperson to the farm to which they were contracted. The stipulated conditions frequently included long hours and, in Florida, punishment for "disrespect" of the employer.[13] Breaking a contract could lead to corporal punishment, or even the contract being sold for a year's worth of labor, or prison time (which, as we will see below, could lead to worse conditions in similar forms of work).

FEES

Each legal violation could lead to fines and court fees, both of which combined with the threat of prison. For people without the means to pay upfront, which was likely to be the position of any recently freed slave, this system essentially led to debt bondage. This phenomenon is current again in the United States. Today, forty-nine states have implemented systems that involve levying fees on people moving through the courts.[14] These fees can compound and increase to levels that eventually result in jail time for those who have not paid them promptly.[15] This judiciary system, like the Black Codes, seems designed to maintain a permanent underclass.

THE TRANSITION FROM SLAVE TO PRISON LABOR

Prison labor has been used throughout the country since the colonial era. Since the abolition of slavery, it has been the only legal form of forced labor. The Thirteenth Amendment abolished "involuntary servitude," but permits prison labor "as a punishment for crime whereof the party shall have been duly convicted." The former slave states' postbellum systematic imprisonment of African Americans capitalized on this loophole. If unpaid

Black labor could no longer be enforced through slavery, laws would be designed to maintain a population of incarcerated Black citizens whose labor could be legally exploited.

The Black Codes created conditions by which Black Americans could be arrested for almost any reason. Upon arrest, they would be assigned either to a plantation, sometimes bypassing the court system, or to prison. Convictions were not necessary to turn formerly enslaved people into prison laborers. Demand for free labor and state revenue fed a demand for prisoners, in turn contributing to trumped-up arrests, against which there was no recourse because due process was not afforded. Although the Black Codes were repealed in most states in 1866, arbitrary arrest and the lack of due process persisted into the twentieth century, and we continue to see it today.

The similarity of this system to slavery was obvious to people then, as it is today. An English traveler to the Southern states wrote in 1871:

> I confess I am more and more suspicious about the criminal justice of these southern states. In Georgia there is no regular penitentiary at all, but an organised system of letting out the prisoners for profit. Some people here have got up a company for the purpose of hiring convicts. They pay $25,000 a year besides all expenses of food and keep, so that the money is clear profit to the state. The lessees work the prisoners both on estates and in mines, and apparently maintain severe discipline in their own way, and make a good thing of it. Colonel P——, who is not very mealy-mouthed, admits that he left the concern because he could not stand the inhumanity of it. Another partner in the concern talked with great glee of the money he had made out of the convicts. This does seem simply a return to another form of slavery.[16]

Georgia was not the only state without a prison to house its convicts; Mississippi, Alabama, and parts of Louisiana also had no prisons. In places without convict leasing, the revenue generated by convict labor constituted approximately half the costs of prisons; in places with convict leasing, the revenue constituted 372 percent of expenses.[17] In other words, convict leasing generated profits for the state at more than two and a half times their expenses.

Prison laborers experienced horrible treatment. Social reformer Clarissa Olds Keeler, who investigated the convict leasing system, wrote in 1910:

> In some States where convict labor is sold to the highest bidder the cruel treatment of the helpless human chattel in the hands of guards is such as no tongue can tell nor pen picture. Prison inspectors find convicts herded together, irrespective of age; confined at night in shackles; housed sometimes, as has been found, in old box cars; packed almost as closely as sardines in a box. During the day all are worked under armed guards, who stand ready to shoot down any who may attempt to escape from this hell upon earth—the modern American bastile. Should one escape, the bloodhounds, trained for the purpose, are put upon his track, and the chances are that he will be brought back, severely flogged and put in double shackles, or worse.[18]

Keeler further describes the physical punishment of convicts and high rates of recidivism in states with lucrative convict leasing programs as a strategy in which re-arrest was incentivized by profit. This perspective is shared by others.

W. E. B. Du Bois quotes a 1908 report by Assistant Attorney General Charles Russell, who said:

> I have no doubt from my investigations and experiences that the chief support of peonage is the peculiar system of State laws prevailing in the South, intended evidently to compel services on the part of the working man. From the usual condition of the great mass of labouring men where these laws are enforced, to peonage is but a step at most. In fact, it is difficult to draw a distinction between the condition of a man who remains in service against his will, because the State has passed a certain law under which he can be arrested and returned to work, and the condition of a man on a nearby farm who is actually made to stay at work by arrest and actual threats of force under the same law.[19]

This image from Bullock County Convict Camp in Alabama shows three guards, two holding guns, on one side of a fence; behind the fence are eighteen prisoners wearing stripes.[20] They are in front of a wagon with

Scene from Bullock Convict Camp, 1929.
Courtesy Alabama Department of Archives and History.

barred sides. The wagon could be moved to different worksites where the
prisoners might cut trees for lumber or produce turpentine. Wagons like
this one were used to move convict laborers between worksites; the imprisoned people slept in the wagons, which were essentially mobile jails. A
wagon like this would sleep twenty, in very crowded conditions, and were
used for convict leasing during and after the end of convict leasing.

States that had no prisons built them when they ended convict leasing.
For example, shortly after ending its convict leasing program in 1894,
Mississippi bought Parchman Farm in 1901 and converted it to the new
Mississippi State Penitentiary to hold Black men; the prison was built by
its own future inmates.[21] Convict leasing resumed at Parchman Farm in
1904. Prisoners sang work songs, some of which set a rhythm for work, for
example, cutting down trees.[22] A smaller section was built to hold white
men, and women's sections were built later. Both sections were segregated
by race into the 1960s; today, two-thirds of Parchman Farm's inmates are
Black. Although convict leasing at Parchman Farm ended in 1942, to this
day, prisoners still work there, where hundreds of their predecessors, some
of whom were worked to death, are buried on the grounds.

Legal prison labor continues today, and scholars have brought popular attention to the injustices of historical and contemporary prison labor in important books like Michelle Alexander's *The New Jim Crow*, David Oshinsky's *Worse Than Slavery: Parchman Farm and the Ordeal of Jim Crow Justice*, Shane Bauer's *American Prison*, and Dennis Childs's *Slaves of the State*. Federal and state prisons pay their incarcerated workers far less than the state's minimum wage, with wages reaching a dollar per hour being rare and some states paying less than a dollar per *day*, but in Alabama, Arkansas, Florida, Georgia, Mississippi, South Carolina, and Texas, the overwhelming majority of prison labor is unpaid.[23] Private prisons pay incarcerated workers between seventeen cents and fifty cents per hour.[24] Some state prisons allow private prison companies to operate their work programs, which reduces the wage to private prison rates. The federal government contracts with three private prison companies: CoreCivic (formerly the Correctional Corporation of America), the GEO Group, and Management and Training Corporation (MTC).[25] They raise their profit margins by employing fewer guards and selling the labor of the inmates. Private prisons contract with private retailers (such as Walmart, Whole Foods, Victoria's Secret, Dell, and Macy's) and food companies producing fish, meat, milk, eggs, and cheese.[26]

Private prisons are intended to profit off prison labor. Private prisons are also traded on the stock market, creating a demand for dividends for shareholders, income that is generated by the prison laborer. This is the contemporary form of convict leasing. Working conditions may be less brutal than the conditions on chain gangs, but prison laborers are not afforded workers' rights. This means that they may be forced to work, to work without breaks, and often without protective equipment.[27] Prison laborers were among those in the most exposed jobs during the new coronavirus pandemic in 2020 and 2021.[28]

Race and sex factor into prison labor. White men are overrepresented in the better paying inmate jobs, while women have been asked for sexual favors in exchange for better job assignments, and transgender and disabled incarcerated people have been denied job assignments.[29] Incarcerated call center workers are chosen not to sound "ghetto" (meaning they sound white when they speak); menial jobs cleaning and in the kitchen are the least well paid, and "the white inmates get the plumbing, electrician, and carpentry jobs [. . .] and the Black and Latino inmates get the jobs like kitchen, yard gang, laundry, clothing, but none of the jobs that can actually train [them] to get a good job on the outside."[30]

While the image popularly conjured by the phrase "human trafficking" is a young girl in sexual servitude, historically and today, the reality is very different. In fact, the main character in the story of forced labor in the United States has been a man or boy of color, alongside many women and girls of color, most frequently toiling on farms and in food production. However, while society as a whole is enthusiastic about the rescue of young girls from sexual degradation, we are less enthusiastic about addressing injustices toward people of color, demonstrated by the decades of toleration of slave labor camps on plantations and compulsory labor in prisons, often doing the same agricultural labor their enslaved counterparts did in centuries past, as at Parchman Farm. We are especially reluctant to perceive men of color as victims.

PART III

TRAFFICKING INTO DOMESTIC WORK

CHAPTER 6

TRAFFICKING INTO DOMESTIC AND CARE WORK TODAY

T HE NEXT TWO CHAPTERS ADDRESS, respectively, trafficking into domestic and care work today and the historical exploitation of people in such work. This chapter includes the personal stories of three survivors of contemporary domestic labor trafficking in different parts of the United States; to understand their stories, it is first helpful to know a little bit about the status of domestic and care work. Domestic work entails cleaning and cooking, while care work includes watching over children and caring for the elderly or people with particular needs. Domestic and care workers include housekeepers, nannies, and home health aides, many of whom are employed in the informal economy. This work is highly gendered and has historically been performed by women; the people in the historical and contemporary cases here are all women.

Women are often not respected for the work they do, and certain types of work tend to be undervalued. Domestic work and care work are examples of this; the lack of value ascribed to this work is apparent in low pay scale. These cleaning and caregiving jobs pay approximately $12 per hour when employees are on the books.[1] The median pay for maids and cleaners is $12.60 per hour or $26,220 per year, and the median for caregivers is $13 per hour or $27,080.[2] This is lower than traditionally male working-class jobs—for example, security guards earn a median of $14 per hour or $31,050 per year, and construction workers earn a median of $18 per hour or $37,890 per year.[3] The pay gaps across these different fields are born out in the general US pay gap: in the US in 2020, women on average earned $0.84 for every dollar earned by men.[4]

US labor law offers little protection to domestic workers. Unlike jobs in most other sectors, domestic work is excluded from workplace safety mandates and from protections against sexual harassment; it was excluded from federal overtime pay requirements until 2013. Very few of these workers have employer-sponsored benefits. These exclusions date back to the New Deal, when white Southern politicians refused to extend the new worker rights to African Americans working on farms and in homes. Both agricultural workers and domestic workers were therefore excluded from the 1935 National Labor Relations Act (NLRA) and the 1938 Fair Labor Standards Act (FLSA). The NLRA assured workers the right to meet to organize and to bargain collectively for better wages and working conditions.[5] The FLSA guaranteed a minimum wage and time-and-a-half overtime pay, as well as outlawing oppressive child labor.[6]

Jean Bruggeman, executive director of Freedom Network USA, said that "US law has created oppressive conditions within [the agriculture and the domestic and care work] industries. Between the lack of labor protections and the immigration system that denies agency of immigrant laborers, that is the perfect intentional creation of abuse and exploitation. This is not an accident."[7] One reason jobs of this kind are subject to such egregious abuses is that the work is necessary but not valued. It is no coincidence that the people who most often perform this work are women, immigrants, and people of color; all three people featured in this chapter hold all these identities.

In 1989, a teenaged Brazilian named Natalicia Tracy came to the United States to work as a nanny in Boston, where she encountered horrific working conditions.[8] Her employers were two married Brazilian doctors with a single child. Tracy had cared for the child in Brazil, living with her own family but traveling with her employer's family on their vacations, and the experience had been good. She was promised that she would be able to continue going to school in the United States, and her employers took care of her visa paperwork.

In Boston, the family paid her one hundred dollars per month to care for the toddler and provided room and board.[9] However, it became clear that the family expected her not only to provide childcare but also to take on new responsibilities: doing all the cooking and cleaning for the household. Her work now took up every waking hour. When the family had guests or visitors from Brazil, she was expected to cook and clean for everyone. When they had another child, her duties expanded again to include the care of that child as well.

Her employers were very controlling. They said that using the dishwasher was too expensive, and that she should wash the dishes by hand. They told her that she could not use the phone to call her family because it was too expensive. They took her name off the mailbox so she could not receive letters. The family wanted Tracy to do unusual and unnecessary tasks, like ironing towels and underwear. She later explained, "In addition to caring for a three-year-old child, I was responsible for all the housework: cooking, washing and ironing. This happened from Monday to Monday with no day off. They didn't let me go to school and then they had a second child, which increased my work and ended my dream of studying English."[10]

"At first, they gave me a room," she said. But upon the arrival of visitors who came to stay at the house, she was moved to a futon mattress on the floor of an enclosed but uninsulated porch through the Massachusetts winter. "The area was protected only by a very thin glass, and when winter came, I had to cover the floor with newspapers and I used the portable heater."[11] Her employers rationed the amount of food they gave her to prepare and made sure not to leave any food for her after they had their meals. The agreement had been that she would be fed at the family's expense. Instead, she was forced to use her own scarce funds to buy food.[12] "[For] food, they only gave me leftovers. Otherwise, I had to buy it. But I could only choose a $1.00 sandwich at McDonald's because my salary was only US$25 weekly."[13] She was not allowed to communicate with her family. "The worst of it was that they prevented me from communicating with my family in Brazil. They said the phone was very expensive and did not allow me to put my name on their home mailbox. At that time, the mailman didn't leave correspondences if the name was not on the list."[14]

When, after a few years, the family returned to Brazil, Tracy decided to stay in the United States, but then discovered that she no longer had regular immigration status. "They took my passport saying they were going to renew my work visa but they never renewed it. I was illegal in the United States." Tracy was desperate, but also resourceful.

> Two years passed and when it came time for them to return to Brazil, I asked to stay in the country. When I walked on the street, unable to speak English with anyone, I even thought it would be better if a car ran over me. So, I learned a few words with a small dictionary I brought in my luggage.[15]

Ultimately, she was able to find another situation that was less exploitative. "In the newspaper I found an ad for a nanny job for an American family. They gave me a room, new clothes, paid for my transportation to go to school and didn't accept my offer to work for free. My salary was $100 per week," four times what she had been paid previously.[16] She stayed in Massachusetts and found a better situation in which her new employer supported her desire for education. Tracy earned a doctoral degree and is now a senior policy advisor in the Occupational Safety and Health Administration.[17]

Natalicia Tracy's trafficking experience is, sadly, not an unusual one.[18] Judith Daluz was thirty-eight years old when she came to New York City from the Philippines in 2005 to work for a diplomat, caring for a child with special needs.[19] Like Tracy, Daluz soon found herself working fifteen-hour days taking care of the house, the cooking, and the child. According to the website of the Damayan Migrant Workers Association (Damayan, for short), which provides services to domestic workers who have been trafficked, Daluz "worked for 14–18 hours a day for $500 a month, cleaned their home with four bedrooms and three bathrooms, washed and ironed their clothes, cooked breakfast and dinner, and took care of the daughter. She wasn't given any days off, her passport was taken, and the mother and daughter physically hit her."[20] Similar to Tracy's ordeal, her work seemed to expand beyond reason; she was told to do all the laundry in the bathtub instead of using the washing machine, including sheets and comforters that needed to be washed frequently because the child would wet the bed. Like Tracy, Daluz was deprived of food. She said, "They don't let me eat much food, because my boss told me, 'Not too much; we are counting how much we cook each day.' If there's a little bit leftover, that's how much I eat. I can't really sleep because I am so hungry in the middle of the night."[21] Her interactions with others were highly scrutinized, so much so that she was not allowed to have friends or go places without her employers, and she was told not to tell anyone about her job situation.

Daluz's employers kept her passport, telling her that they needed it to renew her work visa. When she eventually found the passport, she discovered that they had not renewed her visa. It was at this point that she started making plans to leave. However, visas for immigrant workers like Daluz are linked to their employers; it wouldn't have been easy for her to change jobs and keep her visa. She needed another way out. While grocery shopping one day, Daluz had met and befriended another Filipina, whom she told about her situation. Her friend began to leave food for her with the doorman and also introduced her to an attorney, who helped her document her experiences. Daluz planned her escape and walked out one day, before the family returned from work and school, leaving her key behind. The day Daluz left, in 2006, she had her first real meal in months. Now undocumented, she worked as a nanny and cleaner. Eventually she met people with Damayan. With their help, she filed an application for a T visa. She eventually joined the board of directors of Damayan and reunited in the United States in 2015 with her children who stayed in the Philippines.[22] She is a founding member of Damayan Cleaning Cooperative, a member-owned enterprise.[23]

In 2001, Nena Ruiz, a fifty-five-year-old retired teacher burdened by loan debt for her children's education, was hired by a woman to work as a caregiver for her elderly mother. The elderly woman met Ruiz in the Philippines and traveled back to Sacramento, California, with her. When they arrived in California, however, instead of starting the caregiving job she'd been promised, Ruiz was set to work as a housekeeper for the elderly woman's daughter, taking care of the daughter's house and two dogs in Los Angeles. Her task schedule began before dawn and went until 10:30 p.m., after which she was required to take the dogs out.[24] Ruiz cooked special food for the dogs, though she was only allowed to eat the family's leftovers. She slept on a dog bed in the living room, and her clothes and personal items were stored in the laundry room. Her employer beat her and, just as

Daluz's employer had done, took her passport and refused to give it back. Ruiz recounts:

> At their door they took my passport and everything changed. She pulled my hair. She spanked my head. She punched my mouth. I slept on top of the dog bed because they don't allow me to sleep on the couch because they didn't want to make it dirty. I said it will be a secret of myself, because it embarrassed me.[25]

Ruiz added, "She prevented me to make friends in the neighborhood." However, a teenager in the neighborhood liked to play with the dogs she cared for. "Our neighbor, the thirteen-year-old, wants to play with the dog when I took the dog out. . . . I told the girl about what had happened to me."[26] After Nena confided to the neighbor about her situation, the girl called the police.

Trafficked domestic workers are often forced to pay for their own work expenses, in the same way that agricultural workers are charged for transportation to the fields and the traveling sales crews are charged for their shared motel rooms. Ruiz's employer had charged her for her own airfare to California—and for the elderly woman's roundtrip airfare to the Philippines and back. Ruiz's employer also allowed her visa to expire.

Ruiz said, "Finally one day, we got a knock on the door. It was the police. One of the neighbors had called and said I was being hit. He asked if I wanted to talk with him alone outside, but I was silent and only looked at my boss. Even though my boss treated me cruelly, she was still my boss, and because of my culture, I felt I should obey her. Also, I had no papers, and didn't want to be put in immigrant detention."

Ruiz did not leave that day. However, her employers reported her as an illegal immigrant and the FBI and border enforcement came to investigate her immigration status. When questioned, she told them about her working conditions. She repeated her account to the Filipino Workers Association and the Coalition to Abolish Slavery and Trafficking, two nongovernmental organizations called in to assist her. Her employers had hoped that by reporting Ruiz as an illegal alien, the authorities would take their now problematic employee off their hands and deport her. Instead, they unwittingly launched an investigation into their own trafficking offenses.

Ruiz was fortunate that her case was investigated. Federal investigations into labor trafficking tend to focus on employers who are exploiting people on a larger scale, as was the case with C&C Farms. Trafficking situations of people working as live-in servants or in domestic work typically involve just one or two victims, so they are lower priority.

Ruiz kept a diary recording the details of her yearlong servitude from 2001 to 2002. In it, she noted each day the work she'd done and when she'd been berated or beaten. This diary was the main evidence when she filed a trafficking case and won. The employer and her husband were convicted of involuntary servitude, negligence, and fraud; the employer was also convicted of assault and battery. The employer served jail time, her husband did not, and they were ordered to pay Ruiz more than half a million dollars in civil damages.[27] Ruiz went on to advocate for the passage of California's Domestic Worker Bill of Rights, which extended wage and overtime pay protection to domestic workers in 2014.[28] The Coalition to Abolish Slavery and Trafficking honored Ruiz for her work to help pass this law.[29]

These three women were all eventually able to escape their exploitative situations and help other trafficking victims. Natalicia Tracy's story is particularly inspiring. As she was working to complete her education, she was also becoming an activist. In 2010, she became the director of the Brazilian Worker Center in Massachusetts, which cofounded the Massachusetts Coalition for Domestic Workers that same year. This coalition successfully advocated for the passage of the first Massachusetts law to protect the rights of domestic workers. The Massachusetts Domestic Worker Bill of Rights, passed in 2014, provides much-needed protections for domestic workers, including wage and hour protections, guarantees for overtime pay and accrued paid time off, and special rules about record-keeping, rest, room-and-board costs, and working conditions. This is a model that needs to be emulated by other states.[30] Since 2013, domestic workers in the United States have been included under the FLSA and, consequently, workers who stay on-site for more than 120 hours per week (for example, from Monday morning through Friday evening) must be paid minimum wage for the hours they work. They may be exempt from overtime pay, however, and workers who do not live with their employers for extended periods of time are eligible for overtime pay.[31]

WHY DO PEOPLE STAY?

After hearing the stories of abuse told by domestic workers like Tracy, Daluz, and Ruiz, it may seem incredible that anyone would remain in such a situation. Yet each of these strong women stayed in their situation for months or years. As they have come forward with their stories, they have described multiple reasons why people may remain in such an abusive or exploitative situation.

Practical or material considerations are the most obvious reason people stay, and perhaps the easiest to understand. Natalicia Tracy says, "I worried that if I spoke up, I would get thrown out. The porch was bad, but being out on the street with no English would have been much worse."[32]

Other factors that keep people in exploitative situations are less concrete. Many trafficked people have described their own shame at being victimized. Nena Ruiz, the retired teacher, said, "I really don't tell anybody, I just keep it by myself because, you know, I was so embarrassed."[33] Ruiz worried that people would lose respect for her and her family.[34]

In her account, Tracy drew attention to the unequal power dynamics between an employer and employee. She also stressed the ways in which the American visa system—which predicates immigration status on employment—may prevent people from trying to change their situations:

> My visa was tied to my work with the family. Where would I go if I walked out? I didn't speak English and had no one. I was not getting the education I was promised. Who could I turn to? Many people in these situations are afraid to trust government agencies or the police. I did question things from time to time. But I would get yelled at quickly. Once, the wife told me I shouldn't disrespect her.[35]

Nena Ruiz outlined a similar complex of issues that trapped her in her situation. Along with shame, they included fear of her employer, fear of law enforcement, logistical constraints, and her own lack of funds and resources. "After thirty-two years of teaching, I retired," she said. "Because I have a debt from sending my children to school, I believe the only way to settle my obligation is to work here."[36]

Tracy also described being attached to the boy she cared for. She said that the child would draw pictures for her and comfort her when she was sad.[37] She added, "People don't understand that you can't just walk out.

Even if you are not in physical chains, there are constraints—economic, emotional, social—that keep women like me in place. There's a lot of co-ercion—and denial."[38]

Denial is a complex psychological state of mind that, among other things, includes a determination to carry on, a persistence in the face of adversity, and a need to maintain an appearance of dignity and a sense that things are not as bad as they seem. These elements may be important traits in overcoming hardship, but they can also be leveraged by abusers. The women's employers exploited their human desire to be honorable and to live up to their promises and circumstances.

Judith Daluz described the way simple interactions with the doorman and another domestic worker in the building helped to restore her perspective. She said, "Those small interactions were so important to me, because they helped relieve my isolation and loneliness. They also showed me that things inside the apartment were not normal."[39]

Ultimately, all three had help from unexpected allies: neighbors, acquaintances who became friends, and law enforcement.

LONG-STANDING EXPLOITATION IN CARE WORK AND DOMESTIC WORK

In the popular imagination, caring is an inherently feminine skill. But for all that it is widely undervalued, care work is both essential and demanding. The need for care work can expand in particular situations or stages of life: at birth we are all dependent on the care of others; the elderly may require more care over time; people with disabilities may require a consistent level of care throughout their lives, or at a level that gradually increases, depending on their condition; and people recovering from medical procedures or accidents may temporarily require care in their homes or in institutions.

Domestic work is similarly devalued. In heterosexual relationships, women routinely do more housework than their male partners, even in couples where both partners hold full-time jobs.[40] This disparity was further exacerbated during the coronavirus pandemic beginning in 2020.[41] Hired domestic help and care workers are overwhelmingly women, mostly women of color. About one-third are immigrants. Even in normal circumstances—that is to say, outside of trafficking situations—many live in poverty, earning an average of $12 per hour.[42] Most do not live with their employers, and pay for their accommodation and food from this wage. Even if their income is above the federal poverty line, which is $12,880 per year for a single person and $26,500 for a family of four, they often fail to make enough money to cover their expenses and are forced either to go without necessities or take on debt.[43]

DIPLOMATS

Many trafficked domestic workers are employed by foreign nationals, including diplomats, who enjoy diplomatic immunity that shields them from many criminal charges. This is why Judith Daluz was unable to seek restitution; her employers were diplomats and left the country rather than deal with the possibility of news coverage and any consequences related to their treatment of her. Diplomats are allowed to emigrate to the US with a single servant. Some of these diplomats come from cultures and backgrounds where a large staff works in their family homes. They may come from countries where a distinct servant class still exists, as it did through the early twentieth century in the United States and Europe. When someone from such a background comes to the United States, the burden of running the entire household tends to fall on the single servant permitted under the regulations.

An obvious solution for the foreign nationals is to take on additional help to assist with domestic tasks. It is certainly possible for diplomats, once they arrive in the US, to hire more people, either through an agency or by hiring an individual directly. Though these jobs do not command high wages, such services may feel expensive to people from countries where labor is far cheaper. This is particularly true in the case where more specialized skills are required, such as providing care for a person with a disability. Instead of hiring the extra help they need, some choose to exploit their servants by overworking them or imposing appalling conditions on them.

Foreign workers are particularly vulnerable to exploitation, because if they change jobs they may not be able to maintain their legal immigration status. Workers with irregular immigration status or whose visa is attached to their positions may be threatened with being reported to immigration, making them potentially liable to deportation. Thus, because they are dependent on their employers, they may be subjected to additional forms of control and coercion, particularly if they are live-in servants. As we saw with Daluz and Ruiz, their passports may be taken from them. They may not be allowed to communicate freely with others. They may also be subjected to still more arbitrary, even sadistic measures, such as the restriction of their food intake. Finally, abusive employers may withhold money owed or use a variety of strategies to avoid paying employees in full. A 2019 *New York Times* article reported that "it is estimated that only around 5 percent of domestic workers in the United States are paid on the books."[44]

CHAPTER 7

THE HISTORY OF EXPLOITATION
IN DOMESTIC WORK

I N THE COLONIAL ERA, approximately one-quarter of all indentured servants and convict laborers were women.[1] Gender roles established that female indentured servants were mainly to be engaged in domestic work. Similarly, enslaved girls and women may have been involved in farm-work, but many were employed in domestic work that included childcare, food preparation, and housekeeping. While household work was considered better than working in the fields, domestic work in that era was far more arduous than in most American homes today, as chores like laundry and cooking were far harder without the aid of modern appliances. Through the nineteenth century, domestic work involved demanding physical labor and sometimes hazardous conditions, with laundry and cooking requiring the use of open fires and boiling cauldrons of water. Food preparation involved not just cooking meals but processing raw ingredients—winnowing rice to remove the hull, butchering meat, grinding flour—steps that today are done for us before we purchase these foods. Even the labor-saving machines that did exist then were dangerous: the rollers of the mangle or wringer that were used to wring out laundry could and did crush fingers and hands.

CONDITIONS OF DOMESTIC WORK FOR
SERVANTS AND ENSLAVED PEOPLE

Female indentured servants and convict laborers in domestic work experienced different situations depending on who their masters were. For some people, indenture was simply employment until they were free of their contract. For others, indenture was an abusive and exploitative situation akin to human trafficking today. Elizabeth Abbot, an indentured maid who arrived in Virginia in 1624, ran away before a year was out; she was beaten as punishment and died of her injuries. The people to whom she had been indentured were exonerated.[2] When indentured domestic workers ran away, advertisements were sometimes placed for their return, such as the following:

July 1, 1795

Six-pence Reward.

RAN-AWAY on the 14th instant, from the subscriber, living in Horsham township, Montgomery county, a Servant GIRL, named ELIZABETH LIVINGSTON; had on a linsey petticoat and gown. Whoever takes up the said Servant, shall have the above reward, and no charges.[3]

Many domestic workers were sexually assaulted in their workplaces. Some were repeatedly victimized. Victims could be punished for their own assault: two years of indenture were added to the terms of women who became pregnant in servitude, ostensibly to make up for the time lost as a result of pregnancy. Many were impregnated by their masters.[4] Unmarried women who gave birth were punished for "bastardy," as the blame fell on them for the creation of a person who could become dependent on the colony or state. Punishment was harshest for white indentured women who gave birth to mixed-race children; they could be penalized with an extension of their indenture term for as long as five years.[5]

Enslaved women and girls worked in the fields, took care of children, and kept the house. Domestic work included cooking and cleaning; carding wool, preparing cotton, spinning, and weaving; and various artisanal forms of textile ornamentation, including dying, seamstressing, quilting, embroidering, and other textile ornamentation tasks.

THE DRAMATIC ESCAPE OF ONA JUDGE

One prominent enslaved person who did domestic work during this era was Ona Judge, a dressmaker and lady's maid to Martha Washington.[6] Judge was the daughter of an enslaved seamstress and a white English tailor named Andrew Judge who worked for George Washington at Mount Vernon. She was an accomplished seamstress and accompanied the Washingtons when they moved to the US presidential mansion in New York City after Washington's election. The president's executive residence was later moved to Philadelphia in 1790, where Judge's life was very different from life at Mount Vernon, with opportunities for diversion and entertainment, as well as exposure to abolitionist ideas.

Pennsylvania had in 1780 passed a law ensuring the gradual emancipation of slaves born after the law's passage. However, children born to an enslaved mother still had to work as indentured servants until they reached the age of twenty-eight, at which point they were free, provided they had resided in the state for six consecutive months. Enslaved people under eighteen could apply to be assigned to a "master" until they came of age, and they could not be taken out of state without their own consent. Another section of the new law prohibited enslavers from keeping enslaved people in Pennsylvania for more than six months; Washington exploited a loophole in the law and moved Judge and other enslaved people at the executive residence out of the state periodically, so that they would return as enslaved people and begin anew their six-month waiting period for emancipation.[7] Further cementing his commitment to slavery, Washington also signed the Fugitive Slave Act in 1793, allowing enslavers to recapture enslaved people who had fled to another state, even by force.

After forming her escape plan, Judge fled the Philadelphia residence in 1796, before the Washingtons returned to Mount Vernon. An advertisement was soon posted, offering a ten-dollar reward for her return. Decades later, when interviewed in 1845, Judge explained, "Whilst they were packing up to go to Virginia, I was packing to go, I didn't know where; for I knew that if I went back to Virginia, I should never get my liberty. I had friends among the colored people of Philadelphia, had my things carried there beforehand, and left Washington's house while they were eating dinner."[8] Judge went by ship to New Hampshire, where she was recognized a few months later. Washington sent an emissary to bring her to Philadelphia, who relayed that Judge fled seeking only freedom, and would return if she would be emancipated upon the death of George and Martha Washington. Washington refused to negotiate and twice sent others to recover Judge. When she was informed that someone still intended to recapture her and was willing to use the force allowed by the Fugitive Slave Law, she fled her home to elude him. Judge died in poverty but free, and without regrets.

BREEDING ENSLAVED CHILDREN

After the transatlantic slave trade was banned in 1808, the only way to obtain new slaves in the United States was through reproduction, via children born to enslaved women. By the time the ban was enacted, slavery was essentially self-sustaining in this way. The reproduction of enslaved people was highly desirable for their enslavers, and the fecundity of female slaves was described in terms similar to those used for livestock.[9] Midwives, including enslaved midwives, were paid for their services, and on George Washington's farms, enslaved women were given between four and six weeks off after giving birth.[10]

Some enslaved people formed families and had children, though their family members could be separated and sold. Some enslaved people were bred through rape and through arranged and forced mating. Many enslaved pregnant women who were forced to work up to the last minute of delivery gave birth in the fields, during which a nurse midwife could be called. They were given time to nurse their children, as this was an investment in the future labor of the enslaved child.[11] Enslaved children began work at a very early age, doing light domestic tasks such as fanning flies off the dinner table, and their workload changed and increased as they grew.[12]

INDUSTRIALIZATION AND POSTBELLUM

The expansion of industry changed the nature of traditional women's work, with factory-made fabric reducing the demand for spinning and weaving. During the Industrial Revolution, many white women and new immigrants moved out of domestic work and into factory work. However, after the Civil War, this was not the case for emancipated people in the United States. For example, in Baldwin County, Alabama, white women could find work in the new textile mills, but Black women remained in traditional work like laundering.[13] New freedwomen in domestic work had to learn how much paid time was needed to cover basic expenses like food and other necessities, while also negotiating with former slaveholders on payment and limitations on work hours. Tending their own crops was more lucrative than domestic work, and many women arranged their paid work hours so they would have time for farms and gardens. These boundaries were tested. For example, domestic workers might have to bring their own children to their workplace, where they would leave them to play in the yard, but their employers would sometimes take advantage by giving the children tasks of their own, as they would have before emancipation.[14] In the worst-case scenario, their children were apprenticed to former owners, as described in chapter 5. Wages were low, and Black women left domestic employment temporarily when more lucrative opportunities arose, such as field work in the harvest season. These domestic workers also engaged in cottage industry, selling products that they made, such as butter or starch, sometimes to people they worked for. Before Emancipation, their employers would have gotten these items from the labor of an enslaved person held in their household. This detail seems small but represents a major change in earnings, self-determination, and entrepreneurialism among formerly enslaved people.

Laundry was a large task involving not only washing clothes but also producing soap, making and applying starch, ironing, and carefully handling delicate items. At first, employers provided or paid for soap and starch, but these costs were pushed back onto the washerwomen by the 1880s. It was during this time, the end of the Reconstruction era, that voting rights for Black men were violently rescinded.[15] Losing the right to vote meant the erosion of Black people's civil rights and, with it, the erosion of their negotiating power as workers. The sharecropping system did not pay tenant farmers in cash, so domestic work offered some liquid income, albeit small. The end of the slave economy wrought changes at all levels, and many former enslavers had diminished incomes. Servants were available, but as with other work previously performed by enslaved people, including in agriculture as described in chapter 5, the wages offered were not acceptable to the workers.

It was dangerous for servants to resist their employers' demands for additional labor beyond the parameters of their job. Some servants who resisted were beaten or even killed. One woman named Linda Brown declined to do a load of ironing in addition to field work and was beaten with a hoe; a servant named Eliza Jane Ellison was murdered when she turned down additional tasks not in her contract.[16]

Domestic work continued to be a source of employment for women, particularly Black women, throughout the Jim Crow era. Segregation did not stop at a home's threshold. Vinella Byrd described being a domestic servant during the civil rights era, saying, "The man didn't want me to wash my hands in the wash pan" (that is, the kitchen sink). She was also denied access to the bathroom, so she prepared food without washing her hands. Hazel Rankins said, "I would not only clean the bathroom but I'd take a bath in the bathtub."[17]

PART IV

TRAFFICKING INTO INDUSTRY AND INFRASTRUCTURE

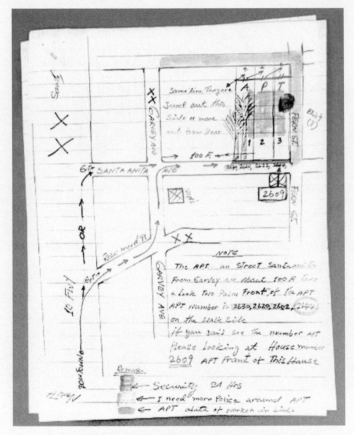

Letter informing California authorities about the El Monte sweatshop, including a map of the site. Courtesy State of California, Department of Industrial Relations, Division of Labor Standards Enforcement.

CHAPTER 8

CONTEMPORARY TRAFFICKING CASES IN INDUSTRY AND INFRASTRUCTURE

T HE TOPIC OF THIS CHAPTER is trafficking into industry, factories, and infrastructure, including the trafficking of the hundreds and possibly thousands of people involved in the cleanup after Hurricanes Katrina and Rita along the Gulf of Mexico. The second chapter in this section examines the role of compulsory labor in historical American industry, including that of enslaved people, contract laborers, and prisoners in the production of natural resources for industry, and it highlights the ways those historical situations are similar to those faced by infrastructure workers today.

From 1988 to 1995, in a makeshift factory in a residential neighborhood in El Monte, California, seventy-two Thai garment workers were held captive: their identification was taken and held by their bosses, they were not allowed to leave, and they were not allowed to communicate directly with their families in Thailand. They were eventually released in 1995 after one of the workers escaped and sent a letter to California's Department of Industrial Relations with a map of the barbed-wire-enclosed factory (as described earlier in chapter 2).[1] Rotchana Cheunchujit, one of the sweatshop employees, described the situation as debt bondage: she owed her traffickers five thousand dollars for her travel from Thailand, a sum she would never be able to pay back while she was earning pennies per garment sewn. Unable to leave the factory, she had to buy her food from a makeshift store on the premises that charged exorbitant prices. Some of her colleagues had been held captive at the factory for seven years.[2] Like Ona Judge, the seamstress and maid to Martha Washington whose story was told in chapter 7, these workers made garments for people much wealthier than they were, they had no say in their work or hours, and, like Judge, they went on to make new lives in the United States after securing their freedom.[3] At the time of their release, there was no path to citizenship or provision to stay in the US for international victims of trafficking. Special accommodations were made so that they could stay in the country, and their case, along with that of the deaf Mexican peddlers in New York City (described earlier in chapter 1) contributed to the realization that it was necessary to address forced labor situations in the US. Before these cases, most Americans did not think about trafficking, and if they did, it was as a problem elsewhere in the world, despite the factors that helped trafficking thrive, in particular our increasingly global economy and the end of large-scale visa programs for temporary workers. These cases were a wake-up call, and, as the twentieth century drew to a close, this sense of urgency led to the passage of the TVPA. However, human trafficking cases continue to persist in industry.

Just a few years after the law's passage, in 2005, traffickers capitalized on the aftermath of Hurricane Katrina. The storm had destroyed homes and damaged infrastructure, including oil rigs, along the Gulf Coast of Louisiana and Mississippi. Thousands of cubic yards of debris had to be cleaned up; homes and other buildings needed to be repaired or demolished for new construction. Cleanup necessitated dealing with human and animal remains, sewage, pollutants, and chemicals. Roads needed to be cleared and repaired; oil rigs required welders and pipefitters.

In the aftermath of the storm, displaced people and the workers who came to the region lived in hotels. Federal emergency money was made available for much of the cleanup. In order to facilitate the cleanup effort, the George W. Bush administration loosened some federal workplace regulations, including occupational safety and health standards and the requirement for construction projects to pay "locally prevailing wages."[4] The wages offered were too low for local workers to live on, so, rather than compel employers to pay more, the federal government relaxed requirements for H-2B visas for temporary non-agricultural foreign workers, who would do the job for lower pay. The Department of Homeland Security also temporarily waived the requirement that employers prove that these foreign workers were permitted to work in the United States, facilitating the hire of many undocumented people. People came from Latin America and the Caribbean, particularly Mexico, Brazil, Honduras, Guatemala, El Salvador, and the Dominican Republic, and even as far away as Thailand and India.[5] Finally, not enough people were assigned to properly oversee government contracts related to rebuilding.[6] These changes and omissions created conditions that led to labor violations and human trafficking. Local workers in Louisiana were replaced with undocumented workers who were paid two dollars less per hour, and with migrant workers with H-2B visas who were paid four dollars less per hour.[7] Even with these depressed wages, many people were still not paid correctly for the hours they worked.

Signal International, an American oil rig company involved in the cleanup, recruited more than five hundred metalworkers from India in 2006, promising permanent US residency for the workmen and their families.[8] These workers paid recruiters' fees totaling over ten thousand dollars for travel costs and visa expenses. The Signal workers were highly literate, educated, and skilled, and yet they were still taken advantage of. When they arrived, their passports were held by the company. They were not paid properly for their work and were housed in overcrowded and substandard conditions, segregated by ethnicity. The workers defied the segregation policy and spoke with their colleagues from other countries and worksites, learning that they were all in similarly terrible circumstances. The workers then organized across ethnicities to better their shared exploitative situation, using their collective power to respond effectively.

After the workers organized and familiarized themselves with US laws, they tried to take their grievances to local law enforcement and the Department of Homeland Security. They explained the labor law violations that had occurred and fraudulent practices they had observed in the recruitment process. Rather than being treated as victims of crime, those who reported their conditions were threatened with deportation. These conditions clearly met the definition of trafficking but, initially, the workers received no support from federal or local law enforcement. Because Louisiana has no state wage and hour laws, the state declined to act.

In response to their seeking better working conditions, the workers soon faced retaliation from Signal International, which, according to the *New York Times*, conspired with immigration agents to use the structure of the guestworker visa system against the workers.[9] Signal's chief operating officer, Ronald Schnoor, attempted to act on an immigration agent's advice to summarily deport workers in 2007, but he was prevented from taking individual workers to the airport by immigration advocates. Shortly after this event, shipyard manager Darrell Snyder emailed his colleagues to say that a different immigration agent had assured him that any workers no longer with Signal would be pursued by immigration authorities.[10] If a person has this type of visa and stops working for their employer for any reason, they become undocumented immediately. Signal fired the people who reported their working conditions, and then called Homeland Security Investigations (HSI), a branch of Immigration and Customs Enforcement, to report that these fired workers were out of regular immigration status. Although this HSI office had on file the labor exploitation complaint made by these very workers, the office complied with Signal and arrested the workers.[11]

Rather than prosecute trafficking wherever they saw it, many of the law enforcement agencies in the Louisiana Human Trafficking Task Force and the New Orleans Human Trafficking Working Group were deputized to enforce immigration law.[12] The Signal human trafficking case got no traction, and in 2008, some of the hundreds of Signal workers staged a hunger strike in Washington, DC, to bring attention to their substandard compensation and dangerous working and living conditions. They also sought to bring attention to Signal's misrepresentation of their employment circumstances and right to potentially remain in the United States, with a focus on the general role of the company as well as that of an attorney working with Signal and the recruiter who brought the workers to the US.[13] The hunger strike received widespread media attention, after which investigations were initiated by the Department of Labor, the Department of Justice, the Occupational Safety and Health Agency, and the Equal Employment Opportunity Commission. The Signal trafficking case and other complaints had suddenly found traction, at least among the federal agencies if not the local ones.

As their case unfolded, some of the workers found work in different locations, and some continued to be persecuted by the government. Twenty-three were arrested by Immigration and Customs Enforcement in North Dakota after a job had been completed; their employer had reported them to ICE for working for a company different from the one that sponsored their visas, and they were arrested. They were then prosecuted for immigration violations by the US attorney for North Dakota, Drew Wrigley, even though he knew about their ongoing trafficking case against Signal.[14] Even when government officials understand that victims of crime are cooperating to prosecute traffickers, as in the case of the former Signal employees, they may deliberately go after those witnesses, further victimizing them.

Ultimately, Signal International was found liable for all charges, and the attorney and recruiter mentioned above were all found guilty under the TVPA and under racketeering statutes. Signal International was ordered to pay $12 million in damages to the workers, while the recruiter and attorney were each ordered to pay $915,000. Signal International later declared bankruptcy. This was only one of multiple labor exploitation cases that arose after the storm: at least 3,750 cleanup workers were identified as potential trafficking victims in the five years following the natural disaster.[15] Some cases concerned working conditions for maids in hotels where workers and displaced people had stayed after the storm; another involved demolition and construction workers involved in clearing debris and repairing damage to buildings. Multiple organizations addressing working conditions were founded from 2006 onward, including the New Orleans Workers' Center for Racial Justice and the Alliance of Guestworkers for Dignity.[16] Trafficking statutes were used with success in some cases, while wage and hour laws were used in others (both types of law can be used on the same case). The most successful cases were those in which workers coordinated protests, demonstrating that self-advocacy was the best approach.[17]

TASK FORCES AND THE CRIMINAL JUSTICE RESPONSE

The United States has anti-trafficking task forces across the country, each assigned to a city or region. These task forces were formed after the creation of the TVPA. Task forces comprise law enforcement agents and local nongovernmental organizations that offer services to trafficked persons. Member organizations may address domestic violence and offer shelter to some victims, or their missions may be guided by geographical location, ethnicity, or economic sector. Law enforcement personnel on task forces often include officers focused on prostitution and drug crimes. The task forces therefore often focus on sex work and prostitution and have rarely investigated labor trafficking, especially when the service providers involved specialize in child protection and/or domestic violence. This was the case with the anti-trafficking task force in Louisiana that formed in 2006: membership included few trafficking survivors who became advocates.[18] In the case of the Indian workers in the cleanup after Hurricane Katrina, members of the recently formed local anti-trafficking task force did not believe that the evidence presented met the standard for human trafficking.[19]

The newly formed organizations like the New Orleans Workers' Center for Racial Justice and the Alliance of Guestworkers for Dignity, along with groups of Signal employees, undertook grassroots know-your-rights trainings in the context of the Katrina cleanup, and advocated for better treatment. Their multi-ethnic labor rights efforts are similar to the Fair Food Program and the Coalition of Immokalee Workers described in chapter 3, in that both employ a human rights approach to trafficking, which includes providing trauma-informed services in the aftermath of the extreme abuses they suffered.

The situations covered in this chapter are similar to others described earlier, bringing to mind the exploitation of young people on sales crews, the irrational amounts charged for domestic workers' travel to the United States, and the dismal accommodations of agricultural workers. Forced and unpaid labor continues to be used to create the structures and products we use every day.

CHAPTER 9

SLAVERY AND PRISON LABOR IN INDUSTRY AND INFRASTRUCTURE

T HE ICONIC IMAGE of American prison labor is that of a chain gang—
men chained together, all wearing striped garments and making a
road. From the photo below, we see how enslaved and prison labor were
intrinsic to building American infrastructure. Much of this work was done
by enslaved people, some of whom were owned by the municipalities who

*A Southern chain gang. From Detroit Publishing Co., between
1900 and 1906, https://www.loc.gov/item/2016803065.*

commissioned the construction projects.[1] Enslaved people built the historic wall that gave its name to New York's Wall Street. They built railroads and public buildings throughout the East Coast. Some of these structures are still in use.

Infrastructure work was dangerous. Enslaved workers died in workplace accidents, in drownings, and of disease. Some were worked to death.

Infrastructure efforts utilizing enslaved labor were administered in different ways. At different moments in history, in Georgia, Mississippi, Tennessee, and Louisiana, state-owned slaves built state-owned railways and roads, cleared waterways, and constructed ports, all for the purposes of moving cotton to places where it would be turned into thread, cloth, fabric, and clothing. As such, these enslaved infrastructure workers built, through state resources, the private wealth of Southern whites.

Even before American independence from Britain, South Carolina mandated that slaveholders send their enslaved workers to work for the colony, building roads, courts, and jails.[2] From 1834 until 1861, the state of Louisiana used enslaved workers to clear waterways and levees and to create water routes that strengthened the state economically, in part by opening land to cotton cultivation. This was deemed a better approach than contracting paid laborers, because many would quit the difficult and dangerous work.[3] The state had initially tried to use prison labor to do this work, but it found that convicts' chains impeded movement and that more investment in structures of control was required than with using the labor of enslaved people. Clearing the water routes and surveying the backcountry was handled by enslaved workers from boats that served as their home and which they had to maintain and manage themselves. One white captain on

WANTED TO HIRE 600 NEGROES
TO WORK on the South & North Alabama and Cen tral Railroads, between Montgomery and Elyton, a Bridging, Track-laying, Grading, getting ties, timbers, &c. for the year 1864.
Apply to Geo. O. Baker, Selma, R. H. Kelly, Lime Station, Shelby county, or the undersigned at Montgomery.
JOHN T. MILNER,
Chief Engineer and Superintendent,
Office in the old Winter Iron Works.
dec 24-d1m.

*Pre-Emancipation advertisement to hire six hundred
"Negroes," presumably including enslaved people for railway work.
Courtesy Alabama Department of Archives and History.*

each boat supervised the enslaved workers, including a cook, a ship's pilot, an engineer, and a mate.[4]

The financial benefits of enslaved labor were calculated by an administrator with the Louisiana Department of Public Labor in 1860, who found that the yearly expense of forty-three white laborers was $43,260, while a crew of the same number of enslaved workers cost $23,422 less. Rather than calculating that the total savings were simply the difference between those figures, he estimated the actual total savings to be $37,475, because he believed that enslaved workers worked harder.[5] Their accomplishments increased the values of land and, through the creation of waterway transport, expanded the options for where free people of means chose to live.

Sometimes public infrastructure, particularly waterways, was seen as counter to the interests of private property, especially near large farms where enslaved people could potentially engage in independent trade outside the interests of their enslavers. At times, infrastructure plans were put off or relocated in response to these concerns.[6] In some cases, business owners used enslaved labor to create their own private infrastructure by which to transport their product. Some businesses were nearly entirely staffed by enslaved people. Where businesses staffed by enslaved people grew, including in the development of roads and waterways and in preparing lumber, the numbers of enslaved people also rose. For example, in one Alabama county, censuses show a steady increase in the numbers of enslaved people and an extreme increase between 1850 and 1860, more than 50 percent, as slave labor was adopted for industrial purposes like sawmills and the necessary means to transport lumber to where it would be used.[7] Railways also employed enslaved people, sometimes hired from enslavers and sometimes owned by the company. Enslaved people were sometimes arrested, but since enslavers did not want to lose their laborers to prison time, they often had them removed from jail. The image below is of a document a railway company filed in an attempt to recover one of its enslaved workers from prison.

Although they supported this state-level use of resources, Southern states resisted national efforts to build interstate and national infrastructure. As slaveholding states, they opposed federal supervision or implementation because they feared threats to legalized slavery. They also sought to avoid increased federal taxation of their assets, including enslaved people and the income generated by their labor; this was a particularly salient concern with

Document of a railway company's attempt to recover from prison a person enslaved by the rail company. Courtesy Montgomery County Archives.

regard to the building of roads and canals, and highlights how the politics of slavery touched on seemingly unrelated issues.[8]

Postbellum, some of this state-level infrastructure as mentioned above in the example of South Carolina, was completed with the forced labor of imprisoned people, using the convict leasing system described in chapter 4. These workers built roads and railways, mined coal, and produced construction materials. Atlanta is the first large city to confront its history of prison labor in infrastructure. A coalition of organizations, including the National Center for Civil and Human Rights, is building a memorial for the convict laborers of Bellwood Quarry, where chain gangs cut the granite that was used to build the city. Atlanta is also converting the site of the Chattahoochee Brick Company, which used prison labor, into a memorial.[9] Scholars in other places are chronicling convict leasing; for example, historians in Tennessee have begun investigating convict leasing sites, including the graveyards of people who died while working in mines, and connecting the names of prisoners to their descendants living today.[10]

Women were included in prison labor and in chain gangs. Most of these women were Black: in the state of Georgia, for instance, between 1908 and 1938, over two thousand Black women and only four white women were forced to work in chain gangs.[11]

Railway owners, mine owners, and manufacturers could rent prisoners to work for them. Convict leasing generated great profits for the business owners, who did not have to pay wages to the prisoners. The leasing fees went to the prison, generating money for the state.

"WE BEG FOR KIND TREATMENT AND FAIL TO GET IT"

Conditions for prison laborers were terrible, and many died in the course of the work. In 1884, Ezekiel Archey and Ambrose Haskins, two Black prison laborers, wrote to the Board of Inspectors of Convicts in Alabama about their poor treatment at Pratt Mines in Jefferson County. In the letter, they describe being prohibited from seeing family visitors who had traveled to visit them, being whipped and receiving other forms of physical punishment, and being given heavier workloads than whites at the coal mine:

> We beg for kind treatment and fail to get it. Please look at the white men and see how many are cutting 5 or 6 ton [sic] coal per day. They are few. They are the men that cause the present trouble + every state officer tries to hold us accountable for the[ir] actions by denying us the privileges of allowing our families to come to see us if our families come.[12]

The restriction on visitation was particularly cruel. Prison laborers were often split from their families and forced to move long distances, a form of family separation very similar to the experiences of many in slavery.

Another letter attributed to Archey further describes poor treatment and working conditions at Pratt Mines.[13] In addition to mentioning their felony record and how it led to them working off their terms, Archey details the scarring and sorely trying conditions of corporal punishment, which include "filth and vermin in the extreme." "Every day some one of us are carried to our ever-lasting rest," he laments. The Board of Inspectors of Convicts ordered the discharge of Archey and John Fannin in January 1887.[14] This individual appeal for justice took years, and calls for systemic change were unheeded.

Letter from Ezekiel Archey and Ambrose Haskins to the Board of Inspectors of Convicts. Courtesy Alabama Department of Archives and History.

Archey and Haskins were not the only people to note the high rate of death among prison laborers. George W. Cable, a white New Orleans native who served in the Confederate Army and later wrote essays condemning Jim Crow, wrote a state-by-state assessment of the convict leasing system across the South, concluding that

if anything may be inferred from the mortal results of the Lease System in other States, the year's death-rate of the convict camps of Louisiana must exceed that of any pestilence that ever fell upon Europe in the Middle Ages. And as far as popular rumor goes, it confirms this assumption on every hand. Every mention of these camps is followed by the execrations of a scandalized community whose ear is every now and then shocked afresh with some new whisper of their frightful barbarities.[15]

CHINESE CONTRACT LABORERS ON RAILWAYS

A quarter of a million "coolies," mostly men, were brought from China to the US between the 1840s and the 1870s.[16] That era's Opium War, in which European countries fought to forcibly sell opium inside China, contributed to instability and hunger there, while ongoing civil unrest in the form of anti-dynastic peasant rebellions meant fighting continued even after the war had concluded. Interethnic strife between Siyi and Hakka people in Guangdong (then known as Canton) also played a part; with so much fighting disrupting the region, agricultural businesses became unsustainable, and many Chinese sought work in other parts of Asia and elsewhere.[17]

After the Opium War, Britain took Hong Kong as a territory, which became home to numerous companies with ties to the west. The Chinese who left Hong Kong and Guangdong emigrated through these companies. Most Chinese who came to the US arrived in California, and the discovery of gold there in 1848 brought many more.

The first Chinese people to arrive in California seem to have been not "coolies" but merchants from the city of Canton who'd been hit by recession in China in 1847 but with enough funds to afford their tickets to the US and set up businesses.[18] Chinese contract laborers, on the other hand, were largely from more rural areas; upon arriving in the city of Hong Kong, they encountered recruiters for Western companies seeking workers.[19] Many Chinese laborers, many of Siyi origin, who went to America seeking gold instead ended up working on the new railroads in the American West.[20] They also rebuilt old track and infrastructure in a South that had been destroyed during the Civil War.[21] They worked in mines and in agriculture in California and in the South, at a time when the planter class was looking for a labor force to replace enslaved labor, as described in chapter 4.

The status of these laborers was reminiscent of indentured servants in that their contracts were time-bound. A key difference was that the

Chinese workers' contracts mandated that the laborers receive set wages and return passage to their place of embarkation after a fixed number of years. However, only approximately a quarter of those who came to work in the US ended up returning to China, even for a short visit.[22]

Contract laborers were primarily recruited from Guangdong and the surrounding region by both Chinese and American contractors, who advanced the cost of passage from Hong Kong to the Americas. The cost of this passage was approximately forty to fifty dollars, four to five times the annual earnings of a Chinese laborer. Through this "credit-ticket" system, the laborers would repay the costs for their passage while working their first job. Upon arrival, one journalist described the newly arrived workers being taken directly from their ship by boat to a railyard, where they were herded into boxcars and transported to the worksite, constantly under vigilant guard. Some workers opened the doors of the boxcars and jumped out, only to die upon hitting the ground.[23]

Increased demand for labor on railways and in mines and in growing cities like San Francisco led to increased importation of and reliance on foreign workers. In 1865, when advertisements for railway workers in California failed to yield the desired number of American laborers, the Central and Union Pacific Railroad Company turned to Chinese miners and farmhands already in California. They were willing to work for the low wages offered, which were about a third of what white workers would accept, but still more than they could earn in China.[24] Once the domestic supply of underpaid Chinese men in the country was exhausted, railway companies turned to recruiters to import additional laborers. The recruiters included some independent American-run operations and the "Six Companies," a group of benevolent associations run by and for Chinese people in California. Between them, they brought tens of thousands of laborers from the regions around China's Pearl River Delta to the American West.

White settlers also went to California with labor contracts, but the railroad companies believed these workers were less likely to fulfill the terms of their contracts than Chinese workers. White workers were more able to walk away from their contracts when they learned of their working conditions and discovered other opportunities. During an 1876 California

State Senate committee hearing about Chinese immigration, governor of California Frederick Low, who had been the US minister to China, explained that the Chinese workers "do not know our laws here, and the companies have such absolute power over them that they keep their contracts. The guilds have absolute power over them here and in their own country."[25] Not only did the American guilds of Chinese contract workers, including the Six Companies, have strong ties with employment agencies in China and Hong Kong; they might have also run them.

When the workers arrived at their camps, they were placed into "gangs" of between twenty-five and one hundred. Each gang worked under a foreman, often of the same ethnicity and from the same part of China as the other members. The recruiting company garnished a part of each worker's wages, and that would continue until the worker paid off his travel debt. US corporations paid the recruiting company, the recruiting company paid the foreman, and the foreman disbursed money to each member of the gang.

The Six Companies also exerted control over workers, particularly with regard to their return to China. Most Chinese workers intended to return, but they could only do so with the blessing of the companies that had recruited them. The Six Companies had agreements with the shipping companies that transported workers across the Pacific Ocean: to gain permission to board the return ship, contract workers were required to show the shipping company a certificate issued by one of the Six Companies confirming that they had paid their debt. The Six Companies also pledged that the bodies of any contract workers who died in the United States would be repatriated to China, which assured that their families would be able to tend the graves of the deceased and fulfill rituals to ensure that they had all they would need in the afterworld.[26] The remains of approximately twelve hundred Chinese workers were repatriated in one shipment after the completion of the Central Pacific Railroad (CPRR) in 1869, unearthed and prepared for shipment by surviving Chinese railway workers.[27]

Despite the arduous working conditions and the low wages, there is evidence that some Chinese laborers found that the arrangement met their needs. Some paid their debt, returned home to China, and later signed on for another contract. Railway managers sought to retain those Chinese workers who stayed on after the initial shock at the severe conditions passed.[28] These workers proved their desirability and became indispensable.

UNREST AND EXPLOITATION ON THE RAILROAD

Railway work was hard and dangerous. Men dug tunnels and laid track across the country, across prairies and through mountains. Workers died in landslides, in avalanches, and in accidents. In both the West and the South, Chinese contract workers faced hostility because of their role in lowering American wages. In multiple incidents, Chinese workers were met with violence from white workers, who violently chased them from their worksites. In the South, freed Blacks who had only just begun to be paid for their work resented the Chinese. Chinese workers were paid so much less that even when they demanded and won raises—as at CPRR, when they won an increase from thirty-one dollars to thirty-five dollars per month in May of 1867—they were still paid less than white men.[29]

The Chinese did not accept exploitation passively. Chinese workers mounted strikes for better conditions in both the South and the West, where workers on the Union and Central Pacific Railroads staged strikes in 1867 and 1868 to demand that they not be beaten, that their hours be shortened to match the hours of white workers, and that they be paid more. After an explosion killed five Chinese laborers and a white man on June 19, 1867, three thousand Chinese workers went on strike all through the CPRR line on June 24. In a predictable reversal, the CPRR sought to hire five thousand formerly enslaved people as replacement workers, but they did not come.[30] A week later, after losing a week's work, Charles Crocker, one of the founders of the CPRR, negotiated with the Chinese workers; as a result, the company offered not to dock the Chinese workers' pay for striking, and most of the workers accepted this offer. They resumed working, and after the company publicly declared victory, it increased their wages.[31]

Later that year, Chinese workers on other railroads engaged in strikes to protest mistreatment and unpaid wages.[32] In the early days of May 1869, the Union Pacific Railroad had stopped paying its workers. The workers responded by holding railroad vice president Thomas Durant hostage for their wages, which were then paid a few days later on May 8.[33]

After the Pacific railroad was completed in 1869, Chinese workers were contracted to work on the Alabama-Chattanooga (AL-CH) railroad after freed Black people had refused to work for the low wages offered. A Dutchman who worked with the Six Companies arranged to bring hundreds of Chinese railway workers from California to Alabama and Tennessee, offering a wage of sixteen dollars per month and meals; the first Chinese railway workers arrived in Alabama in 1870.[34] The owner of the railroad subsequently encountered a credit crisis and was unable to pay workers for several months. Provisions ran short and the Chinese protested, demanding additional rice. (It was common for contracts to specify that Chinese contract workers would be fed food prepared by a Chinese cook.) In this instance, the unpaid employees—white, Black, and Chinese—staged a collective action and "seized the trains."[35] This led to a face-to-face confrontation in which the owner of the railway began to strike workers with a pick handle, killing one and injuring ten others. The railroad ultimately defaulted on its creditors and in 1875 went into receivership (a preliminary stage of bankruptcy that sorts out which assets to sell to repay creditors). At that time, half of the Chinese workers moved south, where they found work on plantations cutting sugarcane and picking cotton.[36] The AL-CH railway company went bankrupt, and the railway was never completed.

THE EMERGENCE OF THE RACIST NATIVIST MOVEMENT

The railroad barons' insistence on using cheap labor, despite having accumulated vast wealth, enough to be able to fully endow universities, is a practice older than the United States itself. Leland Stanford, head of the Central Pacific Railroad and founder of the eponymous university, became committed to hiring Chinese railway workers because they were "contented with less wages."[37] These cost reductions came at the expense of living wages, safe working conditions, and social stability. The fact that people who were exploited this way were Black and Asian helped confirm the white supremacist beliefs of many Americans and inspired their promotion of a racist and nativist platform.

This racist platform culminated in the passage of laws that constrained the immigration of people who would undercut the wages of white workers. The Chinese Exclusion Act of 1882 was one such law; it intended to eliminate the importation of laborers who would undercut the wages of white laborers. At the time, there was no legal path for Chinese people to become citizens, in contrast to the indentured Europeans who had been able to claim citizenship.[38] Few Chinese women lived in the US, because they were excluded from entering if they were presumed to be prostitutes or likely to become public charges. (Chapter 12 has more information about the Page Act, which prohibited the entry of Chinese women to the United States.) The scarcity of Chinese women and widespread laws against interracial marriage severely restricted opportunities for Chinese to marry and have children. However, the passage of the Fourteenth Amendment, with its birthright citizenship clause, in 1868 established that the children of Chinese immigrant workers were American citizens, with all the rights that that carried. Neither the employers of Chinese workers nor workers of European descent were eager to see that happen.[39]

JOHN HENRY, RAILWAY LEGEND AND PRISON LABORER

As discussed earlier in this chapter, much of the railway track in the east was laid by male convicts. One of them was John Henry, a late nineteenth-century folk hero whose legendary, possibly apocryphal, competition with a steam-powered hammer has been immortalized in ballads and work songs. Racing against the machine with his nine-pound hammer, he won the contest but died of a heart attack immediately afterward.[40] The legend highlights the physical strength of the man and the exploitation of his labor. Most Americans know the legend of John Henry, but what is not widely known is the context around him and the role of forced labor in American infrastructure.

The historical John Henry is more tragic even than the legend.[41] At least three locations have been suggested as the site of his death, including in Alabama and West Virginia. The most well documented may be a Black man from the north named John Henry who served in the Union Army and remained in the South, in Virginia, after the Civil War. The head of the Freedmen's Bureau, Charles Burd, enforced the Black Codes described in chapter 5 rather than assisting formerly enslaved people. This John Henry was arrested, perhaps by Burd's men. He was sentenced to ten years in 1866. Few would have lived to see freedom after such a sentence. Henry began working on the Chesapeake & Ohio Railroad as a prisoner in 1868. Steam drills, early jackhammers, and explosives were in use during this time, and approximately a tenth of prison laborers working on railways died from injuries, overwork, malnourishment, disease, and poor treatment each year.

Henry is believed to have died in 1873, and his body would have been returned to the penitentiary in Richmond, Virginia, for burial in a mass grave. In life, John Henry was not a mountain of strength but a malnourished convict of diminutive stature, standing five foot one, who died of overwork—possibly in the form of an accident, silicosis (black lung disease), or even murder. After his truncated life, railway workers sang work songs about him.[42] Railway songs set a rhythm for the dangerous work, intended to keep workers at a regular and safe pace. In contrast to the ballads that tell John Henry's story, the work songs highlight the truth of the tragedy—that he died needlessly and should have slowed down. One version published around 1909 includes these lines:

> *John Henry was hammering on the right side,*
> *The big steam drill on the left,*
> *Before that steam drill could beat him down,*
> *He hammered his fool self to death.*[43]

THE ECONOMIC IMPACT OF PRISON LABOR IN INDUSTRY

In each of these situations, the presence of people forced to work for reduced wages had the effect of lowering wages for all workers in their sector. These less costly labor options were driven by force, coercion, and white supremacy. Prisons made money from the work inmates performed; for example, New Jersey reported that all convicts earned a total of $18,927 compared with expenses of $13,474 in 1851.[44] New Jersey thus generated a profit of $5,453, or 40 percent of the expenditure. In any business, 40 percent would be a compelling margin. While this is an extreme example, it highlights the conflict of interest in states profiting from what is supposed to be an impartial application of the law. The incarcerated aren't the only ones negatively affected by this conflict of interest. In places where prisons have used convict labor to produce the same products made by local companies, local industries have protested. For example, when the Elmira Reformatory in Upstate New York produced brooms and brushes in the 1880s, the nearby manufacturers in the town of Cohoes protested the competition from cheaper prison labor. Some municipalities enacted laws restricting prison production to use only specific types of tools or to ensure that no industry or product made up more than 10 percent of production.[45]

Prison labor continues to be used by corporations, as described in chapter 5. However, consumers can and do protest this practice, both through public protest and in their spending choices.[46] The concluding chapter includes a link to a site that monitors the use of prison labor by publicly owned and traded companies.

PART V

TRAFFICKING
FOR SEX

CHAPTER 10

FLOR'S STORY

THIS SECTION ADDRESSES trafficking for sex, and opens with the story of "Flor," whom I interviewed three times in the course of my work with the Sex Workers Project.[1] Hers is a contemporary case study of trafficking into prostitution. The next chapter describes historical situations involving enslaved people and indentured servants forced to engage in prostitution. Following that chapter are those examining immigration laws that restrict entry on moral grounds, and the Mann Act of 1910, which was applied along racial lines and used politically. The section's concluding chapter looks at new legislative efforts to address trafficking today, including laws that affect communication online and the far-reaching effects of these laws beyond human trafficking.

Flor was born in a small community in a very rural part of central Mexico in the late 1980s. Her family was extremely poor. They did not always have enough to eat, so she sometimes went to sleep hungry. Her family's poverty deepened after her father left. At that point her uncle, her mother's brother, became the man of the house. He violently abused Flor, her mother, and her siblings. Flor had attended a few years of elementary school but not secondary school. Instead, she helped to sell things in the town market, cleaned houses, and worked in the fields to grow food. Her life, marked by limited education and hard work, was typical of girls in her area. However, her family was poorer than most of their neighbors, and her uncle unusually violent.

Unsurprisingly, Flor wanted a better life. Her idea of a better life did not involve riches, but simply having enough food and not being beaten. She had not thought through how she would achieve this but knew her opportunities to improve her life were tied to marriage. Until she married and went to live with her husband, she would continue to live at home with her mother and uncle. This state of affairs was standard for the area, and she did not imagine a different life for herself. What she wanted was to build a life with a loving, affectionate man who lived up to the standard expectations of supporting his family and taking care of his wife.

Flor was fifteen when a neighbor, a woman, introduced her to Alberto. A grown man, more than ten years older than her, he wore fashionable new clothing and drove his own car. Even then, in the early twenty-first century, people in Flor's small town were more likely to own a horse than a car.

He paid attention to Flor, asked her to dinner, invited her to go places with him. Unsure of herself around him, Flor said no at first, but he continued to ask. She found his attentions flattering. She liked being the one he chose to invite. She liked the idea of going on a date with him. Eventually, she accepted his invitation to go with him to his family home to meet his aunt and talk about the possibility of working for her. "And this man [Alberto] appeared, an acquaintance of my neighbor, I went out with him and left the house with him," Flor said. "He said, 'I'm going to take you to my aunt's and she can give you a job.'"

Flor did not think her mother would allow her to go out with Alberto, even though Flor knew him through their neighbor. But Flor was eager to leave home. Without telling her mother, she got in Alberto's car.

Alberto drove far and fast. They drove down mountain roads, past the next town. Her own town had just eight families. This neighboring town was larger, and Flor was familiar with it because her family sometimes went there on market days to sell vegetables. But Alberto continued driving. They passed many more towns, none of which she had ever seen before. She was now farther from home than she had ever been in her life. The roads became wider. They changed from rutted dirt roads to paved roads, then to roads with two lanes, and then with three or four.

As Alberto drove on, she realized she had no idea where she was or how to get home. She understood at that moment that she was dependent upon him to get anywhere. They crossed into the next state. She realized that she would not go home that night. When she told me about leaving with Alberto, Flor said, "I thought that was a really good idea, but it wasn't like that." It was the beginning of her ordeal as a trafficked woman.

Flor realized she would not be going home that night, or ever again. But she also knew then that she could never go home, because, if a small-town girl returns home after staying away for the night, it brings shame on her family. In such a case, the girl is expected to stay with the man she's left with and live with him as his wife. This is why Flor accepted her fate and prepared to live with the man who had seduced and kidnapped her.

Mexican romantic music includes a motif of "seduction" songs about men taking nubile young women from their families. Electa Arenal, professor emerita of Hispanic and women's studies at the Graduate Center of the City University of New York, explained to me, when I was one of her students, that these songs might seem to be about kidnapping and rape to those unfamiliar with Mexican culture, but they are, in fact, "the most romantic songs ever written."[2] They are songs about men and women so in love that they run away together, whatever the consequences. In this culture, "good girls" must never acknowledge their own desire. They cannot admit to desiring a man sexually or romantically, or to wanting to leave their families. But what they can do is to put themselves in a situation where a man can take them away. These songs are unabashedly romantic, in the vein of *Romeo and Juliet*. For example, the second verse of the song "O tú o yo" by José José opens with the lines "Voy a cerrar las puertas y así / Conseguiré guardarte" (I'm going to close the doors and so / I'll get to keep you). The singer goes on about how he does not want her to seek another lover despite his failings, and how he could not live without her.[3] Such songs probably have a strong influence on the way that provincial girls like Flor imagine they will meet the men they will marry and how they will leave their family homes. Flor left an unhappy family home and looked forward to seeing new places and things with a man who was interested in her. She was not afraid. She was happy and relieved and excited to go. She felt a sense of possibility for the future that lifted her heart and her expectations, even as she realized that she had lost control of her situation.

Alberto took her to his family's house in Tenancingo, Tlaxcala, a city of ten thousand. Unbeknownst to Flor, Tlaxcala is a region with a burgeoning sex trade. Flor stayed in Alberto's family's house for a month and was put to work, helping his female relatives with housework and cleaning. Alberto's family was large. There were many children, more than could have belonged to the sisters and in-laws who lived in the house. Flor did not understand whose children they were, but they were all part of the family.

Alberto would visit her at the house but didn't live there himself. She was not permitted to go outside. She was told that it was not safe, that people in the town were violent and would hurt her. It did not seem strange to Flor that she was not allowed out. She did not want to go outside, into an unfamiliar town that she had been told was dangerous. Overall, she felt that she had moved closer to her cultural ideal of being supported by a husband, even though she was expected to work all the time in the house. Nonetheless, Flor was not happy.

> I was put into a room and told not to speak with anyone. I was not allowed to use the phone. They would bring me food into the room where I was staying. During the month that I stayed there, Alberto would come by from time to time. He asked me how I was doing. I told him I was upset and wanted to go home. He said everything was going to be okay. . . .
>
> I was forced to do work in the different houses belonging to his family. I was told to do all the laundry and clean the houses.

Social roles are clearly delineated in Mexican society, and women's roles center on the home: keeping house, cooking, and taking care of children. Being financially supported by a man and not having to work outside the home is the ideal for many women. Moreover, the environment outside the home may be genuinely dangerous. Robbery and violent crimes, including kidnapping, are more common in Mexico than in the United States, especially in the context of the ongoing Mexican drug war and various cartels and paramilitary organizations fighting for territory and resources. Femicide is a problem around the country.

Ana, another Mexican woman I interviewed, articulated these social expectations of women. "In my family," she said, "my mother always told us that when we grow up women should be in the home and have kids and be married and the men should be working."

Flor's mother was heartsick not knowing where her daughter had gone. Initially, her mother knew only that Flor had gotten into a young man's car, a young man not from the area. She asked her neighbors about him, and where Flor might have gone. Gradually, Flor's mother learned enough to know that she should go to Tlaxcala. In the town of Tenancingo, where Alberto's family lived, jobs had dried up more than three generations ago, which is why, in the absence of other economic opportunities, the city has become a hub for forced prostitution.

It is very likely that the neighbor who introduced Flor to Alberto was involved in his family business, and she may have been collaborating with him to recruit another young woman. A woman who arrived in their town with Alberto shared enough information with people there that Flor's mother was able to learn where Alberto was from. This allowed her to do something nearly impossible: find her daughter. Flor's mother had never been out of their state, had never gone beyond a few miles from their home—perhaps no further than the market town Flor mentioned—but now she was going to Tlaxcala. There she found Flor and went to Alberto's family.

Flor's mother explained to her daughter that she could come home. She told Flor that their family would not view her as a disgraced woman and that things at home might change for the better. Although Flor by now knew that she did not want to stay with Alberto, she also knew that her family would lose the respect of their neighbors if she returned as a single woman. She also understood that her return could not do anything to alleviate the violence and poverty she had endured, and that her and her mother's situation could become even worse. Flor accepted her fate with Alberto, living in the large home his family had built and cleaning up after the extended family in their multiple homes.

Flor explained her thinking to me, about why she did not return to her hometown with her mother:

> I was afraid of what my parents would say about my situation—about living with a boy without being married. It was shaming and my family would have been dishonored if I returned to them as a single woman. I had to make my relationship with Alberto work no matter what because

I had nowhere to go. . . . I trusted him to take care of me—I was naive and could not believe he would do anything to harm me. Thus, I was trapped when he eventually became mean and vicious.

Later, shortly after their conversation described above, Flor and her mother had a visit together at Alberto's family's house, with Alberto's family present. At the bus station, as her mother was leaving, she asked Flor to return with her, again. However, Alberto's entire family was there, and even though Flor longed to leave with her mother, she knew she could not. She knew that she was not free to go.

I was scared of the family and what they would do to my whole family if I left with my mother, so I decided to stay with them to protect my own family. I also knew that at the least Alberto would have shamed me and my family if I went back home with my mother.

Things would get worse. Both Alberto and his family members became violent toward her. Then he began pressuring her to travel with him to Guadalajara so that she could sell sex on the street. Prostitution is not a crime in Mexico, but Flor had no interest in it. Cleaning, farming, and selling things in the market were things she had been raised to do, things she had done her whole life. They were acceptable occupations for good women who lacked education and connections. He told her that they had to do it for their future, to build a house for their children. Flor argued that she could do other work, but he only shot her down, angered that she would contradict him. Although they were not officially married, he told her that a wife should obey her husband, that he was in charge of their family. When she resisted, he beat her. She realized then that the man who she thought loved her was abusive, and that he was using her. Her life with him was certainly not, as she'd believed, better than before. She was forced out of the house and taken to another city to sell sex on the street.

After one month, Alberto's cousin forced me to leave the house and sent me to another house in the same city. There, Alberto told me that I owed him because I had been there so long. Alberto and his cousin told me that I was going to work as a prostitute. I told them that I didn't want to do it. He hit me, striking me in the face. He told me that if I didn't work I wouldn't be able to help my family. He didn't tell me how much money I would make, but he said that we would be able to buy a house. The cousin's wife was there and doing the same thing. She told me to do it because Alberto really needed the money.

In the beginning, I didn't accept it when he told me I had to prostitute myself, so he beat me and I had to do it. In Guadalajara I wanted to escape and he threatened me after about two or three months. He threatened me, "Don't think about this. If I don't kill you, I'll get your siblings." They always spoke about the brother that I was closest to and threatened to kill him.

They took me to Guadalajara with two other girls, Maria and Ines. Maria was another wife of Alberto's cousin. Alberto drove his cousin's wife, his brother, and us, the three women, to Guadalajara. We arrived at a hotel. We were then sent to a house where there were about twenty to twenty-five young women from all over Mexico. There were fifteen rooms in the house. Every twenty minutes we would go outside and find a man who we would bring back into the house as a customer. I would have sex with the men and collect the money. We worked from nine a.m. to nine p.m. On average I collected between eight hundred and a thousand pesos per day. All of this money was given to Alberto when we returned to the hotel at night. We were there for three months and then went to Veracruz, where we were forced to do the same for another two months. We then returned to Guadalajara.

Flor went to so many towns and cities that they all ran together in her mind, blurring in time and space: Guadalajara, Veracruz, Matamoros, Mexico City, Tijuana, border towns, major cities, neighborhoods near Mexican military bases. Sometimes Alberto would drive her to the next city but often she would travel by bus. To Flor, the places she passed through all looked the same: she saw only the red-light areas where women in tight clothing solicited on the streets, and the insides of seedy hotels where she would have sex with the men who paid her. The sleeveless minidresses that Flor and the other women wore might not have looked "sexy" compared with the outfits in an American nightclub, but they were far more revealing than the longer sleeves and longer dresses and pants that "good" Mexican women wear, and they worked in neighborhoods where "good" women did not go. Flor would work in one city for a few weeks at a time, and then

Alberto's family would move her on so that she would attract those clients who were seeking new faces.

Being a newcomer carried its own risks. Local people would prey on outsiders, knowing that they were unfamiliar with the area and lacked support or protection. Women in Mexico who sell sex are shamed by others, including the police, who are known throughout the country for corruption and abuse. On the occasions when Flor was robbed or assaulted while doing her work, she could not turn to the police for help.

Although Flor earned a significant amount of money, she never personally benefited from it:

> I was never allowed to keep any of the money I earned. He [Alberto] would take all the money and he always went through my things checking to see if I had any money on me. Whenever I asked for money from him he would get annoyed and say I do not need any money for myself. If I complained that I wanted to go to a movie or something, Alberto would always get mad and say I had to work to make more money to be able to go out. With the money I earned, Alberto built a bedroom and got furniture for our house, and he sent money to his parents in Tenancingo. Alberto refused to let me send any money to my mother. To this day it hurts me a lot that I could never send any money to my family when they needed it a lot.

Flor never had a house in Tenancingo that she saw, but she probably paid for a house with her earnings. Alberto would get her hopes up about a house to manipulate her. He kept Flor under surveillance so that he would know how much money he could expect from her each day. "Alberto and his family knew the people who owned the hotels, so the hotel owners would report the number of customers to Alberto and his family," she said. "Sometimes Alberto would keep track of the number of clients I saw by hanging around."

I asked Flor if she had ever tried to keep any of the money she earned. "One occasion I hid some money, a little part for me. He found it, he beat me a lot, there were no options," she said.

Domestic violence was not legally made a crime in Mexico until 2007; to a large degree, though, violence against women is still tacitly accepted. In this way, the physical violence in Flor's life with Alberto was not so different from what she had experienced when she lived with her family. In both cases, no one around her spoke out against it. Now, however, being a prostitute meant that she was even less able to find any sympathy or protection and was only more vulnerable to violence from others.

> Alberto became more and more abusive. He insulted and humiliated me, called me a dog, hit and beat me. Alberto used to punch me or bang my head against the wall while pulling me by my hair. To this day, I still have migraine headaches sometimes and it feels like my head is being split open. . . . When he beat me sometimes he would force me to have sex with him. Alberto said that he did not care how rough he was being and that I would never find another man. I would tell him he was hurting me, but he seemed to enjoy that. Many times Alberto would beat me and then force me to have sex with him. After beating me he thought having sex with me would calm me down, but of course it would make me feel worse. . . . He would hit me while threatening me.

Several times, Flor became pregnant and was forced to have an abortion. She had wanted to carry each pregnancy to term, and eventually she had a son with Alberto. "Now that I had my son, I was even more scared of leaving Alberto and his family. I did not know what they might do to my son if I left," she said. Once, when Flor did try to leave with her son, she did not get far and was forced to turn back:

> As soon as I entered his house Alberto's mother immediately took my child away and Alberto severely beat me. He insulted me and said vulgar things. Alberto then said that he did not care what I did and that I could leave. His father also said that he had no more use for me. He said I could leave but that I could not take the child with me. They said that knowing that I could never leave my son behind. . . . Alberto said I could leave but that he would keep my child. Therefore, I stayed with him against my wishes so that I would not lose my son forever.

Flor continued to travel from city to city, selling sex in different places across Mexico; her son remained with Alberto's family in Tenancingo. She understood that her son was being used to manipulate her, but she was never certain whether Alberto or his family loved the child and took good care of him, or whether he was simply one more way for them to control her.

TRAVEL TO THE UNITED STATES

Flor had never wanted to travel to the United States, but, after a few years, Alberto insisted. She could earn more money selling sex there than in Mexico. He told her, "This is only temporary. You can do this for only a few years in the US and then we'll have enough money to build a house for ourselves." So Flor entered the US in the Southwest, eventually traveling to New York City.

At first, Alberto was with her. "When Alberto came to the US, he kept my son at his parents' house in Mexico and sent some of the money there," Flor said. "He always warned me that if I told anyone about the fact that I was forced to do prostitution I would never get my son back."

When Alberto was not with Flor, his uncle and brother would watch her. They were not always present, but they knew where she would be and arranged everything. They controlled her movements. When she resisted them, they threatened her and her son and her family. She had suffered enough violence from Alberto and his family to know that these were not idle threats. She did as she was told. They also told her that if she had any encounters with US law enforcement, she would be arrested and treated as a criminal, charged with prostitution and other crimes, and then deported. Flor was terrified of the police, even more than of Alberto's violence and his threats.

In the United States, Flor worked in ethnic brothels alongside other Spanish-speaking sex workers from across Latin America. Many of the women were Mexican like herself. Others were Dominican and Ecuadoran. Many were around her age, in their late teens and early twenties. Many of them had started selling sex before they'd turned eighteen.

According to US law, people who are under eighteen who sell sex are considered victims of trafficking, not criminals. Despite this, minors are still very likely to be arrested while selling sex. In theory, police are trained to identify trafficked persons and assist them instead of arresting them. Unfortunately, brothel raids often lead only to arrest for sex workers, whether trafficked or not. Flor was arrested multiple times on prostitution charges in the United States, including at least twice in New York City. After arrest, she would appear before a judge and pay a fine or be sentenced to time served, meaning time spent in jail after arrest and before conviction. Police never asked her about her experiences or tried to find out her circumstances.

Flor's story comes very close to the stereotypical human trafficking story—a young adolescent girl taken from her family and forced to sell sex, she is eventually identified as a victim of crime and removed from her trafficking situation. Though Flor's story arouses sympathy because she resembles the quintessential trafficking victim that many people imagine, what distinguishes her story is that, multiple times, the authorities arrested her instead of recognizing her as a trafficked person and victim of crime.

Flor's experience is not unusual, however. Other trafficked women who I interviewed for a Sex Workers Project report described being arrested many times, up to ten times in some cases, without ever once being recognized as victims of crime. For Flor, her arrests only confirmed everything that Alberto told her about the police. Her last arrest occurred in New York City, on January 4, 2004. She was in an apartment where she lived with other women whom Alberto's family had coerced into prostitution. She described the moment:

> We were all sleeping in the apartment when the police came in and arrested all of us. They grabbed us and separated us right away. The policeman told me to get some other clothing to take with me. They told me that they knew what we had been doing and that I should cooperate with him. I was very afraid. . . . I was held in immigration detention for two months, and learned that the government wanted to prosecute Alberto and his family, because they had done this to many women, and they had made this a family business.

Unlike her previous arrests by local law enforcement, this arrest was the result of an FBI investigation into Alberto's family. Everyone in the house was arrested. Trafficking is the only crime for which the victim is routinely arrested; victims may be detained as material witnesses if they decline to cooperate with law enforcement investigations.

While in detention, Flor met with attorneys from the Sex Workers Project, who, as part of the legal services they provide to people in the sex trades and people who have been trafficked, helped her apply for a T visa. These applications are reviewed by US Citizenship and Immigration

Services and, as mentioned in chapter 2, applications are more likely to be successful when local police or the FBI attest that the applicant has "cooperated" with law enforcement. This can mean that the person seeking the visa has testified in a prosecution or has shared information with police or the FBI. Unfortunately, some victims are afraid to testify because they fear that their traffickers will hurt their families in retaliation. Others are simply too afraid of law enforcement to speak to them at all.

Their fears are not unreasonable. Women are told by their traffickers that the police will arrest and prosecute them for prostitution-related charges, immigration violations, or other crimes. In most of their encounters with law enforcement, this is exactly what happens.

Trafficking victims may have other reasons for refusing to cooperate with US authorities. Some of the women I interviewed were in love with their trafficker and would not assist in their prosecution. These women typically choose to accept deportation and return to their countries of origin.

Flor, however, was worried about returning to Mexico, and with good reason. She explained in her T visa application she was afraid that she would be forced to return to Alberto's family, that they would know when she arrived in the country, and that they would force her into prostitution again. In part because of this fear, and in part because she had support from attorneys and social workers with the Sex Workers Project, Flor eventually opted to cooperate with the prosecution of Alberto's family members. Flor was not the only victim to make this decision—she and others whom the family had trafficked described their experiences to law enforcement. Alberto himself had already returned to Mexico and avoided travel to the United States when he realized the legal consequences he could face. Indeed, members of his family, including his brothers and sisters-in-law, were convicted based on the evidence shared by Flor and others. They are now in prison in the United States.

Flor continues to live in the New York City area, and her life now is different and better. She cleans houses for a living, and she and her new husband have two children. She is heartbroken about her son in Mexico. Flor has not seen him in eight years, and worries that the money she still sends to support him is not being used for that purpose:

> I am still in contact with Alberto's family because my son is there. They continue to request that I return to them so that I can have my son, and

they keep saying my return to them would solve all of my problems. I always refuse but these conversations are deeply disturbing for me. I also still send money because I want my son to be okay and because Alberto's family say that they will not take care of him if I refuse to send them money. I have no idea if this money actually goes to the upbringing of my child. Alberto's family threaten that they will only give me my child once I build a house for them.

Her son is still used to manipulate her, even now.

Flor also worries about the way that Alberto's family is raising her son. She knows they tell him that she is a "whore" and not a good woman. Since she left Mexico, she has only been able to communicate with him by phone, and then only when they allow it. On their phone calls, he asks her for brand-name clothing and games. She worries not only that he is not being supported by Alberto's family but also about his materialism. She worries that he will be taught to seduce young girls the way she was seduced, that he will victimize other girls and become a pimp and a trafficker like his father.[4]

She did not use these words when she talked about her son, as if afraid that speaking her fears out loud might make them a reality. When I asked direct questions about her son's future, including if she worries that he will join the family business, she nodded or gave brief answers. She was very clear that she hopes he will have a different life, and her greatest hope is that they might one day be reunited.

Being able to stay in the United States has changed Flor's life and allowed her to build a new life for herself, free from the direct control of Alberto and his family. Things are changing in Tlaxcala, too. Today, some of the young women there are in fact able to enrich themselves through sex work: instead of being forced by others to sell sex, they enter the sex industry voluntarily, choosing this line of work among the very limited economic options available to them.

Oscar Montiel Torres, an anthropologist who studies the traffickers in Tenancingo, has written a book on the topic, *Trata de personas: Padrotes, iniciación y modus operandi* (2009), or, in English, *Trafficking in persons: Pimps, initiation and modus operandi*.[5] He has found that men in Tlaxcala have been forcing women into prostitution for at least forty or fifty years, and that the mothers and grandmothers of these men may themselves have been forced to sell sex. Not all the people of Tenancingo are involved in the sex trade, but a few families there have built large homes and significant fortunes this way. These families groom their sons to handle the business. They are taught to seduce young women and to target naive and vulnerable girls. As we saw with Flor, social constraints on girls mean that once a girl has been seduced, it is very difficult for them to return home, leaving them little recourse but to continue to cooperate with their seducer.[6]

Many young women's upbringings in rural Mexico resemble Flor's. They grow up in poverty with very few opportunities. If they stay in their hometown, they will work the land, perhaps sell vegetables or household items, and struggle to earn enough to support themselves and their children. In these tiny towns, men cannot be providers unless they own enough land to run a lucrative farm. Many of these women therefore find themselves without financial or other support, sometimes abandoned by their husbands. Raised in grinding poverty, naive about the way the world works and about sexual matters, these young women are immensely vulnerable to the traffickers of Tenancingo and other towns.

Slowly, however, people are learning to protect themselves. Some of the women who were trafficked in Tlaxcala have gone back to their small hometowns to explain to young women the risks of leaving for the city. They also share information about where to seek help and offer guidance on ways of leaving a bad situation. Montiel Torres, the anthropologist, argues that such peer-to-peer teaching is the best way to alert people to the dangers, and that having this knowledge can help young women protect themselves.

Before the passage of the TVPA in 2000, there would have been no mechanism for Flor to remain in the United States; she would have been deported to Mexico, where she would have remained under the control of Alberto's family. With the passage of the TVPA, US law now considers women like Flor to be victims of trafficking. As such, she should have been offered assistance by the first American police she encountered, but instead she was arrested and prosecuted multiple times. This failure lies in over-reliance on the criminal justice system, which views people in prostitution foremost as criminals, as Flor was treated. Her arrest despite being a *victim* of trafficking made clear that, while the criminal justice system recognizes victims on paper, the emphasis on prosecution can further victimize survivors. After twenty years of training police to recognize trafficked persons in the United States, it is clear that this training is not working out the way it was planned. This is one way in which the criminal justice approach to trafficking fails the people it is meant to help.

GENDER AND SEX TRAFFICKING

Trafficked women who have daughters are in particularly wrenching situations, because their daughters are often forced into prostitution too. For one Mexican woman who had been trafficked in the US and then deported back, the threat of her two daughters being forced into prostitution motivated her to accept a request from American law enforcement to return and testify against her trafficker. Offered a visa to stay, she negotiated to bring her daughters with her, and they emigrated together. They were accompanied by members of the International Organization for Migration, a United Nations agency offering services and advice to governments regarding migrants, refugees, and displaced people.

Such stories of family reunion are rare, but they are most likely to happen to people who fit the identity we imagine of victims of trafficking: they are young foreign women of color. Male victims of sex trafficking are less likely to be helped. This was made clear to me when I was shown materials prepared by two New York City organizations providing services to trafficked persons who entered the US via Mexico, including their clients' redacted affidavits (sworn statements submitted with court documents). Take the case of a young man whose affidavit I reviewed. At the time, he was in prison in New York City and was set to be deported. He originated from a Latin American country (the exact place was redacted to make it impossible to identify him), where his family fell apart after his brother was murdered. At age eleven, he ended up traveling with a man with whom he worked in the fields during the day. At night, this man dressed him as a girl and locked him in a room with men who abused him sexually and physically. He ran away and eventually met someone who helped him cross the border to the United States, where he traded sex in his early teens. He stayed with a man in New York who forced him into prostitution. This went on for years before he ran away and survived by trading sex on the streets. He was arrested, and being over seventeen, was charged as an adult for various crimes including entering the country illegally. Had he been a woman, it is more likely that, having been forced to sell sex, he might have been recognized as a trafficking survivor, possibly sooner, and organizations that assist survivors of trafficking could have offered legal support, appointments with a therapist, and other services before he was set to be deported.

There are thousands of homeless minors who trade sex in New York City, approximately half of whom are boys; some are immigrants. Beyond a few small groups, there are no prominent organizations campaigning and assisting male survivors of trafficking into the sex trade. For example, the Sex Workers Project has two attorneys who address such cases. The male survivors are less likely to receive the services and assistance offered to victims of such crimes because they are less likely to be seen as victims; those not born in the US are more likely to be seen as illegal immigrants who have broken the law and therefore deserve punishment and deportation. There are a tiny number of shelter beds available to boys, and almost none for men. Homophobia and transphobia have affected the ways trafficking victims are identified, and while the language of TVPA is gender neutral, the same cannot be said of its implementation.[7]

PROSTITUTION OF ENSLAVED AND INDENTURED WOMEN

I N THE ANTEBELLUM ERA, "fancy girls" were fair-skinned, enslaved Black women sold for "implicitly sexual purposes."[1] While most enslaved people were forced to labor in agriculture and industry, some were specifically marketed for sexual purposes. This was a distinct abuse separate from the sexual assault that could befall any enslaved woman or girl and was separate from the practice of forcing enslaved women to birth children who would be the next generation of slaves. Fancy girls were typically more costly than other enslaved people. The illustration on the next page, a photograph of a bill of sale for a fancy girl named Clary, purchased by Robert Jardine for fifty pounds in Virginia in 1806, shows a comparatively high price paid for the young woman.

Some fancy girls were purchased for the use of a single person. Others were forced to work in brothels, similar to the ways enslavers would contract out the labor of the enslaved people they owned. Prostitution was legal at this time; New Orleans regulated prostitution starting in 1857, delineating red-light districts as spaces where it was allowed, and selling licenses to prostitutes and their landlords. In some of these brothels, enslaved women were forced to sell sex. For enslaved women and girls in prostitution, there was no legal recourse; the law was used to enforce the involuntary servitude of all enslaved people. It remained that way until the passage of the Thirteenth Amendment in 1865, which ended the involuntary servitude of all enslaved people in the United States.

Know all men by these Presents that we the Subscribers have Bargained, Sold Transferred and delivered, and by these Presents doath Bargain & Sell, Transferd and deliver unto Robert S. Jardine a negro Girl Slave named Clary for the Consideration of Fifty Pounds Current Money of Virginia us in hand paid the Receipt whereof we do hereby Acknowledge We do bind our selves, our heirs, Executors & Administrators to warrant and defend the said Slave named Clary unto the said Robert S Jardine his heirs Executors Administrators and Assigns for ever against the Claim or Claims of any Person or Persons watsoever In witness whereof we have hereunto set our hands, and Seals, this 15th Day of January One Thousand Eight Hundred & Six.

Bill of sale for a girl named Clary, purchased by Robert Jardine for fifty pounds. Collection of the Smithsonian National Museum of African American History and Culture.

These unfortunate enslaved women were not the only people forced to work in brothels. From 1850 through 1924, women comprised less than 5 percent of the Chinese population of the United States.[2] But even a seemingly invisible population as small as this one was seen as a source of vice. Of the Chinese women living in San Francisco in 1870, it was said that "less than one hundred were respected members of the community." The remainder, almost six hundred, were prostitutes, apparently in conditions akin to bonded indenture.[3] While historians do not agree about male Chinese contract laborers' levels of independence, with some historians seeing the laborers' situations as largely coercive and others highlighting their agency, there is general consensus that female Chinese prostitutes were in bonded servitude.[4] A few of the Chinese women who arrived between 1849 and 1854 were able to be independent and even entrepreneurial—in their culture, girls and young women of low birth were able to emigrate voluntarily to work in prostitution abroad, and thereby contribute to their families' upkeep. After 1854, Chinese women brought to the United States were more likely to have been sold by their families (girls were less valued for their labor and because their offspring would not carry their familial line). Alternatively, their families might arrange a contract for the indenture of a girl.[5] One such contract opens:

> The contractee Xin Jin is indebted to her master/mistress for passage from China to San Francisco and will voluntarily work as a prostitute at Tan Fu's place for four and one-half years for an advance of 1,205 yuan to pay this debt. There shall be no interest on the money, and Xin Jin shall receive no wages. At the expiration of the contract, Xin Jin shall be free to do as she pleases.[6]

The contract goes on to specify that if she becomes pregnant, a year will be added to her bondage (as was seen with the indentured women in the American colonies described in chapter 4), and that if she runs away, the amount spent to find and retrieve her will be added to her debts.[7] Unlike the treatment of male laborers described in chapter 9, Chinese women's remains were not repatriated.

While this contract was terrible for the indentured woman, some of her compatriots were worse off, having been essentially sold as chattel and treated as such.[8] Other women were kidnapped, typically by Chinese men returning from America who promised these women gold or marriage or a job, much in the same vein as Alberto and his promises to Flor in chapter 10. Between 1852 and 1873, the Hip Yee Tong (a secret society sometimes involved in criminal activity) imported six thousand women from China, destined for American brothels.[9] Japanese women also entered the country after being similarly deceived, sometimes just before a boat left for America; some of them passed through Hong Kong or Singapore en route, were sold again, and put on Chinese ships.[10] As we shall see in the next chapter, after the Page Act of 1875 and the Chinese Exclusion Act of 1882 banned most emigration from China, the practice of paying bribes to enter the United States became more common, as did bribes to the police to protect criminals. Everyone involved except the trafficked women made more money with each new anti-immigration law.[11]

CHAPTER 12

MORALITY IN IMMIGRATION RESTRICTIONS

CHINESE IMMIGRATION AND THE PAGE ACT

The very first law restricting immigration to the United States was the Page Act of 1875.[1] Horace F. Page, the California representative who introduced the act, claimed to be defending the United States against cheap Chinese labor and "immoral" Chinese women. White people at the time believed that both male and female Chinese immigrants were working in involuntary servitude—the men as laborers and the women in prostitution.[2] (It is important to note that legal restrictions on prostitution were enacted only as recently as 1917, in response to sexually transmitted infections undermining the US war effort during World War I.) Page wanted to exclude "undesirable" immigrants: forced laborers from many parts of Asia, women from China and Japan who might engage in prostitution, and people who were convicts in their native country. Ironically, these migration restrictions, which effectively banned Chinese women from entering the United States, may have promoted what today would be called trafficking by making it impossible for Chinese women to enter the country legally. The Page Act led to the bribery of officials both before the women embarked and upon arrival in California.[3] These bribes added to costs borne by the traveler, including those in debt bondage. The Page Act also further decreased the already small numbers of Chinese women entering the country, and, historically speaking, when men greatly outnumber women, paid sexual transactions abound. In this situation, where only a few hundred Chinese women lived in a community of tens of thousands of Chinese men, a logical ramification was that some sold sex and others were bonded in prostitution.

SEXUAL MORALITY ASPECTS OF IMMIGRATION LAW

Predictably, since powerful American employers benefited from cheap immigrant labor, the labor aspects of the Page Act were not enforced as strictly as the restrictions on women. This pattern would be repeated in subsequent laws and their implementation. Later immigration acts also addressed prostitution in an effort to exclude "immoral" people from entering the United States. The Immigration Act of 1903, motivated primarily by the desire to bar anarchists from the United States after the assassination of President William McKinley by an American-born anarchist, also included provisions to exclude people with epilepsy and importers of prostitutes. The Immigration Act of 1907 prohibited immigration by people who were likely to become dependent on the state ("public charges"), including "imbeciles" and people unlikely to be able to earn a living, as well as people deemed immoral: bigamists, anarchists, and women suspected of prostitution.

The 1924 Immigration Act extended the restrictions of the Chinese Exclusion Act to most of Asia, and imposed quotas on Asian, African, and European immigrants in such a way as to promote immigration by white people, primarily from Northern Europe. A quota was also set for immigration overall, of which 85 percent was reserved for arrivals from Northern and Western Europe. The clear (but unstated) goal was maintaining a white-majority population in the United States.

THE CONTEXT OF IMMIGRATION AND CHANGING LAWS

The late nineteenth and early twentieth centuries saw widespread panic among white Americans over "white slavery," a term referring to the forced prostitution of white women. It initially reflected a mixture of different fears of the time, including jobs lost to new immigrants, the rapid urbanization and industrialization of society, accompanying changes in morality, and increased immigration from southern Europe.

"White slavery" is a phrase with a long history and a constantly changing meaning. In the first half of the nineteenth century, it referred to

Puck cover *"Will the White Slave Have a Lincoln?"* depicting
a man labeled *"independent labor"* being whipped while tied to a post
labeled *"organized tyranny."* Note the factory in the background.
By S. D. Ehrhart, Puck, v. 57, no. 1475 *(June 7, 1905).*

indentured servants in bondage. Amid increasing industrialization in the
second half of the nineteenth century, the meaning shifted to refer to wage
labor. Factories, including textile and clothing factories, were becoming
major employers of poor white people, around the same time that prison
labor was being used to replace slave labor in the agricultural South. Factory

work employed many but paid poorly. This second use of the phrase was contemporary to Marx's economic analysis in *Capital* (published in 1867), in which he repeatedly compared Black slavery to wage labor.

Over time, however, the focus of the term narrowed. "White slavers," often imagined as foreigners, became popular "folk devils" in urban legends and conspiracy theories in which criminal gangs kidnapped white women and girls and forced them into sexual servitude. Activist campaigns in the late nineteenth century and early twentieth century pushed Congress to take action against this new form of "white slavery," which largely existed only in the public imagination of white Americans. Accordingly, the era's immigration laws, as described earlier in this chapter, focused increasingly on prostitution and "white slavers." By the 1890s, the Chinese were feared less as job stealers and more as opium sellers and white slavers.[4] White women were cautioned against entering Chinese laundries lest they face "kidnapping, druggings, and sexual abuse."[5] Such was the plot of movies like *In a Chinese Laundry* (1897), in which a male Chinese laundry worker unsuccessfully hits on a young white woman picking up her laundry.[6] Two more films from the same studio, Biograph, *A Chinese Opium Joint* (1898) and *A Raid on a Chinese Opium Joint* (1900), depicted white women in opium dens lounging alongside a Chinese drug merchant. While interracial relationships horrified some whites and were not allowed under anti-miscegenation laws, these relationships were inevitable considering the small numbers of Chinese women and thousands of Chinese men working in the United States.

Fear of Chinese white slavers gradually waned, and by the start of the twentieth century, white slavers were more commonly portrayed as Jewish.[7] At that time, the term was used to mean prostitution, rape, and female sexual servitude.[8] In 1910, these fears culminated in the passage of a new federal law, the "White Slave Traffic Act" (also called the Mann Act after its author, Representative James Mann of Illinois). This act famously made it a crime to transport women across state lines for "immoral purposes," specifically debauchery and prostitution, but through wording vague enough to be applied to nearly all extramarital sex. While previous legislative efforts to limit human movement had required travel passes, restricted emigration of indebted workers, or imposed general immigration quotas, this new law focused entirely on sexual behavior.

WHO BENEFITED FROM SHIFTING THE FOCUS FROM WORK TO SEX?

American reformers and legislators changed their focus from labor to morality, specifically women's sexuality, during the late nineteenth and early twentieth centuries, spanning the Victorian and Progressive eras. The laws enacted to address human trafficking and their application reflected this shift in focus. Focusing on sex deflected attention away from the working conditions and wages of the period. The late nineteenth century saw rapid industrialization, a lack of workplace safety regulations, and many, many workplace accidents and deaths—approximately one hundred workplace deaths per day in the last twenty years of the nineteenth century. This was a time of labor organizing and strikes, with mixed results. In this context, the moral panic of "white slavery" served the interests of a capitalist establishment. It helped to distract attention from larger societal issues by offering an alternative narrative that was sensational and sexy. It smoothed the passage of anti-trafficking laws like the Mann Act and its sequels, which were immediately applied in political, racist, or sexist ways to serve a larger agenda of social and political control, particularly over women's sexuality and the numbers of immigrant arrivals. Propaganda, which uses emotionally provocative images and stories to redirect attention, was part of this process.

The image on the next page, showing a blond girl behind bars, is meant to generate sympathy for the person in the picture. The image was published both inside and on the cover of a 1910 book entitled *Fighting the Traffic in Young Girls; or, War on the White Slave Trade*. The combat metaphors in the title alert the reader to the theme of sexual danger to children. The cover also includes a quote—"For God's sake, do something!"—and it reads, below the image, "The Greatest Crime in World History." In this case, the narrative of a girl in trouble was used to foment concern about an unspecified but implied sexual threat to girls.

Another image from this book shows the entrance to a dance hall. The drawing and its caption position the dance hall as the "brilliant entrance to hell itself," with "blazing lights, gaiety, and apparent happiness," and showing people dancing. Note the daily and weekly room rates posting, implying that rooms were available for rent by the day, for a quick sexual encounter, or by the week, perhaps for prostitute residents. The book's editor, Ernest A. Bell, was the first secretary of the Illinois Vigilance Association,

"MY GOD! IF ONLY I COULD GET OUT OF HERE."
The midnight shriek of a young girl in the vice district of a large city, heard by two worthy men, started a crusade which resulted in closing up the dens of shame in that city. (See page 450.)

Illustration from Fighting the Traffic in Young Girls; or, War on the White Slave Trade. *From Ernest Albert Bell*, Fighting the Traffic in Young Girls (*G. S. Ball, 1910*).

DANGEROUS AMUSEMENTS—THE BRILLIANT ENTRANCE TO HELL ITSELF.
Young girls who have danced at home a little are attracted by the blazing lights, gaiety and apparent happiness of the "dance halls," which in many instances leads to their downfall. (See page 112.)

The drawing posits the dance hall as the "brilliant entrance to hell itself" with "blazing lights, gaiety and apparent happiness." Note the daily and weekly room rates posting. From Ernest Albert Bell, Fighting the Traffic in Young Girls; or, War on the White Slave Trade (G. S. Ball, 1910).

and the book includes a report by the Chicago Vice Commission. Similar books looking at the sex trades with simultaneous intrigue and repulsion were published during the Progressive Era (1897–1920). The Chicago Vice Commission also produced reports about prostitution and "perverted" activities including cross-dressing and homosexual acts; among them was a titillating report about what today might be called gay subculture.[9] This fascination with activities that were disapproved of was a hallmark of the Progressive Era, during which numerous laws addressing trafficking in women were passed.

IMMIGRATION ASPECTS OF THE MANN ACT OF 1910

The Mann Act is best known for the enforcement of its interstate trafficking aspects, but it also included aspects related to immigration. These immigration aspects of the Mann Act were twofold: the law was used both to reject potential immigrants (much like its predecessors, the Immigration Acts of 1903, 1907, and 1910) and to deport people who had arrived within the previous three years. The Mann Act specifically targeted immigrant women and girls involved in prostitution and included provisions for their deportation, saying:

> Every person who shall keep, maintain, control, support, or harbor in any house or place for the purpose of prostitution, or for any other immoral purpose, any alien woman or girl within three years after she shall have entered the United States from any country, party to the said arrangement for the suppression of the white slave traffic [agreement between the United States and other powers for the repression of the trade in white women, 1908], shall file with the Commissioner-General of Immigration a statement in writing setting forth the name of such alien woman or girl, the place at which she is kept, and all facts as to the date of her entry into the United States, the port through which she entered, her age, nationality, and parentage, and concerning her procuration to come to this country within the knowledge of such person.[10]

The law asked for a lot of information about foreign-born women and girls involved in prostitution, although the exchange of sex for money was not a crime when the act was passed, and it set up a system for reporting such instances to the government. This facet of the Mann Act reflected the social anxiety about women and girls crossing borders.

AGREEMENT BETWEEN THE US AND OTHER POWERS FOR THE REPRESSION OF THE TRADE IN WHITE WOMEN

The white slavery panic from which the Mann Act arose was not limited to the United States. A less well-known international agreement, forged in 1904 between the US, the nations of Europe, and Brazil, preceded the Mann Act and addressed a different kind of movement: women's emigration from Europe and North America to former colonies such as Argentina, Chile, and Uruguay, some of which were richer than their former colonizers. The aim of this agreement was to ensure that white women and girls—and only white women and girls—who had been lured into the sex trades in foreign countries would be able to return to their countries of origin.

The racism of the agreement is notable, and this concern about white women's movements may have been rooted in fears that they would travel independently. Such women were seen as "adventuresses" seeking to enrich themselves through relationships with men. It was also feared that they would be forced into prostitution in Buenos Aires or other wealthy international cities. Clearly, the United States was not alone in its fear of its white women and girls being exploited by the "other."

To this day, immigration laws continue to be used to address sexual morality. Race remains a factor in the enforcement of both immigration and prostitution law, with greater scrutiny paid to people of color. Non-citizens entering the United States are asked whether they have ever engaged in prostitution. If they reply that they have, even in legal prostitution, or if immigration agents somehow identify them as having engaged in prostitution, they are not admitted to the country. Facial recognition software is used by law enforcement, including Immigration and Customs Enforcement, and this has led to the identification of some sex workers and their being turned away at the US border.[11]

CHAPTER 13

THE MANN ACT
AND "WHITE SLAVERY"

T HE MANN ACT, best known for its prohibition on interstate travel for "immoral purposes," quickly entered into the American conscious-ness and was frequently referenced in early twentieth-century culture in theater, literature, and cartoons. These cultural references did one of two things: They demonstrated the danger of arrest whenever a girl or woman crossed a state line, even for a mundane reason, as in F. Scott Fitzgerald's *Tender Is the Night* and illustrated in the 1914 cartoon reproduced on the following page in which a woman asks, "Are you going to see me home to Jersey tonight?"[1] Or, they advanced a rescue narrative—the fantasy of saving a trafficked girl in trouble, as in the play *The Lure*, and in movies like *Traffic in Souls* and *The Inside of the White Slave Traffic*.

IMPACT OF THE MANN ACT

As discussed in the previous chapter, the "white slavery" problem that the Mann Act was created to address was more imaginary than real. There is no evidence to suggest that large numbers of young white women were being kidnapped or enslaved. Nevertheless, the act had enormous cultural conse-quences. Its outsize impact stemmed from the fact that it referred broadly to "immoral purposes" and could thus be used to address sexual activity unrelated to "white slavery": sex across racial lines, adultery, and prostitution.

A woman who traveled from one state to another with a man or to meet up with a man other than her husband could face charges for violating the

*"Are you going to see me home to Jersey tonight?" / "Think I want to get
pinched under the White Slave law?" The cartoon refers to the use of the
Mann Act against couples who were not involved in prostitution.
Glenn O. Coleman,* The Masses, *February 1914.*

act.[2] Although the law was ostensibly intended to protect women, most of
the people charged under the Mann Act were in fact women, particularly
those who arranged their own travel.

The Mann Act was the first of several federal trafficking reform efforts
of the twentieth century, and it set the pattern for later legislation. Subsequent trafficking laws followed the precedent of the Mann Act in that
they addressed sex in one way or another while excluding other types of
trafficked workers.

The Mann Act specifically targets interstate commerce because, as a federal law, it cannot regulate what happens within a single state. Similar laws were passed at the state level around the country prohibiting the transportation of women within the state, if, for example, extramarital sexual activity was suspected to be the driving purpose for the undertaking.

SEXIST ENFORCEMENT OF THE MANN ACT

The Mann Act was soon extended from its initial focus on prostitution and applied to other sex acts. Although a court first ruled in 1911 that the Mann Act specifically addressed commercial sex, a highly publicized case of two men, Drew Caminetti and Maury Diggs, led to a 1917 Supreme Court ruling that the Mann Act applied also to consensual adult acts and acts involving minors.[3] Caminetti and Diggs were two politically connected men who had been tried and convicted under the Mann Act after traveling from California to Nevada with their extramarital partners. The men appealed their convictions, but the guilty verdict was upheld by the US Supreme Court, which ruled that the "immoral purposes" named in the Mann Act included adultery and sex outside marriage.[4] This held without regard for the age of the partners or whether the sex was consensual, and even if no payment or exchange had occurred.[5] This ruling opened the door to more prosecutions of women. In 1915, a court ruled that women could be arrested for "conspiracy" for "agreeing to go along on the trip," heightening the threat of women's normal social interactions being ruled criminal.[6] Seventeen years later, in 1932, this burden was lessened by another case ruling that women had to be involved beyond merely agreeing to travel. In the interim between these cases, the numbers of Mann Act cases annually jumped from approximately three hundred to approximately five hundred; thousands of women and their boyfriends were charged with conspiracy for making plans and traveling, or for consenting to travel.[7] One source of motivation for this enforcement strategy was that the new Bureau of Investigation (forerunner to the FBI) wanted to develop a reputation for addressing crime and thereby justify the expenditure on the new agency's budget.

In 1922, the government reported that white slave gangs had been eradicated. Of course, the existence of white slave gangs had never been substantiated: most Mann Act cases had been brought against individuals rather than crime rings.[8] Instead of declaring victory, the Bureau of Investigation expanded its interstate policing efforts to catch prostitutes and "pimps."[9] After a temporary dip in Mann Act convictions in 1923, they proceeded to ramp up.[10]

RACIST ENFORCEMENT OF THE MANN ACT

The Mann Act was almost immediately used against Black men, particularly celebrities who had sexual relationships with white women. The act's notion of "immoral purposes" was extended to include interracial sex as "immoral." Notable examples involved Jack Johnson, an early twentieth-century Black boxer who married and dated white women and was prosecuted twice under the act. He was first tried in 1912 for traveling from Minneapolis to Chicago with Lucille Cameron, a white woman.[11] Cameron did not implicate Johnson in her testimony; they married after he was acquitted. But the case's determined prosecutor, assistant US district attorney Harry Parkin, searched for other white women Johnson may have transported in order to bring a second Mann Act case against him. He found Belle Schreiber. In 1910, Johnson had given Schreiber money to move to Chicago and set up her own business.[12] Johnson was tried for transporting Schreiber, who cooperated with the prosecution, and this time, he was convicted.

Parkin made explicit the racist motivation behind the trial, stating: "This negro, in the eyes of many, has been persecuted. Perhaps as an individual he was. But it was his misfortune to be the foremost example of the evil in permitting the intermarriage of whites and blacks."[13] Johnson, who had married two white women in succession, could not be prosecuted for intermarriage under any existing law in Illinois, where he lived.[14] But the Mann Act handed a racist prosecutor a tool that he could use to convict a Black man for a different crime entirely—"transportation of an individual for immoral purposes."

Such targeting of prominent African American men coincided with a renewed interest in a revisionist portrayal of the Civil War. Groups like the United Daughters of the Confederacy advocated for the veneration of the Confederacy and erected statues of Confederate generals across the American South. At the same time, lynchings of Black people by white mobs enforced white supremacy through racist terrorism. White lynch mobs murdered African Americans for the simple act of voting or for alleged infringements like vagrancy, robbery, and assault; a quarter of lynchings happened when Black men were accused of having made sexual overtures to white women.[15] The racist enforcement of the Mann Act was part of a broader white supremacist pattern.

Another prominent victim of the Mann Act was musician Chuck Berry. In 1958, Berry was first arrested with Joan Mathis, a white woman, while traveling across state lines from Kansas to Missouri. Mathis stated that she "had not been molested" and no Mann Act charges were filed.[16]

In 1959, shortly before a scheduled performance in the border town of El Paso, Berry was in Ciudad Juarez, Mexico, where he met a fourteen-year-old girl from Arizona named Janice Escalanti. Escalanti had left the Apache reservation where she had grown up and had worked as a prostitute and as a waitress. Berry brought her from Mexico to St. Louis, Missouri, to work as a hat-check girl in his nightclub. They traveled together and purportedly engaged in sex during the two-week trip to Missouri. She worked in his club for only a few days before Berry fired her for leaving the coat-check area during her shift. He bought her a bus ticket back to El Paso, but she wanted to go to her native Yuma, Arizona, which would have been an additional 500-mile trip. Instead of using the ticket Berry had given her, she stayed in St. Louis and turned to prostitution.[17] In her frustration about being 1,500 miles from home, she called the Yuma police, and they told her to wait for the St. Louis police. Both Escalanti and Berry were arrested—Escalanti for prostitution and Berry for "transportation of an individual for immoral purposes."[18] The police chose to bring charges against Berry for the earlier Mathis incident at the same time. Berry was acquitted in the Mathis case, in part because she testified in his defense. Berry expressed his gratitude that Mathis "chose to open herself to what was then considered indignity by declaring that she was in love with a Negro."[19] But Berry was convicted in the Escalanti case. In an unusual turn of events, the case was retried because of the overt racism of the court. The judge had emphasized race with regard to Berry's interactions with white women; for example, he asked one witness, "By Mr. Berry, do you mean this Negro, the defendant?"[20] The judge also inquired about a hotel in Colorado where Berry stayed by asking, "Is it patronized by white people?" Berry was convicted during the second Escalanti trial as well, and he ultimately served twenty months in prison.[21]

During both of Berry's trials, Escalanti was detained at the Home of Sisters of the Good Shepherd in St. Louis because she was a witness. When she was finally returned to her native Arizona, instead of being brought to the reservation where she'd grown up, she was kept in juvenile detention, possibly until she was eighteen years old.

Racist enforcement was double-edged: the Mann Act was used exceedingly rarely in cases involving women of color.[22]

POLITICAL ENFORCEMENT OF THE MANN ACT

J. Edgar Hoover was director of the Bureau of Investigation from 1924 until 1935; the bureau then became the FBI, which he led until 1972. During his tenure, he used the bureau for political purposes and personal vendettas, exploiting (among other statutes) the flexibility and range of the Mann Act. Hoover led many Mann Act raids in which prostitutes were arrested and sought to attract publicity around them. For example, in a Baltimore area raid in 1937, 137 people were arrested, but there were no Mann Act arrests—the Mann Act was merely a pretext.[23] Hoover also used these raids to gather information on suspected anarchists and communists. He instructed agents to include sources of data such as address books, especially those containing prominent persons, in "administrative" files, which he sometimes leaked to the press.[24]

Hoover sought a Mann Act case against the actor Charlie Chaplin in 1944 because of the entertainer's overt communist sympathies and purported immorality. The basis of the case was that Chaplin had paid for train tickets for his mistress and her mother to travel from Los Angeles to New York in 1942. When their affair ended the following year, the now former mistress went to gossip columnists with her story. This drew public attention and led to the prosecution of Chaplin under the Mann Act.[25] Even though Chaplin was acquitted, his public image and career were unsalvageable, and he relocated to Europe.[26]

The Mann Act has been amended multiple times to make it gender neutral and to align it more with current mores. In 1978, it was amended to apply to the interstate transportation of boys under the age of eighteen for sexual purposes.[27] In 1986, the *Final Report of the Attorney General's Commission on Pornography* (also known as the *Meese Commission Report*) recommended that the Mann Act be amended to use gender-neutral language.[28] This recommendation was implemented via the Child Sexual Abuse and Pornography Act of the same year. This act was bundled with another amendment limiting the Mann Act only to acts that were criminal in the jurisdiction where they were committed, removing the phrase "any other immoral purpose" and replacing it with "any sexual activity for which any person can be charged with a criminal offense."[29] While these changes have restricted the political use of this law, the Mann Act remains in force over a century after its passage.

THE MANN ACT IN THE TWENTY-FIRST CENTURY

In June 2022, R. Kelly, a Grammy-winning R&B singer-songwriter and producer, was sentenced to thirty years in prison after being convicted in a high-profile trial on multiple charges related to human trafficking, child pornography, kidnapping, and forced labor in pornography, including violations of the Mann Act, in 2020.[30] He was convicted of similar crimes in September 2022. Kelly is both perpetrator and victim, as he was subjected to repeated sexual abuse as a young child. His case is interesting because his race was not weaponized as in twentieth-century cases with famous Black plaintiffs. Historically, the Mann Act was more commonly used to prosecute African American men who had sexual relationships with white women; in R. Kelly's case, both he and his victims are African American. The prosecutions moved forward with the extensive cooperation and support of African American women who are part of the Time's Up movement to end sexual abuse and harassment in the entertainment industry.[31]

Jeffrey Epstein, the infamous financier who cultivated friendships with rich and powerful men while consorting with young women, was charged with trafficking before his death in 2019. In 2006, Palm Beach police had arrested him on charges related to prostitution of a minor; he pleaded not guilty. In 2008, he pleaded guilty to charges involving sex with minors and served thirteen months in prison in Florida, registered as a sex offender, and paid restitution to thirty-six victims identified by the FBI.[32] Epstein was arrested in July 2019 and died in jail five weeks later while awaiting trial on trafficking charges.

Epstein had a long personal and professional relationship with British socialite Ghislaine Maxwell. After his death, Maxwell became the main target of civil and criminal cases already underway; to that point, she had not been charged with any crime. An attorney for Maxwell, David Oscar Markus, said that Maxwell essentially served in lieu of Epstein himself: "Epstein died. They need someone. . . . If there was real evidence, she would have been charged long ago."[33]

Maxwell was convicted in New York in 2021 of a variety of charges dating back to the 1990s, including Mann Act charges. Maxwell's situation is interesting not only for replacing Epstein as a criminal target upon his death but also because her trial was disrupted in January 2021 by QAnon conspiracy theorists who believe, without any basis, that Democrats are involved in a Satanist pedophile sex trafficking ring. In this way, QAnon hysteria recalls the hysteria about white slavery gangs. In 2022, she was sentenced to twenty years in prison and is appealing the conviction.[34]

In 2020, Joel Greenberg, tax collector of Seminole County, Florida, was charged with Mann Act violations related to sex trafficking involving a minor. According to the charges, the crimes occurred over the course of three years, when the victim was between the ages of fourteen and seventeen. Greenberg had improperly used his access to the state database of driver's licenses to look up information about women with whom he had sexual relationships. He frequently abused his position, at one point posing as a police officer to pull over a woman, claiming that his tax collector badge was a sheriff's badge. He also delivered valuable contracts to close contacts and started a technology company whose only purpose seemed to be billing his government office for services. He had also used his position to create false identification documents made from confiscated driver's licenses. Upon his arrest, authorities found in Greenberg's work vehicle a backpack containing fake IDs and materials to make more.[35] Because of the severity of the charges, Greenberg has cooperated with law enforcement. In the course of this cooperation, Greenberg, who is a confidant of the conservative representative Matt Gaetz of Florida, told law enforcement that he and Gaetz "had encounters with women who were given cash or gifts in exchange for sex," possibly related to allegations that Gaetz had had sex with a seventeen-year-old.[36] Greenberg pleaded guilty to six felony charges including sex trafficking of a minor, identity theft, stalking, fraud, and bribery; in a deal with prosecutors, twenty-seven other charges were dropped.[37] In January 2022, a woman associated with Gaetz received immunity for cooperating with investigators, contributing to expectations that the congressman may face charges.[38] Greenberg's sentencing has been postponed in light of his cooperation in the case against Gaetz; at the time of writing, it remains to be seen whether Gaetz will be charged with sex trafficking under the Mann Act or any other law.[39]

The essential vagueness of the Mann Act, with its references to ill-defined terms such as "white slavery" and "immoral purposes," allowed it to be exploited for political, sexist, and racist reasons. Even today, anti-trafficking initiatives are often bedeviled by something of the same vagueness, with similar results, such as the frequent arrest of sex workers in what are labeled anti-trafficking raids but in which no survivors of trafficking are identified. Even as the legal terminology has shifted from "traffic in women and children" to "trafficking in persons," trafficking and sex work are often conflated, sometimes intentionally in order to answer to the political or moral agenda of interested parties—from historical examples of racist prosecutors who opposed interracial relationships and a federal government that wished to exclude ethnicities and occupations deemed undesirable, to today's religious ideologues promoting a patriarchal social order and anti-sex-work feminists, both raising money using salacious imagery.

CHAPTER 14

TWENTY-FIRST-CENTURY EFFORTS
TO COMBAT HUMAN TRAFFICKING

MANY OF THE twenty-first century anti-trafficking initiatives led by legislators and advocacy organizations have reproduced key features of historical attempts to address "white slavery." These include the use of sensationalist and emotive promotional campaigns (as in Exodus Cry's videos), performative concern for women's safety disguising a moral agenda against sex work (as with SWERF organizations such as CATW), and the promotion of laws and policies restricting sexual behavior (as by the religious right). The language and imagery these initiatives use often makes a sharp distinction between idealized victims, typically women and children, who deserve protection, and "bad girls" who get what they deserve.

These elements are all present in the TVPA. Although this landmark law has helped many trafficked people, it is in other ways deeply flawed, such as in how it separates sex trafficking from the larger category of labor trafficking (described in chapter 2). Yet the TVPA is also the first law in more than a century that also addresses the full spectrum of trafficking situations—not only sex but also labor. (The last such law was passed in 1867 and banned peonage, a form of debt bondage.)[1]

SEX AND LABOR IN THE TRAFFICKING
VICTIMS PROTECTION ACT

As described in chapter 2, the TVPA addresses force, fraud, and coercion in labor and the sex trades, including physical violence, rape and sexual abuse, imprisonment, psychological abuse, and threats, including threats to harm others. Despite the inclusion of labor in the TVPA, current anti-trafficking efforts in law enforcement perpetuate the historical focus on sex. Most anti-trafficking raids since the TVPA was passed have been conducted at brothels or massage parlors, typically those employing Asian and Latina women. Far fewer anti-trafficking raids have been at workplaces such as factories, slaughterhouses, and corporate farms. In the words of Suzanne B. Seltzer, an attorney for survivors of trafficking and partner at Klasko, Rulon, Stock & Seltzer, LLP, "No one is raiding a factory looking for trafficking victims; they are looking for illegal immigrants."[2] Yet these are the types of industries where the greatest number of labor violations have been identified. And this emphasis on brothels and massage parlors has not been useful for identifying trafficked persons in the sex industry.

In 2009, as part of a report published by the Sex Workers Project, in line with the research agenda I initiated upon its founding, I interviewed fifteen women who had been trafficked.[3] Many told me they had been arrested multiple times, in some cases up to ten times, before being identified as a trafficking victim.[4] Only one, upon being arrested, had ever been asked whether she had been coerced into sex work.[5] Even in raids that claim to be looking for victims of crime, law enforcement officers approach people in the sex industry as criminals first and foremost. This is partly why trafficking raids today, much like Hoover's Mann Act prostitution raids described in the previous chapter, include arrests of many sex workers but identify few survivors of trafficking. In the same 2009 report, service providers and advocates who assist trafficked persons described law enforcement taking a racial approach, focusing on Korean brothels in particular.[6]

TRAFFICKING COURTS

Some local judicial systems address trafficking with special courts. Trafficking courts are similar to other special courts, such as "drug court" or "prostitution court"; all are intended to divert people arrested from prison time. Trafficking courts were created in 2013 by a judge in Queens, New York, who wanted women arrested for prostitution not to be punished but to receive helpful services. Where trafficking courts exist, everyone arrested for prostitution goes through them. Arrested people who have been trafficked into other economic sectors are not required to go through these special courts; in this way, trafficking courts go beyond conflation and explicitly equate prostitution with trafficking. For example, New York State's description of Human Trafficking Intervention Courts says, "Human traffickers exploit vulnerable domestic and foreign nationals both in the United States and abroad by compelling victims to engage in commercial sex."[7] Police forces frequently use the term "trafficking" when they mean prostitution.

Trafficking courts exist around the country. First-time offenders are not sentenced to jail, but instead are mandated to attend sessions with an organization offering social services. Sessions may include yoga, counseling with a social worker, or drug treatment. In New York City, offenders are typically expected to attend six sessions, but the number of sessions is at the discretion of a judge. After six months, if they have not been arrested for prostitution again, their records are sealed. People who miss a session can be mandated to attend additional sessions or even sentenced to jail time.

Unfortunately, these court-mandated sessions are onerous for many. For example, one woman described having to drop out of her first semester of college in order to attend her sessions. The value of the courts has also been questioned. Leaders of the National Survivor Network oppose trafficking courts and the arrest of victims because they see better results when people are able to exit trafficking situations without going through the criminal justice system. Special courts have not resolved the problematic relationship between law enforcement and trafficked persons.

Not all victims of trafficking are treated equally. Male and transgender victims of all types of trafficking are less likely to be referred to service providers because they are not perceived as victims; they are not the stereotypical "women and children" or "women and girls" that most people imagine when they hear the word "trafficking." Homophobia plays a role in the way men and boys are not thought of as possible victims of crime. The perception that trafficking refers to sex makes it difficult for people under eighteen years old in other labor sectors to be identified as trafficked. For example, as mentioned in chapter 2, the federal government's National Child Abuse and Neglect Data System (NCANDS) also shows a biased focus on sex. NCANDS, which gathers reports of child abuse and neglect from across the United States, limits its reporting codes about trafficking to only two choices: "sex" and "other." NCANDS should include all industries because, as we've seen, trafficking happens in a wide variety of sectors.

FOSTA-SESTA

Today's anti-trafficking efforts continue to be mixed with problematic attempts to constrain the sex trades. At times, these efforts are devoid of any anti-trafficking component, as shown by campaigns in the 2010s to close the website Backpage.com and Craigslist's "Adult Services" section, both of which provided platforms on which sex workers and clients could find each other. These were the platforms first affected during the initial efforts by conservative politicians and SWERFs to limit sex workers' and their clients' use of the internet. Both sites endured attacks from elected officials: in 2020 Craigslist's "Adult Services" was condemned in a letter from the attorneys general of seventeen states, after which the page was closed by the site's founder. Backpage was attacked by both of Arizona's senators—at that time John McCain and Jeff Flake—in part because the owners of the site were based in their state. The proprietors of the site had started Backpage in 2004 with advertising content that included massage parlor ads and ads placed by sex workers.

In 2018, Backpage was seized by the federal government and became the target of a federal lawsuit in which the owners of the site were charged with pimping. These charges were not upheld because Section 230 of the Communications Decency Act specified that an online platform cannot be held accountable for what others post.[8] However, this stipulation has changed with the passage of an anti-trafficking law supported by SWERFs in partnership with right-wing Christians. This law, the FOSTA-SESTA package (Fight Online Sex Trafficking Act, the House bill, and the Stop Enabling Sex Traffickers Act, the Senate bill), passed in 2018.[9] The law was supported by Representative Chris Smith (R-NJ), the Coalition Against Trafficking in Women, and Professor Donna Hughes, all of whom share an anti-sex-work stance. FOSTA-SESTA makes it illegal to facilitate or support sex trafficking and extends the definition of "support" to include websites that advertise sexual services. Section 3 of the bill reads:

> The bill amends the federal criminal code to add a new section that imposes penalties—a fine, a prison term of up to 10 years, or both—on

a person who, using a facility or means of interstate or foreign commerce, owns, manages, or operates an interactive computer service (or
attempts or conspires to do so) to promote or facilitate the prostitution
of another person.[10]

This law overrode the provisions in Section 230. Now platform owners and hosting services can be held accountable for what others post on
their sites. The law's use of the term "facilitate" is vague and can be widely
interpreted. Though the title of this law seems to address trafficking, the
focus is in fact on prostitution; this law holds websites responsible for
any acts of prostitution that result from their content (such as classified
listings). Through the override of Section 230, FOSTA-SESTA equates
prostitution with trafficking and has led to the closure of many sites where
sex workers advertised, such as the directories NightShift and CityVibe.[11]
Some sex workers who had previously advertised online have turned to
soliciting on the street, where they are more likely to be arrested and less
likely to be able to verify clients' identities and screen for safety. Before
FOSTA-SESTA, some sites had included pages accessible only by sex
workers, where information about clients could be shared, including dangerous clients to avoid. Without such resources, their working conditions
have become much more dangerous.

The law has also had a chilling effect on online discourse. Many sites
that once connected people who shared common sexual interests have shut
themselves down. One such site, Pounced.org, catered to people who cos-
play as anthropomorphic animals (sometimes called "furries"). A wiki site
for the furry community says that Pounced had hosted over seventy-one
thousand users and over thirteen thousand personal ads.[12] Although the
site was not associated with prostitution or trafficking, the people who
maintained it feared being targeted under FOSTA-SESTA. Pounced.org
administrators explained their risks thus:

> The problem is, with limited resources and a small volunteer staff, our
> risk for operating the site has now significantly increased. Now if some-
> one posts an ad looking to exchange sex for something to pounced.org,
> and we don't catch it, is that facilitating prostitution? Is it enough to
> simply re-train our volunteer staff and update our terms of service? . . .
> We now can be held accountable for the actions of others using our

service. This bill is a poor trade off, it makes all service operators bear increased liability for the actions of their users or act as censors to their speech in exchange for targeting a few malicious services.[13]

They explained that prior to this new law, "we didn't frequently have to pay for lawyers, and we ate this cost when we did." Shutting down a message board for *fear* that its operators *might* be charged with sex offenses under this law is the epitome of a chilling effect on speech. The Pounced administrators explained this well, highlighting that large corporations could cope with these changes but that communities on the margins lack the resources necessary:

In many ways this bill targets small sites like ours directly, it favors organizations with the resources to invest in filtering technology, paid staff and legal support staff. It is less of an impediment for big organizations, while doing significant harm to small organizations like ours, which service niche communities like ours. Our larger competitors are not likely to find a large market in servicing the furry community, and so our community will suffer.[14]

As yet, there is little case law related to FOSTA-SESTA. In part, this is because the law is so new. Another reason may be that websites targeted under FOSTA-SESTA lack the resources to mount a defense and may choose to close down or accept a plea bargain rather than go to court. However, two people who have been affected by the law have described their experiences for me.[15]

Luka,[16] a sex worker, described the ways law enforcement has been used to shut down websites where men like him advertise their sexual services, both before and after the passage of this new law. Before FOSTA-SESTA, he said, "I was meeting on all sorts of platforms and ways, including Rentboy, Craigslist, Backpage, Rentmen, Seeking Arrangement, street work, and dancing at a club and meeting clients there." Rentboy and Rentmen focused on male sex workers, while Craigslist and Backpage were used by sex workers of every gender. Craigslist and Backpage required very low investment to post advertisements in their sex work classifieds; after being targeted by the federal government with the threat of or actual trafficking charges, both have given up their adult services listings. Craigslist gave up their adult services section voluntarily and Backpage was seized by the federal government even before the passage of FOSTA-SESTA.

According to Luka, FOSTA-SESTA has affected men less than women. While the Rentboy shutdown led to a public uproar among sex workers and their supporters, platforms on which women advertise sex work services, he says, "get shut down all the time; one gets shut down every year," starting before FOSTA-SESTA was passed, and more frequently now.

Luka explained that law enforcement in general and anti-trafficking enforcement specifically has not targeted men's sites the same way: "Backpage was the only one I used that was affected [by FOSTA-SESTA] and it wasn't my primary or secondary" source of clients. Luka now advertises on websites hosted outside the United States. He has found ways to be creative using dating and hookup sites, and he was privileged enough to take a hiatus in 2020 and 2021 in an effort to keep safe during the coronavirus pandemic.

Transgender sex workers have had a different experience. Many transgender people had relied on low-cost platforms like Craigslist and Backpage to advertise. My second interview subject, Ceyenne Doroshow, is a long-standing and renowned transgender activist in New York City.[17] She is the founder of G.L.I.T.S., an organization that helps offer both transitional and permanent housing to members of the transgender community, including formerly incarcerated people. Ms. Doroshow described the ways this new law has adversely affected sex workers, especially street-based sex workers and transgender people:

> I've been a sex worker for over thirty years, having gone from street work for survival to online work. Street work was extremely dangerous. Sometimes it was fun and exciting, but very dangerous. Online work gave me and my community the time to work behind the scenes and screen clients and to advertise safely. Countless people were independent and now they can't do sex work carefully and safely. . . . SESTA robbed us of that. People were literally starving. Some became homeless. Some had to move in with others, and that is harmful. . . . This put a whole community in harm's way nationally.

Ms. Doroshow blames anti-sex-work, anti-trafficking advocates for the new law and its effects, saying, "Anti-trafficking people say all sex workers are trafficked, but no one looked at the single mom or the young person going to college and supporting themselves. What about the harm that the law has caused? Worrying about walking while trans—I am worrying about even more now. We are in darkness, this law literally pushed us back on the streets."

Studies report that between 22.3 percent and 47 percent of transgender people experience immense employment discrimination.[18] Many turn to the sex trades for income. Doroshow explained that with fewer options for sex workers to advertise, financial hardship for transgender people has become more extreme. She said, "We used to pick and choose our clients but now we have to barter. You used to make three hundred, four hundred, five hundred dollars but now clients are not willing to pay that much because we can't advertise." She went on to say that

> people are doing strange things for change—going the extra, they are forced into being unsafe. Because [of] our protections through the internet and [not] being able to advertise in a safe and sustainable way, sex workers now have to do extra stuff to make money because they are not able to advertise the way they used to! They are being asked to have unprotected sex, sex without condoms . . .

The advertising platforms that still exist require a greater monetary investment on the part of sex workers and require them to show government-issued identification. Doroshow explained, "Not everyone can pay for upscale advertising; these platforms exist. Not everyone is willing to give up their government name to make money."

FOSTA-SESTA has not led to the identification of survivors of trafficking, but it has increased the burden on sex workers. The law also affects many more people than sex workers because of its chilling effect on online speech.

Despite the problematic consequences of FOSTA-SESTA, as of this writing there is a similar bill that Congress may soon discuss. The Eliminating Abusive and Rampant Neglect of Interactive Technologies (EARN IT) bill, sponsored by Senator Lindsey Graham (R-SC), would require tech businesses to surveil users to identify child sexual abuse material (CSAM), or what might be more familiarly known as child pornography. The bill would also require platforms and service providers to remove their encryption, eroding privacy protections against intrusions by both businesses and governments.[19] The Electronic Frontier Foundation opposes the bill for its overreach against online privacy and for an excessive kind of breadth that would chill online speech. It is similar to the argument in the Pounced letter about FOSTA-SESTA's impact, but this legislation would have far greater reach. The bill would empower a new federal committee that includes law enforcement agencies with the authority to eliminate sites' ability to provide secure, private, encrypted communication, "as long as [the committee] could claim that its recommendations somehow aided in the prevention of child exploitation. Those laws could change and expand unpredictably, especially after changes in the presidential administration."[20] The EARN IT bill is the latest example of how narratives about the protection of children from sexual issues are used to promote authoritarian control.

A BETTER APPROACH

The TVPA was introduced in the last year of the twentieth century, and, along with its re-authorizations and FOSTA-SESTA, it represents the major legislative responses to trafficking in the twenty-first century. The TVPA has had mixed results; provisions for people trafficked for labor have been underutilized, and trafficking victims in both sex work and labor have been subject to arrest instead of receiving the assistance guaranteed by this law. FOSTA-SESTA has chilled speech about sexuality and simultaneously forced the most marginal sex workers to solicit clients in more dangerous venues.

The core problem is that legislation has still to adequately address the real needs of human trafficking survivors. Sadly, it seems that there is no political will to prioritize survivors over other competing interests, including political ends and the private agendas of people against the existence of sex work.

A better approach can be seen in the Survivors of Trafficking Attaining Relief Together (START) Act of New York State, passed in 2021. The START Act allows people with criminal records to vacate criminal convictions that occurred in relation to having been trafficked; attorneys call this process "vacatur." A previous New York State law had permitted vacatur only for acts of prostitution, but many trafficking victims have been forced to commit other crimes, including theft and robbery. For example, a person I interviewed was forced to steal baby formula from drug stores. This is the sort of criminal conviction that can now be vacated by START, enabling the survivor to clear their record and thus find better employment. Additionally, for immigrant victims, the START Act's removal of criminal charges means that these crimes would not count against survivors' applications to become citizens. Yet another obstacle that comes with a criminal record is the barrier to finding housing, which this law also removes. Finally, educational access can also be affected, because some criminal charges eliminate eligibility for some federal student aid, including Pell Grants. This law is a model for other states and the federal government to adapt.

WHAT KIND OF HELP IS TRULY HELPFUL?

T HE STORIES IN THIS BOOK have shown individuals in the US being trafficked into major sectors across the American economy: agriculture, manufacturing, sales, the sex trades, and domestic work. We have also seen how laws ostensibly meant to stop such trafficking have overwhelmingly focused on policing women's sexual behavior, particularly with regard to prostitution. This focus on sexual behavior comes at the detriment of people trafficked in other sectors—their exploitation has been overlooked for the past century and longer. This has two consequences: First, people trafficked in sectors other than sex are not reliably given legal protection, and a response, if there is one, is usually delayed. Second, people in the sex trades have been overpoliced. People trafficked into the sex trades are highly likely to be arrested for prostitution-related crimes, but arrest does not usually alleviate their problems or lead to the provision of social services. Upon arrest, they may instead be fined or appear in front of a judge who, in the best-case scenario, may sentence them to time served in pretrial detention. Alternatively, they may go through a Human Trafficking Intervention Court and be mandated to attend sessions in social services areas such as yoga and counseling but receive no support toward safe employment or a path to regular immigration status.

Current criminal justice models have proven to be inadequate for assisting victims of trafficking because they replicate the punitive and racially driven systems of indentured servitude, chattel slavery, and compulsory labor. These laws and policies, new permutations on an old theme, reflect not the needs of the people who have been hurt in modern-day slavery but rather the desires of the people who make the rules. While unscrupulous anti-trafficking campaigns encourage us to look primarily for girls in sexual servitude, there are adults of all genders, many of color, toiling in all kinds of work situations that meet the definition of trafficking. These victims are less likely to receive help because we do not see them as trafficked, blinkered by inaccurate information.

This focus on sex shields many traffickers from consequences, as well as people who benefit indirectly from compulsory labor in its myriad forms. The focus on sex also obscures the historical roots of labor exploitation, promoting a corporate anti-labor agenda. Real people are being harmed by structural oppression—wage stagnation among the lowest-paid workers, real wages reduced to poverty levels, capitalist enterprises subsidized by the state as federal benefits fill the shortfall between a living wage and what employers are prepared to pay. People can be distracted from these issues by the literally sexier idea of sex trafficking, and the gratifying idea of the rescue. Some would-be rescuers are law enforcement officers trying to break up what they believe is a trafficking ring, no matter that the people the officers are determined to rescue tell them they are not in need of help.

For example, in 2019, billionaire Robert Kraft, owner of the New England Patriots football team, was arrested for soliciting prostitutes at a massage parlor in South Florida. The local police had been surveilling the parlor as part of a trafficking investigation, and they told major news outlets that they had broken an international sex trafficking ring. The Asian women who worked at the massage parlor did not describe themselves this way. Instead, they said that they had simply taken a job, relocating to Florida for better weather. But, as a *Vanity Fair* article reported, "it was somehow easier for law enforcement officers in South Florida to believe that the women had been sold into sex slavery by a global crime syndicate than to acknowledge that immigrant women of precarious status, hemmed in by circumstance, might choose sex work."[1] After the media hoopla, there was no trafficking case, and the women either went to jail, were kept under house arrest, or were handed over to ICE, reminiscent of the way that the Mann Act was used against the women it was purported to protect.

Operation Underground Railroad is an organization explicitly centered on rescue narratives, and is run by a Utah man named Tim Ballard, who claims to have been an agent with the Department of Homeland Security but whose employment there has not been confirmed. Operation Underground Railroad raises funds to make films depicting heroes saving children and promotes stories of its personnel undertaking such rescues. In one instance, the organization funded a law enforcement sting in which officers pretended to be children online, and then paid off a man who was falsely smeared in the press as a pedophile upon his arrest. Operation Underground Railroad is enthusiastic in its rescue stunts but is less concerned about the children involved after a dramatic rescue has been completed. There have been questions about whether the organization has helped any children at all, and whether, in its promotion of rescuing children, it has created a demand for children in trafficking situations, contributing to the problem rather than combating harm. Operation Underground Railroad is currently under investigation by multiple federal agencies.[2]

The narrative of a girl in trouble is very compelling, but some girls are seen as more sympathetic victims than others, reflecting the existing social hierarchy: media coverage of missing persons prioritizes stories about white women and girls, with far less attention paid to women of color and men who have disappeared.[3] A media study determined that television outlets and other media tend to publicize cases about which the police share information, and that the police most often share information about white women and girls.[4] This reflects the racially stratified social order that US law enforcement—first through slave patrols and later the police—was historically created to enforce, as well as the gender roles in which men and boys are not perceived as possible victims. This phenomenon also occurs in human trafficking, such as with the disproportionate attention to white victims, as happened with the women from former Soviet states who appeared on the *New York Times'* front page in 1998.

Unscrupulous anti-trafficking campaigns are often sensationalist and even voyeuristic. Lurid and sexualized descriptions of the horrors faced by trafficked persons are used to generate sympathy, but also to retain interest. As in advertising, sex sells. Some of the images that campaigns use are nonsensical, such as naked women packaged like groceries in glass jars and plastic wrap. Others are blatantly racist, such as that of a white adolescent girl whose mouth is covered by large, dark-skinned hands.[5] These manipulative fundraising appeals do not offer help but instead validate the feelings of people who give to these campaigns.

These are superficial campaigns that may succeed at raising funds but are not informed by evidence or the voices of survivors. They certainly do nothing to address the harder issues coming on the horizon, such as the new front lines of trafficking created by the climate crisis. (Climate change is rendering disasters like Hurricane Katrina more and more common; exploitation during its cleanup is discussed in chapter 8.)[6]

WHAT KIND OF HELP IS TRULY HELPFUL?

To craft effective solutions, the key question to ask is, *What kind of help is truly helpful?* The people who can best answer this question are survivors themselves; most people in trafficking situations rescue themselves. People leaving such situations need practical support: foremost, they need a place to live, preferably in long-term transitional housing. Six months is a generous length of time to offer for transitional housing in the US, but it is not usually enough time to secure a permanent place to live. Every individual case is different, and survivors may need months to address trauma, then get a job, and finally save up for a place to live; this process could take a year or even two.

Survivors also need material support. Those in low-paying jobs may benefit from job training and placement. English language classes are helpful for some. Many ethical organizations help survivors; the best of them use a human rights framework and offer trauma-informed services. A trauma-informed perspective recognizes that traumatic experiences can have long-term effects. Service providers meet survivors where they are, and do not try to scare them into, for example, testifying in court or cooperating with a prosecution.

The Biden administration has introduced the National Action Plan to Combat Human Trafficking, which focuses on workers' rights, emphasizes evidence-based practices, increases funding for survivors' housing, and includes acting on input from survivor leaders who have themselves experienced human trafficking.[7] This is a real change from the previous administration's focus on "immployment," or workplace audits and arrests of workers if they are found to be out of regular status.[8] Such a focus had less to do with combating trafficking than with combating immigration.

There continues to be too great a reliance on police in anti-trafficking, such that sex workers are overpoliced and law enforcement stings do not result in the identification of trafficked persons.[9] One answer is to rely on community groups and service providers, and to bring in law enforcement only when other avenues have failed and an in-depth investigation is necessary to reach victims. Freedom Network USA, a coalition working to ensure that trafficking survivors have access to justice, safety, and opportunity, recommends changing the composition of anti-trafficking task forces to replace law enforcement with community partners, particularly groups that are led by, employ, and are directly in communication with the communities at risk, such as agriculture and domestic workers. Jean Bruggeman, executive director of Freedom Network USA, explained,

> This community-based organization model is more effective than funding law enforcement to infiltrate a community where there is little to no trust and the community is actually fearful of law enforcement. Most people in trafficking situations are held in the scheme through fear of law enforcement and fear of immigration agents, the very systems that are trying to infiltrate and identify victims. This is destined to fail.[10]

Again and again, survivors have told me, "We can rescue ourselves"; this means that saviors are not needed or wanted. Assistance, on the other hand, is welcome, and most people get out of their situations with help from acquaintances, colleagues, and service organizations. People who have escaped sex trafficking are most likely to find help from the people they know from their jobs and those who offer them money, transportation, a cell phone to use, and/or a place to stay.[11]

WHAT YOU CAN DO TODAY

Many people want to help those in the distressing situations I have described in the previous chapters. Ethical shopping is an imperfect avenue—avoiding trafficking in supply chains is difficult, and impossible to do completely—nonetheless, there are things that can be done right now by people like you and me.

- If you suspect a trafficking situation, call a labor union in the relevant economic sector, if one exists, or call the nearest member organization of Freedom Network USA.[12]

- If you interact with a person you suspect may be in a trafficking situation, help them contact a Freedom Network member.
- Buy from companies that participate in the Fair Food Standards Council (FFSC) and do not support companies that do not. This information is easy to access from their website at www.fairfood standards.org/resources/participating-buyers.[13] Where there are few buyers listed, it is worth asking management where you currently shop to consider joining the FFSC.
- Avoid products made with prison labor, and do not invest in private prison corporations. A not-for-profit organization tracking prison labor, Worth Rises, offers a spreadsheet of corporations sorted into degree of involvement and levels of potential as effective targets for activism. The spreadsheet is available at worthrises.org.[14]
- If you choose to donate money to anti-trafficking organizations, choose those, like members of Freedom Network USA that offer direct services to trafficked persons using a human rights framework, and that organize workers to prevent trafficking.[15] Community-based organizations and labor organizers are also good donation options. The organizations that helped people included in this book include these:
  - Brazilian Worker Center
  - Coalition to Abolish Slavery and Trafficking
  - Coalition of Immokalee Workers
  - Damayan
  - Fair Food Program and Fair Food Standards Council
  - Human Trafficking Legal Center
  - International Human Rights Clinic of George Washington University Law School
  - New Orleans Workers' Center for Racial Justice
  - Safe Horizon
  - Sex Workers Project at the Urban Justice Center
- Organizations that offer services to survivors of trafficking may benefit from volunteers and pro bono legal services. These organizations employ people in a variety of roles, doing work that some readers may find gratifying. The Human Trafficking Legal Center (legalcenter.org) is one such organization that coordinates pro bono legal services for trafficked persons.

ACKNOWLEDGMENTS

M Y GRATITUDE EXTENDS to many people, foremost among whom are Marlyn Perez, "Flor," Natalicia Tracy, Jo Weldon, and all survivors who have shared their stories.

This book was improved immensely by my editor, Catherine Tung, and copyeditor Brian Baughan.

Louise Litt gave me invaluable advice. Gillian Beebe explained particular legal issues and offered a lovely place to work.

The Coalition of Immokalee Workers and the Fair Food Program were invaluable, especially Marley Monacello, Judge Laura Safer Espinoza, Laura Germino, Julia Perkins, and Matt Stark Blumin. Susan French of the International Human Rights Clinic's Anti-Trafficking Project at George Washington University Law School was extremely generous with her time and expertise. Lynly Egyes and Stacie Jonas shared insight and information based on their work experience. The Zinssers encouraged my inclusion of care work, and Maryann gave me specific insight available only to someone who had been a care worker for a lifetime.

Volunteers with the Alabama Department of Archives and History, supervised by Meredith McDonough and working with Amelia Chase, have achieved an enormous feat and provided a critical service in digitizing tens of thousands of historical materials. Dallas Hanbury, Montgomery County Archivist, offered both services and relevant reading recommendations. Melynda Barnhart, Weiben Wang, Angela Jones, Eugenia Corvera Poiré, and others helped me access materials. Kate Griffith, Shannon Gleeson, Leanne McCallum, Persio Pereyra, and others pointed me to new articles and information.

Sections about terminology that appear in this book were presented at Ryerson University's conference on Contextual Perspectives on "Human

Trafficking" in Toronto on November 29, 2012, during which Anna-Louise Crago, Francesca Degiuli, Amanda Glasbeek, Juliet November, and Emily van der Meulen offered their insights and suggested resources. Prior to my presentation, Kevicha Echols, Jean Halley, Laurie Pea, and Cris Sardina contributed comments that led to invaluable improvements.

The chapter "From Slavery to Prison and Peonage" was presented at Columbia University's Seminar for the Study of Women and Society, during which I benefited immensely from attendees' responses, including those from Melinda Chateauvert, Samantha Majic, Laura McTighe, Emily Sohmer Tai, and Billur Avlar.

Tracy Quan, Marisa Day, and the Lucky Gallery of Weirdos continue to encourage me with wit and hospitality. This book would not have been possible without the stalwart Angus McIntyre.

NOTES

INTRODUCTION: DOWN THE RABBIT HOLE

1. My publications are available on my website, https://www.melissa ditmore.com.

2. Juhu Thukral, Melissa Ditmore, and Alexandra Murphy, *Behind Closed Doors*, Sex Workers Project, Urban Justice Center, 2005.

3. Ditmore, *The Use of Raids to Fight Trafficking*, Sex Workers Project, Urban Justice Center, 2009.

4. "Garment Worker Protection Act Frequently Asked Questions," California Department of Industrial Relations, https://www.dir.ca.gov/DLSE /GarmentFAQs, accessed May 5, 2022.

5. The nongovernmental organization Clean Clothes Campaign has an enormously informative website with information about particular companies, what a living wage would mean for workers, and what practical things consumers who support the equitable treatment of workers should try to do. See https://cleanclothes.org.

6. Personal correspondence, March 18, 2022.

7. Amy Luft, "Protest Planned in Front of Pornhub HQ in Montreal on International Women's Day," CTV News, March 6, 2020, https://montreal .ctvnews.ca/articles-by-amy-luft/protest-planned-in-front-of-pornhub-hq -in-montreal-on-international-women-s-day-1.4842226?cache=%3FclipId %3D375756%3FautoPlay%3Dtrue; Tarpley Hitt, "How Did a Film by a Shady Anti-Porn Group with Trump Ties End Up on Netflix?" *Daily Beast*, October 22, 2020, https://www.thedailybeast.com/how-did-a-film-by-a-shady -anti-porn-group-with-trump-ties-end-up-on-netflix, accessed April 10, 2022.

8. Exodus Cry, https://exoduscry.com and https://exoduscry.com/our solution, accessed April 10, 2022.

9. Gemma Ahearne, "Puritan Movement," *Plastic Dollheads* (blog), June 15, 2019, https://plasticdollheads.wordpress.com/2019/06/15/puritan-movement/; Samantha Cole, "The Crusade Against Pornhub Is Going to Get Someone Killed," *Motherboard*, April 13, 2021, https://www.vice.com/en/article/n7bj9w /anti-porn-extremism-pornhub-traffickinghub-exodus-cry-ncose.

10. Tarpley Hitt, "Inside Exodus Cry: The Shady Evangelical Group with Trump Ties Waging War on Pornhub," October 16, 2020, updated November

2, 2020, *Daily Beast*, https://www.thedailybeast.com/inside-exodus-cry-the
-shady-evangelical-group-with-trump-ties-waging-war-on-pornhub; Luft,
"Protest Planned in Front of Pornhub HQ in Montreal on International
Women's Day."

11. Benjamin Nolot, "Kids Getting Exposed to Hardcore Porn Is a Ca-
tastrophe We CAN Fix," *New York Post*, August 12, 2021, https://nypost.com
/2021/08/12/kids-getting-exposed-to-hardcore-porn-is-a-catastrophe-we
-can-fix.

12. Cole, "The Crusade Against Pornhub Is Going to Get Someone
Killed."

13. Cole, "The Crusade Against Pornhub Is Going to Get Someone
Killed."

14. Claire Provost and Lara White, "Revealed: The US 'Christian Funda-
mentalists' Behind New Netflix Film on Millennial Sex Lives," Open Democ-
racy, https://www.opendemocracy.net/en/5050/revealed-christian-group
-netflix-spring-break-sex, accessed April 10, 2022.

15. Julian Mark, "A Southwest Flight Attendant Suspected Human Trafficking. It Was Just a Mixed-Race Family Flying to a Funeral," *Washington Post*,
November 8, 2021, https://www.washingtonpost.com/nation/2021/11/08
/southwest-human-trafficking-suspicions-mary-maccarthy.

16. Melinda Chateauvert, *Sex Workers Unite: A History of the Movement from
Stonewall to Slutwalk* (Boston: Beacon Press, 2013), 63.

17. David J. Langum, *Crossing Over the Line: Legislating Morality and the
Mann Act* (Chicago: University of Chicago Press, 1994).

18. Pamela Donovan, *No Way of Knowing: Crime, Urban Legends, and the
Internet* (New York: Routledge, 2004).

19. US Department of Agriculture, Economic Research Service, "Ag and
Food Sectors and the Economy," https://www.ers.usda.gov/data-products/ag
-and-food-statistics-charting-the-essentials/ag-and-food-sectors-and-the
-economy, accessed May 5, 2022.

20. Interview and personal correspondence, March 23, 2022.

21. US Department of State, *2021 Trafficking in Persons Report: United
States*, https://www.state.gov/reports/2021-trafficking-in-persons-report
/united-states, accessed May 21, 2022.

22. Gerard Albert, "Cindy McCain Talks Preventing Human Trafficking
Ahead of Super Bowl," January 13, 2020, Health News Florida, https://health
.wusf.usf.edu/health-news-florida/2020-01-13/cindy-mccain-talks-preventing
-human-trafficking-ahead-of-super-bowl.

23. Correspondence with Erin Albright, November 22 2021.

24. Flor is a pseudonym used to protect her anonymity.

CHAPTER 1: YOUNG AMERICANS ON TRAVELING SALES CREWS

1. US Department of Labor, "Workers Under 18," https://www.dol.gov
/general/topic/hiring/workersunder18.

2. Darlena Cunha, "Trapped into Selling Magazines Door-to-Door," *The
Atlantic*, April 20, 2015, https://www.theatlantic.com/business/archive/2015/04
/trapped-into-selling-magazines-door-to-door/388601.

3. See, for example, this Better Business Bureau page of customer reviews for D & T Connection, Inc., of Georgia: https://www.bbb.org/us/ga/atlanta/profile/magazine-sales/d-t-connection-inc-0443-11002475/customer-reviews, accessed August 13, 2021.

4. Cunha, "Trapped into Selling Magazines Door-to-Door."

5. Ian Urbina, "For Youths, a Grim Tour on Magazine Crews," *New York Times*, February 21, 2007, https://www.nytimes.com/2007/02/21/us/21mag crew.html.

6. Nick Morgan, "Anti-Scam Activist Wins," *Mail Tribune*, January 14, 2016, https://www.mailtribune.com/crime-courts-and-emergencies/2016/01/14/anti-scam-activist-wins/.

7. "New Plan to End Solicitor Abuses; Registering Magazine Crews by Better Business Bureaus to Make Program Effective," *New York Times*, October 11, 1948, https://timesmachine.nytimes.com/timesmachine/1948/10/11/85286252.html, accessed July 1, 2021.

8. Ron Devlin, "Magazine Sales Enmesh Youths in Murky World," *Morning Call*, June 17, 1984, www.mcall.com/news/mc-xpm-1984-06-17-2418037-story.html, accessed August 12, 2021.

9. US Congress, Senate Committee on Governmental Affairs, *Exploitation of Young Adults in Door-to-Door Sales: Hearing Before the Permanent Subcommittee on Investigations of the Committee on Governmental Affairs.* (Known hereafter as *Exploitation of Young Adults in Door-to-Door Sales: Hearing Before the Permanent Subcommittee on Investigations of the Committee on Governmental Affairs.*)

10. "Fatal Crash Left Permanent Scars, Exposed Abusive Industry," *Pioneer Press*, August 16, 2015, https://www.twincities.com/2015/08/16/fatal-crash-left-permanent-scars-exposed-abusive-industry/, accessed July 1, 2021.

11. See examples of ads from the 1980s on page 126 (Attachment 10) of *Exploitation of Young Adults in Door-to-Door Sales: Hearing Before the Permanent Subcommittee on Investigations of the Committee on Governmental Affairs.*

12. See an example of a newer ad from around 2007 in "Life on a Magazine Crew," *New York Times*, February 20, 2007, https://www.nytimes.com/video/us/1194817097685/life-on-a-magazine-crew.html.

13. "Outside Sales Hiring Immediately," Craigslist.com, https://harrisburg.craigslist.org/sls/d/summerdale-outside-sales-hiring/7473967202.html, accessed May 7, 2022.

14. F. T. Norton, "2 Face Human Trafficking Charges in Teen Kidnapping," *Star News Online*, August 13, 2014, https://www.starnewsonline.com/article/NC/20140813/News/605045087/WM; Meg Kissinger and Dave Umhoefer, "Van Disaster Was Just Last Stop on a Hellish Trip," *Milwaukee Journal Sentinel*, June 4, 1999, http://archive.jsonline.com/news/wisconsin/282757451.html, accessed July 1, 2021.

15. National Human Trafficking Hotline, "Sales Crews, Peddling & Begging Rings," https://humantraffickinghotline.org/what-human-trafficking/labor-trafficking/sales-crews-peddling-begging-rings, accessed July 2, 2021.

16. *Exploitation of Young Adults in Door-to-Door Sales: Hearing Before the Permanent Subcommittee on Investigations of the Committee on Governmental Affairs*, p. 22.

17. *Exploitation of Young Adults in Door-to-Door Sales: Hearing Before the Permanent Subcommittee on Investigations of the Committee on Governmental Affairs*, p. 20.

18. *Exploitation of Young Adults in Door-to-Door Sales: Hearing Before the Permanent Subcommittee on Investigations of the Committee on Governmental Affairs*, p. 22.

19. Cunha, "Trapped into Selling Magazines Door-to-Door."

20. *Exploitation of Young Adults in Door-to-Door Sales: Hearing Before the Permanent Subcommittee on Investigations of the Committee on Governmental Affairs*, p. 24.

21. *Exploitation of Young Adults in Door-to-Door Sales: Hearing Before the Permanent Subcommittee on Investigations of the Committee on Governmental Affairs*, p. 22.

22. *Exploitation of Young Adults in Door-to-Door Sales: Hearing Before the Permanent Subcommittee on Investigations of the Committee on Governmental Affairs*, p. 21.

23. "Life on a Magazine Crew."

24. "Life on a Magazine Crew."

25. Urbina, "For Youths, a Grim Tour on Magazine Crews."

26. *Exploitation of Young Adults in Door-to-Door Sales: Hearing Before the Permanent Subcommittee on Investigations of the Committee on Governmental Affairs*, p. 41.

27. "Life on a Magazine Crew."

28. Urbina, "For Youths, a Grim Tour on Magazine Crews."

29. *Exploitation of Young Adults in Door-to-Door Sales: Hearing Before the Permanent Subcommittee on Investigations of the Committee on Governmental Affairs*, p. 22.

30. *Exploitation of Young Adults in Door-to-Door Sales: Hearing Before the Permanent Subcommittee on Investigations of the Committee on Governmental Affairs*, pp. 19–20.

31. *Exploitation of Young Adults in Door-to-Door Sales: Hearing Before the Permanent Subcommittee on Investigations of the Committee on Governmental Affairs*, pp. 196–97.

32. *Exploitation of Young Adults in Door-to-Door Sales: Hearing Before the Permanent Subcommittee on Investigations of the Committee on Governmental Affairs*, pp. 19–20.

33. "Life on a Magazine Crew."

34. *Exploitation of Young Adults in Door-to-Door Sales: Hearing Before the Permanent Subcommittee on Investigations of the Committee on Governmental Affairs*, p. 197.

35. National Human Trafficking Hotline, "Sales Crews, Peddling & Begging Rings."

36. *Exploitation of Young Adults in Door-to-Door Sales: Hearing Before the Permanent Subcommittee on Investigations of the Committee on Governmental Affairs*, pp. 77 and 196.

37. *Exploitation of Young Adults in Door-to-Door Sales: Hearing Before the Permanent Subcommittee on Investigations of the Committee on Governmental Affairs*, p. 21.

38. *Exploitation of Young Adults in Door-to-Door Sales: Hearing Before the Permanent Subcommittee on Investigations of the Committee on Governmental Affairs*, p. 22.

39. Kissinger and Umhoefer, "Van Disaster Was Just Last Stop on a Hellish Trip."

40. Norton, "2 Face Human Trafficking Charges in Teen Kidnapping."

41. Caroline Curran and Christina Haley, "UPDATED: Missing North Dakota Sisters Found in Wilmington; Two Men Charged with Kidnapping, Human Trafficking," *Port City Daily*, August 13, 2014, https://portcitydaily.com /local-news/2014/08/13/missing-north-dakota-sisters-found-in-wilmington -two-men-charged-with-kidnapping-human-trafficking/, accessed August 12, 2021.

42. National Runaway Safeline, "Home Free," https://www.1800runaway .org/youth-teens/home-free, accessed March 3, 2022.

43. *Exploitation of Young Adults in Door-to-Door Sales: Hearing Before the Permanent Subcommittee on Investigations of the Committee on Governmental Affairs*, pp. 25–26.

44. Virginia Pelley, "Human Trafficking: Mag Crew Kid at Your Door Could Be Victim," *Al Jazeera English*, February 24, 2015, http://america .aljazeera.com/articles/2015/2/24/human-trafficking-victim-mag-crew-kid -at-door.html, accessed July 8, 2021.

45. *Exploitation of Young Adults in Door-to-Door Sales: Hearing Before the Permanent Subcommittee on Investigations of the Committee on Governmental Affairs*, p. 22.

46. "Magazine Subscription Company Has a History of Complaints," WECT News 6, August 15, 2014, https://www.wect.com/story/26282044 /magazine-subscription-company-has-history-of-complaints/, accessed August 12, 2021.

47. Better Business Bureau, "Customer Reviews: Midwest Circulation LLC," https://www.bbb.org/us/mo/osborn/profile/subscription-agents/midwest -circulation-llc-0674-99150659/customer-reviews#o, accessed March 3, 2022.

48. "Fatal Crash Left Permanent Scars, Exposed Abusive Industry."

49. Devlin, "Magazine Sales Enmesh Youths in Murky World."

50. Urbina, "For Youths, a Grim Tour on Magazine Crews."

51. *Exploitation of Young Adults in Door-to-Door Sales: Hearing Before the Permanent Subcommittee on Investigations of the Committee on Governmental Affairs*, pp. 202–11.

52. Associated Press, "Cowles and Hearst Accused by F.T.C. in Magazine Sales," *New York Times*, January 22, 1971, https://www.nytimes.com/1971 /01/22/archives/cowles-and-hearst-accused-by-ftc-in-magazine-sales.html, accessed August 13, 2022.

53. Pelley, "Human Trafficking."

54. *Exploitation of Young Adults in Door-to-Door Sales: Hearing Before the Permanent Subcommittee on Investigations of the Committee on Governmental Affairs*, p. 57.

55. Wisconsin Department of Workforce Development, "Wisconsin Regulation of Sales Crews," https://dwd.wisconsin.gov/er/laborstandards/work permit/travelsales.htm, accessed March 3, 2022.

56. "Traveling Door-to-Door Super Cleaner Sales," www.facebook.com /DoortoDoorSoapSales, accessed July 8, 2021.

57. Ojito, "For Deaf Mexicans, Freedom After Slavery and Detention."

58. Ian Fisher, "17th Arrest Made in Case of Deaf Mexican Peddlers," *New York Times*, August 2, 1997, https://www.nytimes.com/1997/08/02/nyregion /17th-arrest-made-in-case-of-deaf-mexican-peddlers.html.

59. Mirta Ojito, "Deaf Mexicans Are to Remain as Witnesses," *New York Times*, August 3, 1997, https://www.nytimes.com/1997/08/03/nyregion/deaf -mexicans-are-to-remain-as-witnesses.html.

60. Ojito, "Deaf Mexicans Are to Remain as Witnesses."

61. Jo Weldon's website is http://www.joweldon.com.

CHAPTER 2: SEX AND LABOR IN THE TRAFFICKING
VICTIMS PROTECTION ACT

1. National Museum of American History, "El Monte," https://american history.si.edu/sweatshops/el-monte, accessed May 7, 2022. A picture of the apartment complex is included.

2. Michael Specter, "CONTRABAND WOMEN—a Special Report; Traffickers' New Cargo: Naive Slavic Women," *New York Times*, January 11, 1998, https://www.nytimes.com/1998/01/11/world/contraband-women-a-special -report-traffickers-new-cargo-naive-slavic-women.html, accessed October 26, 2021.

3. Israel Women's Network, "Trafficking in Women to Israel and Forced Prostitution," *Refuge* 17, no. 5 (November 1998), https://refuge.journals.yorku .ca/index.php/refuge/article/view/21990/20659, accessed May 7, 2022.

4. The United States signed the Protocol to Prevent, Suppress and Punish Trafficking in Persons, Especially Women and Children, supplementing the UN Convention on Transnational Organized Crime, on November 15, 2000, and ratified the Optional Protocol in 2005. For more information, see the United Nations Treaty Collection, Protocol to Prevent, Suppress and Punish Trafficking in Persons, Especially Women and Children, supplementing the UN Convention Against Transnational Organized Crime, https://treaties.un .org/pages/ViewDetails.aspx?src=TREATY&mtdsg_no=XVIII-12-a&chapter =18&clang=_en.

5. Ditmore, *The Use of Raids to Fight Trafficking in Persons*.

6. Vitale, *The End of Policing*, chap. 2.

7. Conversations with Senator Thurmond's staff in my lobbying capacity with the Human Rights Caucus, 2000.

8. Melissa Ditmore and Marjan Wijers, "The Negotiations on the UN Protocol on Trafficking in Persons: Moving the Focus from Morality to Actual Conditions," *Nemesis* (2003): 4; Jo Doezema, "Now You See Her, Now You Don't: Sex Workers at the UN Trafficking Protocol Negotiation," *Social & Legal Studies* 14, no. 1 (March 2005): 61–89, https://doi.org/10.1177 /0964663905049526.

9. ACLU, "As a Result of ACLU Litigation, Trump Administration Ends Policy Prohibiting Immigrant Minors from Accessing Abortion," news release, September 29, 2020, https://www.aclu.org/press-releases/result-aclu-litigation -trump-administration-ends-policy-prohibiting-immigrant-minors, accessed May 12, 2002; Hannah Levintova, "Trump's DOJ Lawyers Just Made a Shocking Argument about the Right to Abortion," *Mother Jones*, October 18, 2017, https://www.motherjones.com/politics/2017/10/trumps-doj-lawyers-just-made -a-shocking-argument-about-the-right-to-abortion, accessed May 30, 2022; Tessa Stewart, "Trump's Anti-Abortion Refugee Program Chief Has Been

Removed from His Post," November 19, 2018, *Rolling Stone*, https://www
.rollingstone.com/politics/politics-news/scott-lloyd-removed-o-r-r-755468,
accessed May 30, 2022.

10. Interview with author, May 10, 2022.

11. The NCANDS language in section 106(d)(17) of CAPTA subsection
(b)(2)(B)(xxiv) requires "provisions and procedures requiring identification and
assessment of all reports involving children known or suspected to be victims
of sex trafficking." The relevant definition of "sex trafficking" for this section is
"the recruitment, harboring, transportation, provision, obtaining, patronizing,
or soliciting of a person for the purpose of a commercial sex act." I thank Dr.
Hanni Stoklossa for bringing this to my attention.

12. Information in this paragraph is from correspondence with Lynly
Egyes, legal director, Transgender Law Center, March 25, 2022.

CHAPTER 3: IN THE DEVIL'S GARDEN

1. Most of the information about Marlyn Perez's experiences comes from
interviews and Doe v. Tapia-Ortiz, Case No: 2:14-cv-206-FtM-38MRM (M.D.
Fla. Feb. 10, 2017). There are ninety-three documents listed in the case docket,
and the documents used for this chapter are the original complaint (document
1 in the docket) and documents 44 (amended complaint) and 78 in the docket,
which include a revised complaint (accessed through Bloomberg Law database), and document 91 (the transcript of the damages hearing from August 16,
2016). The documents refer to Jane Does 1 and 2 and John Does 1 through 5.
I have made these public documents available on the informative website for
this book: https://unbrokenchains.com. Resources cited in footnotes throughout this chapter are included at http://www.unbrokenchains.com/in-the-devils
-garden.

2. For before-and-after pictures—one, taken April 2019, of the pre-existing
border fence; the other, taken January 2020, of a section of Trump's border
wall—see Robert Farley, "Trump's Border Wall: Where Does It Stand?," Fact-
Check.org, December 12, 2020, https://www.factcheck.org/2020/12/trumps
-border-wall-where-does-it-stand, accessed January 5, 2021.

3. Lorne Matalon, "Extending 'Zero Tolerance' to People Who Help
Migrants Along the Border," *All Things Considered*, National Public Radio,
May 28, 2019, https://www.npr.org/2019/05/28/725716169/extending-zero
-tolerance-to-people-who-help-migrants-along-the-border, accessed January
5, 2021.

4. Beverley Bidney, "Project to Restore Devil's Garden to Natural State,"
Seminole Tribune, January 26, 2016, https://seminoletribune.org/project-to
-restore-devils-garden-to-natural-state, accessed February 25, 2021.

5. Patsy West, "Abiaka, or Sam Jones, in Context: The Mikasuki Ethnogenesis Through the Third Seminole War," *The Florida Historical Quarterly* 94,
no. 3 (2016): 366–410, http://www.jstor.org/stable/24769276.

6. South Florida Water Management District, "Quick Facts on . . . Sam
Jones/Abiaki Prairie C-139 Annex Restoration Project," Splash!, March 2016,
https://www.sfwmd.gov/sites/default/files/documents/spl_sam_jones.pdf,
accessed February 25, 2021.

7. Itemization of deductions and hours worked is required under the Migrant and Seasonal Agricultural Worker Protection Act of 1983. More information and forms related to the act are available from the Department of Labor at https://www.dol.gov/agencies/whd/agriculture/mspa.

8. Interview with Judge Laura Safer Espinoza, director of the Fair Food Program, October 3, 2019; Human Rights Watch, *Cultivating Fear*.

9. Interview with Marlyn Perez, November 2, 2019.

10. Coalition of Immokalee Workers, "$3.5 Million Settlement Closes the Books On Yet Another Forced Labor Case in Florida's Fields . . . ," February 21, 2017, https://ciw-online.org/blog/2017/02/devils-garden-case, accessed November 16, 2020.

11. Fair Food Program, *2021 Fair Food Program Report*, September 2021, https://indd.adobe.com/view/2e8c5302-3772-4122-a6a7-f345d4801a16.

12. Gerardo Reyes-Chavez, "Coalition's Efforts Go Beyond Better Pay for Farmworkers," *Naples Daily News*, August 28, 2011, http://archive.naplesdaily news.com/opinion/perspectives/gerardo-reyes-chavez-guest-commentary -coalitions-efforts-go-beyond-better-pay-for-farmworkers-ep-39-342838542 .html, accessed November 16, 2020.

13. Ditmore and Thukral, "Accountability and the Use of Raids to Fight Trafficking."

14. Susan French, a highly qualified law professor and former human trafficking prosecutor in the Department of Justice's Civil Rights Division, was the lead counsel, working with the Miami-based law firm Stroock & Stroock & Lavan. The Human Trafficking Legal Center, a Washington, DC-based or-ganization, facilitated the identification of the law firm. VIDA Legal Assistance also offered pro bono services on immigration cases.

15. The total damages sought were based on calculations of amounts awarded per violation of the Migrant and Seasonal Agricultural Worker Protection Act, along with considerations of wage and hour violations and violations of the Trafficking Victims Protection Act, as well as the battery, false imprisonment, and sexual harassment charges. The damages requested also included punitive damages. Susan French and the legal team are to be com-mended for contributing to the development of a way to calculate damages in trafficking cases, based on unpaid wages and precedent rulings on damages.

CHAPTER 4: INDENTURE, SLAVERY, AND CONTRACT
LABOR IN AGRICULTURE

1. Smith, *Colonists in Bondage*, 336.

2. Information in this paragraph is from Kenneth Morgan, "English and American Attitudes Towards Convict Transportation 1718–1775," *History*, 72, no. 236 (October 1987): 416–31, http://www.jstor.org/stable/24415748.

3. Mittelberger, "Journey to Pennsylvania."

4. Galenson, "The Rise and Fall of Indentured Servitude in the Ameri-cas," 10.

5. "Law Regulating Marriage of Indentured Servants, 1643," William Waller Hening, ed. (New York: R. & W. & G. Bartow, 1823), 1:252–53, https://

encyclopediavirginia.org/entries/law-regulating-marriage-of-indentured
-servants-1643, accessed January 17, 2022.

6. Maureen Meyers, "From Refugees to Slave Traders: The Transformation of the Westo Indians," in *Mapping the Mississippian Shatter Zone: The Colonial Indian Slave Trade and Regional Instability in the American South*, ed. Robbie Franklyn Ethridge and Sheri Marie Shuck-Hall (Lincoln: University of Nebraska Press, 2009), 81–103.

7. Brent Tartar, "Bacon's Rebellion, the Grievances of the People, and the Political Culture of Seventeenth-Century Virginia," *Virginia Magazine of History and Biography* 119, no. 1 (2011): 2–41, http://www.jstor.org/stable /41059478.

8. Benjamin Franklin, *Autobiography of Ben Franklin* (New York: Henry Holt, 1916), chap. 3, "Arrival in Philadelphia," 41–55.

9. *Minutes of the Council and General Court of Colonial Virginia* (1640), ed. H. R. McIlwane (Richmond: Library of Virginia, 1924), 466–67; "General Court Responds to Runaway Servants and Slaves, 1640," Encyclopedia Virginia, https://encyclopediavirginia.org/entries/general-court-responds-to -runaway-servants-and-slaves-1640, accessed January 17, 2022.

10. Richard Wojtowicz and Billy G. Smith, "Advertisements for Runaway Slaves, Indentured Servants, and Apprentices in the *Pennsylvania Gazette*, 1795–1796," *Pennsylvania History: A Journal of Mid-Atlantic Studies* 54, no. 1 (1987): 34–71, http://www.jstor.org/stable/27773159.

11. Kulikoff, *Tobacco and Slaves*, 295–96, cited in Righi, "The Right of Petition," 42.

12. Cloud and Galenson, "Chinese Immigration and Contract Labor in the Late Nineteenth Century," 22–42.

13. Galenson, "The Rise and Fall of Indentured Servitude in the Americas," 13.

14. Rönnbäck, "Were Slaves Cheap Laborers?," 721–41.

15. Rönnbäck, "Were Slaves Cheap Laborers?," 732.

16. Rönnbäck, "Were Slaves Cheap Laborers?," 721–41.

17. Fisher, "'Why Shall Wee Have Peace to Bee Made Slaves,'" 91–114,

18. Sweet, "The Thirteenth Colony in Perspective," 435–60.

19. Mark Stelzner and Sven Beckert, *The Contribution of Enslaved Workers to Output and Growth in the Antebellum United States*, Washington Center for Equitable Growth, June 2021, p. 25, https://equitablegrowth.org/working -papers/the-contribution-of-enslaved-workers-to-output-and-growth-in-the -antebellum-united-states.

20. David Williams, *Bitterly Divided: The South's Inner Civil War* (New York: The New Press, 2010).

21. Sven Beckert, *Empire of Cotton: A Global History* (New York: Alfred A. Knopf, 2014).

22. Sven Beckert and Seth Rockman, eds., *Slavery's Capitalism: A New History of American Economic Development* (Philadelphia: University of Pennsylvania Press, 2016).

23. An Act Concerning Servants and Slaves, Virginia, 1705.

24. Ross Kimmell, "Freedom or Bondage: The Legislative Record," Maryland State Archives, https://msa.maryland.gov/msa/speccol/sc5300/sc5348/html/chap3.html, accessed January 17, 2022. This page quotes the text from *Archives of Maryland*, ed. William Hand Browne et al. (in progress; Baltimore, 1883 to date), I, pp. 533–34.

25. Curriculum Concepts International, "Slave Market," Mapping the African American Past, https://maap.columbia.edu/place/22.html, accessed January 17, 2022.

26. "Blacks Before the Law in Colonial Maryland," Maryland State Archives.

27. Act of the Commonwealth of Virginia 1669. Cited in William Waller Hening, ed., *The Statutes at Large; Being a Collection of All the Laws of Virginia, from the First Session of the Legislature in the Year 1619*, 2 vols. (New York: R. & W. & G. Bartow, 1823). The text of this act was reproduced by Channel Thirteen, *Slavery and the Making of America*, https://www.thirteen.org/wnet/slavery/experience/living/docs1.html, accessed January 17, 2022.

28. "Field Labor," and "Tom," George Washington's Mount Vernon, https://www.mountvernon.org/george-washington/slavery/field-labor. The website currently dedicated to Mount Vernon (www.mountvernon.org) includes a database of people who were enslaved at Mount Vernon. An amazing and unique resource, the database includes their names, the work they did, and the information sources for each entry. The URL for the Database of Mount Vernon's Enslaved Community is https://www.mountvernon.org/george-washington/slavery/slavery-database.

29. "Field Labor," "Priscilla and Penny," and "A Day in the Life of an Enslaved Field Worker," George Washington's Mount Vernon.

30. "Field Labor," George Washington's Mount Vernon. More information about the life of a field worker is available at https://www.mountvernon.org/george-washington/slavery/field-labor.

31. South Carolina Department of Archives and History, Miscellaneous Records of the Secretary of State (main series), OO: 387, 398 (October 8 and 11, 1770). Cited by Nic Butler, "Self-Purchase: The Price of Freedom from Slavery," Charleston County Public Library, February 28, 2020, https://www.ccpl.org/charleston-time-machine/self-purchase-price-freedom-slavery, accessed January 17, 2022. This is a transcript of episode 147 of *Charleston Time Machine*, available at https://soundcloud.com/user-242710718/episode-147-self-purchase-the-price-of-freedom-from-slavery?utm_source=www.ccpl.org&utm_campaign=wtshare&utm_medium=widget&utm_content=https%253A%252F%252Fsoundcloud.com%252Fuser-242710718%252Fepisode-147-self-purchase-the-price-of-freedom-from-slavery.

32. Colleen M. Elliot and Louise A. Moxley, eds., *The Tennessee Civil War Veterans Questionnaires*, vols. 1–5 (Easley, SC: Southern Historical Press, 1985), vol. 3, 1057. Quoted in Keri Leigh Merritt, *Masterless Men: Poor Whites and Slavery in the Antebellum South* (Cambridge: Cambridge University Press, 2017), 5.

33. Krauthamer, *Black Slaves, Indian Masters*.

34. Krauthamer, *Black Slaves, Indian Masters*, 80–82.

35. Krauthamer, *Black Slaves, Indian Masters*, 83–84.

36. Krauthamer, *Black Slaves, Indian Masters*, 85–87, 89.

37. Krauthamer, *Black Slaves, Indian Masters*, 89–91.

38. Krauthamer, *Black Slaves, Indian Masters*, 91–92.

39. Krauthamer, *Black Slaves, Indian Masters*, 139–41.

40. Special Field Orders, No. 15, Headquarters Military Division of the Mississippi, January 16, 1865, Orders & Circulars, series 44, Adjutant General's Office, Record Group 94, National Archives; William A. Gladstone, collector, *William A. Gladstone Afro-American Military Collection: Special Field Orders, No. 15, Headquarters, Military Division of the Mississippi, by Major General W. T. Sherman*, 1865, manuscript/mixed material, Library of Congress, https://www.loc.gov/item/mss83434256; Foner, *Reconstruction*. While freedmen in the east were eager to benefit from this offer, Lincoln's successor, President Andrew Johnson, rescinded the land grant and reinstated ownership to the former owners who had seceded from the union.

41. Melinda C. Miller, "'The Righteous and Reasonable Ambition to Become a Landholder': Land and Racial Inequality in the Postbellum South," *Review of Economics and Statistics* 102, no. 2 (2020): 381–94, https://doi.org/10.1162/rest_a_00842.

42. Foner, *Reconstruction*, 214.

43. Brooks, "'John Chinaman' in Alabama," 21.

44. Murray and Herndon, "Markets for Children in Early America," 356–82; Jernegan, *Laboring and Dependent Classes in Colonial America*, 162–64, cited in Murray and Herndon, "Markets for Children in Early America: A Political Economy of Pauper Apprenticeship," *Journal of Economic History* 62, no. 2 (2002); 356–82, http://www.jstor.org/stable/2698184.

CHAPTER 5: FROM SLAVERY TO PRISON AND PEONAGE

1. "Historic Documents," Slavery by Another Name website, PBS, http://www.pbs.org/tpt/slavery-by-another-name/themes/historic-documents.

2. Gutman, *The Black Family in Slavery and Freedom*, 402.

3. Mary Niall Mitchell, *Raising Freedom's Child: Black Children and Visions of the Future After Slavery* (New York: New York University Press, 2008).

4. Foner, *Reconstruction*, 201.

5. Lew Wallace's report to Maryland General Assembly, Document J in the Maryland State Reports for 1865 entitled "Communication from Major General Lew Wallace in Relation to the Freedmen's Bureau to the General Assembly of Maryland," 1865.

6. Hadden, *Slave Patrols*, 198.

7. Foner, *Reconstruction*, 209.

8. Francis B. Simkins and Robert H. Woody, *South Carolina During Reconstruction* (Chapel Hill: University of North Carolina Press, 1932), 48–50; 39th Congress, 2d Session, Senate Executive Document 6, 218–19; cited in Foner *Reconstruction*, 200.

9. McConnell, *Negroes and Their Treatment in Virginia from 1865 to 1867*, 30–31.

10. McConnell, *Negroes and Their Treatment in Virginia from 1865 to 1867*, 30–33.

11. Colleen M. Elliot and Louise A. Moxley, eds., *The Tennessee Civil War Veterans Questionnaires*, vols. 1–5 (Easley, SC: Southern Historical Press, 1985), vol. 3, p. 966. Quoted in Keri Leigh Merritt, *Masterless Men: Poor Whites and Slavery in the Antebellum South* (Cambridge: Cambridge University Press, 2017), 5.

12. Quoted in McConnell, *Negroes and Their Treatment in Virginia from 1865 to 1867*, 48.

13. Foner, *Reconstruction*, 200.

14. "State-by-State Court Fees," "Guilty and Charged" special series, National Public Radio, May 19, 2014, http://www.npr.org/2014/05/19/312455680/state-by-state-court-fees.

15. "As Court Fees Rise, the Poor Are Paying the Price," "Guilty and Charged" special series, National Public Radio, 2014, www.npr.org/2014/05/19/312158516/increasing-court-fees-punish-the-poor.

16. Campbell, *White and Black*, 384.

17. Matthew J. Mancini, "Race, Economics, and the Abandonment of Convict Leasing," *Journal of Negro History* 63, no. 4 (1978): 339–52.

18. Keeler, *American Bastiles*, 7–8, and quoted in Du Bois, *Black Reconstruction in America 1860–1880*, 699.

19. *Occasional Papers*, American Negro Academy, no. 15, p. 10. Quoted in Du Bois, *Black Reconstruction in America 1860–1880*, 696.

20. Bullock County is in eastern Alabama and was part of the area from where Indigenous Creek people were uprooted and forced west to Indian Territory, in what is now Oklahoma, so that the land could be taken over by whites and turned into cotton farms worked by enslaved people, as described in chapter 4.

21. David Oshinsky, *Worse Than Slavery: Parchman Farm and the Ordeal of Jim Crow Justice* (New York: Free Press, 1996).

22. Alan and John Lomax collected songs of prison laborers at Parchman Farm. The Lomax Digital Archive includes audio recordings of prisoners singing work songs and photographs from Parchman Farm and other prisons; see https://archive.culturalequity.org. Some video footage can be seen in this clip from the documentary *Lomax the Song Hunter* at https://www.youtube.com/watch?v=Yw2O8hdlpfQ, accessed March 10, 2022.

23. American Civil Liberties Union and the University of Chicago Law School Global Human Rights Clinic, *Captive Labor: Exploitation of Incarcerated Workers*, June 15, 2022, 55-58, https://www.aclu.org/report/captive-labor-exploitation-incarcerated-workers, accessed July 30, 2022

24. Vicki Peláez, "The Prison Industry in the United States: Big Business or a New Form of Slavery?" Global Research, March 31, 2014.

25. Louisa Valentin, "The First Step to Stopping Corporations from Profiting from Prison Labor in the United States," Transnational Institute, March 30, 2021, https://www.tni.org/en/article/the-first-step-to-stop-corporations-from-profiting-from-incarceration-in-the-united-states, accessed July 30, 2022.

26. American Civil Liberties Union and the University of Chicago Law School Global Human Rights Clinic, *Captive Labor*, 43; H. Claire Brown, "How Corporations Buy—and Sell—Food Made with Prison Labor," *The*

Counter, May 18, 2021, https://thecounter.org/how-corporations-buy-and-sell -food-made-with-prison-labor/, accessed July 30, 2022; Caroline Winter, "What Do Prisoners Make for Victoria's Secret?" *Mother Jones*, July/August 2008, www.motherjones.com/politics/2008/07/what-do-prisoners-make -victorias-secret; Jennifer Alsever, "Prison Labor's New Frontier: Artisanal Foods," *Fortune*, June 2, 2014, http://fortune.com/2014/06/02/prison-labor -artisanal, accessed March 2, 2015.

27. Caitlin Seandel, "Three Strikes and You're Hired," Ella Baker Center, June 27, 2013, http://ellabakercenter.org/blog/2013/06/prison-labor-is-the-new -slave-labor. This original link no longer functions; a PDF of this piece is available at https://worldwithoutmoneyarg.files.wordpress.com.

28. American Civil Liberties Union and the University of Chicago Law School Global Human Rights Clinic, *Captive Labor*, 14–15 and 48.

29. American Civil Liberties Union and the University of Chicago Law School Global Human Rights Clinic, *Captive Labor*, 53.

30. American Civil Liberties Union and the University of Chicago Law School Global Human Rights Clinic, *Captive Labor*, 52.

CHAPTER 6: TRAFFICKING INTO DOMESTIC AND CARE WORK TODAY

1. Heidi Shierholz et al., *Domestic Workers Chartbook*.

2. "Maid and Housekeeper Salary," *U.S. News & World Report*, https://money .usnews.com/careers/best-jobs/maid-and-housekeeper/salary, accessed May 14, 2022; "Personal Care Aide," *U.S. News & World Report*, https://money .usnews.com/careers/best-jobs/personal-care-aide, accessed May 14, 2022.

3. "Security Guard Salary," *U.S. News & World Report*, https://money.usnews .com/careers/best-jobs/security-guard/salary, accessed March 23, 2022; "Con-struction Worker Salary," *U.S. News & World Report*, https://money.usnews .com/careers/best-jobs/construction-worker/salary, accessed March 23, 2022.

4. Barroso and Brown, "Gender Pay Gap in U.S. Held Steady in 2020."

5. National Labor Relations Act of 1935, 29 U.S.C. §§ 151–169, accessible from the National Labor Relations Board at https://www.nlrb.gov/guidance /key-reference-materials/national-labor-relations-act.

6. The text of the FLSA is available at https://uscode.house.gov/view .xhtml?path=/prelim@title29/chapter8&edition=prelim, accessed December 29, 2021.

7. Interview and personal correspondence with author, March 23 and 24, 2022.

8. Indie Lens Storycast, "Hitting the Road with CareForce One: The CareForce One Travelogues Ep. 1," YouTube, May 1, 2018, https://www .youtube.com/watch?v=wkJotlGCGMc, accessed April 17, 2022.

9. Tracy, "I Am a Survivor of Human Trafficking: Natalicia's Story."

10. Marques Travae, "From Nightmare to American Dream: Trafficked, Exploited Brazilian Domestic Becomes Professor at US University," *Black Brazil Today*, December 4, 2013, https://blackbraziltoday.com/from-nightmare -to-american-dream, accessed April 17, 2022.

11. Travae, "From Nightmare to American Dream."

12. Tracy, "I Am a Survivor of Human Trafficking: Natalicia's Story."

13. Travae, "From Nightmare to American Dream."

14. Travae, "From Nightmare to American Dream."

15. Travae, "From Nightmare to American Dream."

16. Travae, "From Nightmare to American Dream."

17. "Natalicia Tracy, Senior Policy Advisor," US Department of Labor, Occupational Safety and Health Administration, https://www.osha.gov/aboutosha/biography/tracy, accessed April 17, 2022.

18. See, for example, Daluz, "I Am a Survivor of Human Trafficking: Judith's Story"; Ruiz, "I Am a Survivor of Human Trafficking: Nena's Story."

19. Splinter Video, "'I'm Free': A Domestic Worker Who Escaped Human Trafficking Tells Her Story," *Splinter*, July 7, 2017, https://splinternews.com/i-m-free-a-domestic-worker-who-escaped-human-traffic-1796728421, accessed December 28, 2021.

20. "Labor Trafficking Survivor and Leader Reunites with Four Children After 10 Years," Damayan, n.d., https://www.damayanmigrants.org/news3/2018/1/7/labor-trafficking-survivor-and-leader-reunites-with-four-children-after-10-years, accessed April 17, 2022.

21. Splinter Video, "'I'm Free.'"

22. Don Tagala, "Pinay Trafficking Victim Reunited with Family in US," ABS-CBN News, February 20, 2015, https://news.abs-cbn.com/global-filipino/02/20/15/pinay-trafficking-victim-reunited-family-us; Splinter Video, "'I'm Free.'"

23. Abigail Savitch-Lew, "Filipina Trafficking Survivors Launch a Co-op—and They Own Their Jobs," *Yes!*, December 23, 2015, https://www.yesmagazine.org/economy/2015/12/23/these-filipina-trafficking-survivors-launched-a-co-op-and-they-own-their-jobs, accessed April 17, 2022.

24. Ruiz, "I Am a Survivor of Human Trafficking"; Richard Verrier, "Sony Pictures Exec, Wife Liable in Labor Lawsuit," *Los Angeles Times*, August 27, 2004, https://www.latimes.com/archives/la-xpm-2004-aug-27-fi-slave27-story.html.

25. Coalition to Abolish Slavery and Trafficking, "NENA Portrait of a Survivor," YouTube, June 10, 2014, https://www.youtube.com/watch?v=jovZXAsEADA, accessed April 17, 2022.

26. Coalition to Abolish Slavery and Trafficking, "NENA Portrait of a Survivor."

27. Verrier, "Sony Pictures Exec, Wife Liable in Labor Lawsuit."

28. California Department of Industrial Relations, "The Domestic Worker Bill of Rights," https://www.dir.ca.gov/dlse/DomesticWorkerBillOfRights.html, accessed March 10, 2022; Coalition to Abolish Slavery and Trafficking, "NENA Portrait of a Survivor."

29. Coalition to Abolish Slavery and Trafficking, "NENA Portrait of a Survivor."

30. Massachusetts Domestic Workers Coalition, https://www.massdomesticworkers.org/mcdw, accessed October 10, 2021.

31. US Department of Labor, "Fact Sheet #79B: Live-in Domestic Service Workers Under the Fair Labor Standards Act (FLSA)," September 2013, https://www.dol.gov/agencies/whd/fact-sheets/79b-flsa-live-in-domestic-workers.

32. Tracy, "I Am a Survivor of Human Trafficking: Natalicia's Story."

33. Coalition to Abolish Slavery and Trafficking, "NENA Portrait of a Survivor."

34. Ruiz, "I Am a Survivor of Human Trafficking: Nena's Story."

35. Tracy, "I Am a Survivor of Human Trafficking: Natalicia's Story."

36. Coalition to Abolish Slavery and Trafficking, "NENA Portrait of a Survivor."

37. Tracy, "I Am a Survivor of Human Trafficking: Natalicia's Story."

38. Tracy, "I Am a Survivor of Human Trafficking: Natalicia's Story."

39. Daluz, "I Am a Survivor of Human Traffickin": Judith's Story."

40. Bianchi et al., "Housework," 55–63.

41. Multiple news articles reported this phenomenon, including Jo Craven McGinty, "Covid-19 Raised Housework Demands and Women Carried More of the Burden," *Wall Street Journal*, May 21, 2021, https://www.wsj.com /articles/covid-19-raised-housework-demands-and-women-carried-more-of -the-burden-11621589410, accessed August 17, 2021; Terry Gross, "Pandemic Makes Evident 'Grotesque' Gender Inequality in Household Work," *Fresh Air*, National Public Radio, May 21, 2020, https://www.npr.org/2020/05/21/860091230 /pandemic-makes-evident-grotesque-gender-inequality-in-household-work, accessed August 17, 2021.

42. Shierholz et al., *Domestic Workers Chartbook*.

43. Department of Health and Human Services, "2021 Poverty Guide- lines," https://aspe.hhs.gov/topics/poverty-economic-mobility/poverty -guidelines/prior-hhs-poverty-guidelines-federal-register-references/2021 -poverty-guidelines, accessed March 11, 2022.

44. Lauren Hilgers, "Out of the Shadows," *New York Times Magazine*, Feb- ruary 21, 2019, https://www.nytimes.com/interactive/2019/02/21/magazine /national-domestic-workers-alliance.html.

CHAPTER 7: THE HISTORY OF EXPLOITATION IN DOMESTIC WORK

1. Kenneth Morgan, "English and American Attitudes Towards Convict Transportation 1718–1775," *History* 72, no. 236 (1987): 416–31, http://www .jstor.org/stable/24415748.

2. Martha W. McCartney, *Virginia Immigrants and Adventurers, 1607–1635: A Biographical Dictionary* (Baltimore: Genealogical Publishing, 2007), 77.

3. Richard Wojtowicz and Billy G. Smith, "Advertisements for Runaway Slaves, Indentured Servants, and Apprentices in the Pennsylvania Gazette, 1795–1796," *Pennsylvania History: A Journal of Mid-Atlantic Studies* 54, no. 1 (1987): 45, http://www.jstor.org/stable/27773159.

4. Jones, *American Work*, 72–73, cited in Brandon Paul Righi, "The Right of Petition: Cases of Indentured Servants and Society in Colonial Virginia, 1698–1746" (master's thesis, College of William and Mary, 2010), 42.

5. Raleigh-Adams, *Orders, Wills, Etc. 1706–1708*, cited in Righi, "The Right of Petition," 35.

6. Information about Ona Judge from Jessie Macleod, "Ona Judge," George Washington's Mount Vernon, https://www.mountvernon.org/library /digitalhistory/digital-encyclopedia/article/ona-judge, accessed May 14, 2022.

7. Letter from Tobias Lear to George Washington, April 24, 1791, National Archives, https://founders.archives.gov/documents/Washington/05-08 -02-0099, accessed May 14, 2022.

8. T. H. Adams, "Washington's Runaway Slave, and How Portsmouth Freed Her," *Granite (NH) Freeman,* May 22, 1845, reprinted in Frank W. Miller, *Portsmouth New Hampshire Weekly,* June 2, 1877, quoted in Macleod, "Ona Judge."

9. Sheldon, "Breeding Mixed-Race Women for Profit and Pleasure," 741–65.

10. Sara Collini, "The Labors of Enslaved Midwives in Revolutionary Virginia," in *Women in the American Revolution: Gender, Politics, and the Domestic World,* ed. Barbara Oberg (Charlottesville: University of Virginia Press, 2019).

11. John W. Blassingame, ed., *Slave Testimony: Two Centuries of Letters, Speeches, Interviews, and Autobiographies* (Baton Rouge: Louisiana State University Press, 1977), 380, 382–83, 476–77.

12. Jackson, "Rosy, Possum, Morning Star," 133.

13. Lakwete, "The Eclectic Industrialism of Antebellum Baldwin County," 3–39.

14. Thavolia Glymph, *Out of the House of Bondage: The Transformation of the Plantation Household* (New York: Cambridge University Press, 2003).

15. Glymph, *Out of the House of Bondage,* 179.

16. Glymph, *Out of the House of Bondage,* 199–200.

17. Information in this paragraph is from Katherin van Wormer, "Maid Narratives," Virginia Commonwealth University, Social Welfare History Project, https://socialwelfare.library.vcu.edu/eras/maids-narratives, accessed May 23, 2022.

CHAPTER 8: CONTEMPORARY TRAFFICKING CASES
IN INDUSTRY AND INFRASTRUCTURE

1. Grieder, "These Dark Satanic Mills," 205–6; Chisolm-Straker and Chon, *The Historical Roots of Human Trafficking*; Erin Blakemore, "20th-Century Slavery Was Hiding in Plain Sight," *Smithsonian Magazine,* July 31, 2020, https://www.smithsonianmag.com/smithsonian-institution/20th-century -slavery-california-sweatshop-was-hiding-plain-sight-180975441, accessed September 29, 2021.

2. Blakemore, "20th-Century Slavery Was Hiding in Plain Sight."

3. Jessie Macleod, "Ona Judge," George Washington's Mount Vernon, https://www.mountvernon.org/library/digitalhistory/digital-encyclopedia /article/ona-judge, accessed May 14, 2022; Blakemore, "20th-Century Slavery Was Hiding in Plain Sight."

4. US Department of Labor, Memorandum Number 199, September 22, 2005. This is an appendix to the Department of Homeland Security's Hurricane Katrina Threshold-Rescind Memo of October 28, 2005, https://www.dhs .gov/publication/archived-far-deviations, accessed May 28, 2022; Olam and Stamper, "The Suspension of the Davis-Bacon Act and the Exploitation of Migrant Workers in the Wake of Hurricane Katrina," 145–80.

5. Administration for Children and Families Office on Trafficking in Persons & National Human Trafficking Training and Technical Assistance Center,

Trafficking Prevention and Disaster Response, February 2018, https://nhttac.acf
.hhs.gov/sites/default/files/2020-02/Trafficking%20Prevention%20and%20
Disaster%20Response%20Literature%20Review.pdf, accessed March 30, 2022.

6. US Government Accountability Office, "Hurricane Katrina: Improving
Federal Contracting Practices in Disaster Recovery Operations," May 2006,
https://www.gao.gov/assets/gao-06-714t.pdf, accessed March 30, 2022.

7. McCallum, "Reflections from the Field," 26, 32.

8. David v. Signal International, LLC (2012), 08-1220-SM-DEK, US
District Court for the Eastern District of Louisiana.

9. Julia Preston, "Suit Points to Guest Worker Program Flaws," *New York
Times*, February 10, 2010, https://www.nytimes.com/2010/02/02/us/02immig
.html, accessed August 1, 2022.

10. Preston, "Suit Points to Guest Worker Program Flaws."

11. Hepburn and Simon, *Human Trafficking Around the World*.

12. McCallum, "Reflections from the Field," 36.

13. Julia Preston, "Workers on Hunger Strike Say They Were Misled on
Visas," *New York Times*, June 7, 2008, https://www.nytimes.com/2008/06/07
/washington/07immig.html, accessed April 1, 2022.

14. Hepburn and Simon, *Human Trafficking Around the World*.

15. Stephanie Hepburn, "Dispatches: Labor Conditions in New Orleans,"
Americas Quarterly, July 22, 2010, https://www.americasquarterly.org/fulltext
article/dispatches-labor-conditions-in-new-orleans, accessed April 1, 2022.

16. McCallum, "Reflections from the Field," 24.

17. McCallum, "Reflections from the Field," 21–41.

18. McCallum, "Reflections from the Field," 24–25.

19. McCallum, "Reflections from the Field," 30.

CHAPTER 9: SLAVERY AND PRISON LABOR IN INDUSTRY
AND INFRASTRUCTURE

1. Aaron Hall, "Slaves of the State: Infrastructure and Governance
Through Slavery in the Antebellum South," *Journal of American History* 106,
no. 1 (2019): 19–46.

2. Ryan Quintana, "Slavery and the Conceptual History of the US State,"
Journal of the Early Republic 38, no. 1 (2018): 82, doi:10.1353/jer.2018.0004.

3. Aaron R. Hall, "Public Slaves and State Engineers: Modern Statecraft
on Louisiana's Waterways, 1833–1861," *Journal of Southern History* 85, no. 3
(2019): 531–76.

4. Hall, "Public Slaves and State Engineers," 547.

5. The author of the report was Duncan Reed, chief engineer of the Board
of Public Works, State of Louisiana, *Annual Report of the Chief Engineer* (1860),
10–15, quoted in Hall, "Public Slaves and State Engineers," 573.

6. Petition of Nathaniel Heyward and Others Requesting That a Public
Landing May Not Be Established on Their Plantations, December 4, 1806,
Item No. 92, Series S165015, Legislative Papers, SCDAH. Cited by Quintana,
"Slavery and the Conceptual History of the US State," 84.

7. Lakwete, "The Eclectic Industrialism of Antebellum Baldwin County,"
3–39.

8. Daniel M. Mulcare, "Restricted Authority: Slavery Politics, Internal Improvements, and the Limitation of National Administrative Capacity," *Political Research Quarterly* 61, no. 4 (2008): 671–85.

9. Information in this paragraph is from Adina Solomon, "Atlanta Reckons with the Convict Labor That Built the City," *Next City*, January 18, 2022, https://nextcity.org/urbanist-news/atlanta-reckons-with-the-convict-labor -that-built-the-city, accessed April 2, 2022.

10. Abby Lee Hood, "Tennessee Professors and Historians Uncover History of Convict Leasing in the State," *Tennessee Lookout*, October 6, 2021, https://tennesseelookout.com/2021/10/06/tennessee-professors-and-historians -uncover-history-of-convict-leasing-in-the-state/, accessed July 28, 2022.

11. Haley, "'Like I Was a Man,'" 56.

12. Letter from Ezekiel Archey and Ambrose Haskins, convict laborers at Pratt Mines in Jefferson County, Alabama, to Reginald Dawson, president of the Alabama Board of Inspectors of Convicts, Alabama Department of Archives and History Digital Collections, http://digital.archives.alabama.gov /cdm/singleitem/collection/voices/id/5417/rec/2.

13. Letter from a convict laborer at Pratt Mines in Jefferson County, Alabama, to Reginald Dawson, president of the Alabama Board of Inspectors of Convicts, Alabama Department of Archives and History Digital Collections, http://digital.archives.alabama.gov/cdm/singleitem/collection/voices/id/5414 /rec/1.

14. Order from the Alabama Board of Inspectors of Convicts to Comer and McCurdy of Pratt Mines in Jefferson County, Alabama, for the discharge of convict laborers Ezekiel Archey and John Fannin, Alabama Department of Archives and History Digital Collections, http://digital.archives.alabama.gov /cdm/singleitem/collection/voices/id/5418/rec/3.

15. Cable, "The Convict Lease System in the Southern United States," 597. Also quoted in Du Bois, *Black Reconstruction in America 1860–1880*, 699.

16. Kwong, *Forbidden Workers*, 42–43.

17. Mei, "Socioeconomic Origins of Emigration," 463–501.

18. Mei, "Socioeconomic Origins of Emigration," 476.

19. Mei, "Socioeconomic Origins of Emigration," 480–82.

20. Mei, "Socioeconomic Origins of Emigration," 463–501.

21. Brooks, "'John Chinaman' in Alabama," 5–36.

22. Mei, "Socioeconomic Origins of Emigration," 486.

23. Chang, *Ghosts of Gold Mountain*, 53.

24. Cloud and Galenson, "Chinese Immigration and Contract Labor in the Late Nineteenth Century," 24.

25. California State Senate 1878 Committee Hearing, 77. Cited in Cloud and Galenson, "Chinese Immigration and Contract Labor in the Late Nineteenth Century," 25.

26. Chang, *Ghosts of Gold Mountain*, 47.

27. Chang, *Ghosts of Gold Mountain*, 228, 243.

28. Chang, *Ghosts of Gold Mountain*, 138–39.

29. Chang, *Ghosts of Gold Mountain*, 150.

30. Chang, *Ghosts of Gold Mountain*, 153.

31. Chang, *Ghosts of Gold Mountain*, 156–57.

32. Chang, *Ghosts of Gold Mountain*, 159.

33. Chang, *Ghosts of Gold Mountain*, 205.

34. Brooks, "'John Chinaman' in Alabama," 17.

35. Brooks, "'John Chinaman' in Alabama," 20, quotes Lucy M. Cohen, *The Chinese in the Post–Civil War South: A People Without a History* (Baton Rouge: Louisiana State University Press, 1984), 94; *Memphis Daily Appeal*, June 16, 1871; A. B. Moore, "Railroad Building in Alabama During the Reconstruction Period," *Journal of Southern History* 1, no. 4 (November 1935): 433–34.

36. See James A. Ward, ed., *Southern Railroad Man: Conductor N. J. Bell's Recollections of the Civil War Era* (DeKalb: Northern Illinois University Press, 1994), 47–78, quoted in Brooks, "'John Chinaman' in Alabama," 19. Half of the railway workers seem to have remained on the railroad, and were not paid for their labor (Brooks, "'John Chinaman' in Alabama," 20).

37. Chang, *Ghosts of Gold Mountain*, 85.

38. Kwong, *Forbidden Workers*, 142, 76. The Naturalization Act of 1790 limited citizenship to people from or descended from Western Europe.

39. However, the destruction of birth records in San Francisco's 1906 earthquake created the possibility for Chinese immigrant men to bring their children to the US from China: with no way for authorities to disprove claims of the children's birth on US soil, the children became US citizens. The "slots" for these "paper children," as they were called, were frequently sold until new immigration policies enacted during the civil rights movement eliminated this system in 1965. Kwong, *Forbidden Workers*, 93–95.

40. Many artists have recorded ballads about John Henry, including Harry Belafonte, Johnny Cash, Justin Townes Earle, and Leadbelly. The Library of Congress summarizes the song's legacy and provides links to two recordings: "John Henry," https://www.loc.gov/item/ihas.200196572, accessed April 8, 2022.

41. Information about the life of John Henry is from Scott Reynolds Nelson, *Steel Drivin' Man: John Henry, the Untold Story of an American Legend* (New York: Oxford University Press, 2006).

42. An audio recording of a work song is available from the Library of Congress: Stetson Kennedy, Herbert Halpert, and Harold B. Hazelhurst, "John Henry," audio, Jacksonville, FL, 1939, https://www.loc.gov/item/flwpa 000035, accessed May 20, 2022.

43. A reproduction of "John Henry, the Steel Driving Man," published by W. T. Blankenship, possibly in 1909, can be viewed at "John Henry (Blankenship Version)," FolkSongIndex.com, http://www.stephengriffith.com/folksong index/john-henry-blankenship-version, accessed May 15, 2022.

44. Robert T. Devlin, "Various Reformatory and Penal Institutions of the United States," *Report of the State Board of Prison Directors, California* (Sacramento: State Printing Office, 1890), 136, cited in Miller, "At Hard Labor," 97, 100.

45. Z. R. Brockway, *Fifty Years of Prison Service* (Montclair, NJ: Patterson Smith, 1969), 240, cited in Miller, "At Hard Labor," 103.

46. Whitehouse, "Modern Prison Labor," 89–+.

CHAPTER 10: FLOR'S STORY

1. "Flor" is a pseudonym used to protect her identity.

2. Arenal was the director of the Women's Studies Program at the Graduate Center of the City University of New York while I studied there, and we discussed many things, including my research on sex work and human trafficking, on multiple occasions between 1998 and 2001. I vividly remember her describing these songs, because her explanation was diametrically opposite my interpretation of them.

3. The video for "O tú o yo" by José José is available online: YouTube, https://www.youtube.com/watch?v=9ZSV2l1mF2I, accessed May 16, 2022.

4. Human Smuggling and Trafficking Center, *Tenancingo Bulletin #11*.

5. Montiel Torres, *Trata de personas*.

6. Human Smuggling and Trafficking Center, *Tenancingo Bulletin #9*.

7. US Department of State, *2021 Trafficking in Persons Report: United States*, https://www.state.gov/reports/2021-trafficking-in-persons-report/united -states, accessed May 21, 2022.

CHAPTER 11: PROSTITUTION OF ENSLAVED AND INDENTURED WOMEN

1. Alecia Long, *The Great Southern Babylon: Sex, Race, and Respectability in New Orleans, 1865–1920* (Baton Rouge: Louisiana State University Press, 2004), 2.

2. Chang, *Ghosts of Gold Mountain*, 177.

3. Chang, *Ghosts of Gold Mountain*.

4. In their article "Chinese Immigration and Contract Labor in the Late Nineteenth Century," Cloud and Galenson highlight the coercive conditions of this population, while Chang's *Ghosts of Gold Mountain*, on Chinese men in California in the nineteenth century, emphasizes their self-determination and ability to change workplaces. However, Chang emphasizes the lack of autonomy of Chinese women in prostitution in the same era.

5. Information in this paragraph is from Hirata, "Free, Indentured, Enslaved," 3–29.

6. Hirata, "Free, Indentured, Enslaved," 15.

7. Hirata, "Free, Indentured, Enslaved," 16.

8. Hirata, "Free, Indentured, Enslaved," 9–10.

9. Hirata, "Free, Indentured, Enslaved," 10.

10. Ichioka, "Ameyuki-San," 1–21.

11. Hirata, "Free, Indentured, Enslaved," 3–29.

CHAPTER 12: MORALITY IN IMMIGRATION RESTRICTIONS

1. Jan C. Ting, "'Other Than a Chinaman': How U.S. Immigration Law Resulted from and Still Reflects a Policy of Excluding and Restricting Asian Immigration," *Temple Political and Civil Rights Law Review* 4 (Spring 1995): 301–15.

2. Chang, *Ghosts of Gold Mountain*.

3. Hirata, "Free, Indentured, Enslaved," 10.

4. Frederick K. Grittner, *White Slavery: Myth, Ideology, and American Law* (New York: Garland, 1990), 47.

5. David J. Langum, *Crossing Over the Line: Legislating Morality and the Mann Act* (Chicago: University of Chicago Press, 1994), 47.

6. John Haddad, "The Laundry Man's Got a Knife!," *Chinese America: History and Perspectives—Journal of the Chinese Historical Society of America* (2001): 34–35.

7. Pamela Donovan, *No Way of Knowing: Crime, Urban Legends and the Internet* (New York: Routledge, 2004).

8. Grittner, *White Slavery*, 119.

9. Vice Commission of Chicago, *The Social Evil in Chicago: A Study of Existing Conditions with Recommendations* (Chicago: Gunthorp-Warren, 1911), 296–97.

10. US Statutes at Large (1910), vol. 36: 827, quoted in Mark Thomas Connolly, *The Response to Prostitution in the Progressive Era* (Chapel Hill: University of North Carolina Press, 1980), 57–58. The full text can be accessed from "The Full Text of the Mann Act," PBS, https://www.pbs.org/kenburns /unforgivable-blackness/mann-act-full-text, accessed October 14, 2021.

11. Rivkah Brown, "How Facial Recognition Software Is Being Used to Target Sex Workers," *New Statesman*, May 31, 2019, updated September 9, 2021, https://www.newstatesman.com/science-tech/2019/05/how-facial -recognition-is-being-used-to-target-sex-workers-2, accessed July 29, 2022.

CHAPTER 13: THE MANN ACT AND "WHITE SLAVERY"

1. Jessica Pliley, "Any Other Immoral Purpose: The Mann Act, Policing Women, and the American State, 1900–1941" (doctoral dissertation, Ohio State University, 2010); David J. Langum, *Crossing Over the Line: Legislating Morality and the Mann Act* (Chicago: University of Chicago Press, 1994), 247; Rachel Schreiber, "Before Their Makers and Their Judges: Prostitutes and White Slaves in the Political Cartoons of the 'Masses' (New York, 1911–1917)," *Feminist Studies* 35, no. 1 (2009): 161–93.

2. Langum, *Crossing Over the Line*, 10.

3. Langum, *Crossing Over the Line*.

4. Langum, *Crossing Over the Line*, 97–138.

5. Grittner, *White Slavery*, 141; Langum, *Crossing Over the Line*, 113.

6. Langum, *Crossing Over the Line*, 10.

7. Beckman, "The White Slave Traffic Act," 106–22. Beckman analyzed 156 records of women imprisoned for Mann Act violations from the opening of the first federal prison for women in 1927 through 1937, which represented 87 percent of women convicted and incarcerated for Mann Act violations during that time, and Beckman found that the law prosecuted women who were engaging in noncommercial sexual behavior and women who were the victims under the law.

8. Langum, *Crossing Over the Line*, 156–57.

9. Langum, *Crossing Over the Line*, 168; Jessica R. Pliley, *Policing Sexuality: The Mann Act and the Making of the FBI* (Cambridge, MA: Harvard University Press, 2014).

10. White Slave Traffic Act Convictions, 1911–1938, O. John Rogge to Julian Rosenberg, October 18, 1939, DOJ Mann Act Records, Box 2626,

National Archives, College Park, MD. Cited in Pliley, "Any Other Immoral Purpose," 180.

11. Langum, *Crossing Over the Line*.

12. Langum, *Crossing Over the Line*, 183.

13. "US Jury Finds Johnson Guilty; May Go to Prison," *Chicago Tribune*, May 14, 1913, quoted in Langum, *Crossing Over the Line*, 185.

14. Many states had laws against racial intermarriage, but Illinois had repealed its law against miscegenation decades earlier. However, the prosecutor's comments indicate that interracial marriage was not accepted by all.

15. Equal Justice Initiative, *Lynching in America*.

16. Langum, *Crossing Over the Line*, 186.

17. Pegg, *Brown Eyed Handsome Man*, 117.

18. US Court of Appeals for the Eighth Circuit—295 F.2d 192 (8th Cir. 1962), Charles Edward Anderson Berry, Appellant, v. United States of America; Pegg, *Brown Eyed Handsome Man*. This book is an excellent source about Berry's legal cases because it includes a great deal from court documents.

19. *Chuck Berry: The Autobiography* (New York: Harmony Books, 1987), quoted in Langum, *Crossing Over the Line*, 187.

20. Pegg, *Brown Eyed Handsome Man*, 127, 129–30.

21. US Court of Appeals for the Eighth Circuit—283 F.2d 465 (8th Cir. 1960), Charles Edward Anderson Berry v. United States of America; Langum, *Crossing Over the Line*, 186–88; Grittner, *White Slavery*, 181.

22. Pliley, "Any Other Immoral Purpose," 240–43.

23. Langum, *Crossing Over the Line*, 169–70.

24. Langum, *Crossing Over the Line*, 171.

25. Langum, *Crossing Over the Line*, 192.

26. Grittner, *White Slavery*, 150.

27. Pub. L. No. 95–225, § 3. 92 Stat. 7. 8–9 (1978) (codified at 18 U.S.C. § 2423 [1982]).

28. US Attorney General's Commission on Pornography, *Final Report of the Attorney General's Commission on Pornography* (Nashville, TN: Rutledge Hill Press, 1986), https://archive.org/details/finalreportofattoooounit.

29. Langum, *Crossing Over the Line*, 249–50.

30. Troy Closson, "R. Kelly's 30-Year Sentence Was the End of a Long Downfall for the Former Superstar," *New York Times*, June 29, 2022, https://www.nytimes.com/2022/06/29/nyregion/r-kelly-the-disgraced-rb-superstar-is-sentenced-to-30-years.html?searchResultPosition=1.

31. Joe Coscarelli, "R. Kelly Faces a #MeToo Reckoning as Time's Up Backs a Protest," *New York Times*, May 1, 2018, https://www.nytimes.com/2018/05/01/arts/music/r-kelly-timesup-metoo-muterkelly.html, accessed September 23, 2021. #MeToo was started by Tarana Burke, an African American woman, in 2006 to highlight sexual violence experienced by women of color and poor women and girls. The #MeToo hashtag exploded in 2017 when women actors used the hashtag to highlight sexual harassment and abuse in the entertainment industry. Black Lives Matter (BLM) arose in 2013 in response to police violence against African American people. Both movements were begun by African Americans in response to problems faced by

African Americans. These distinct movements overlap, and both are driven by African American women—#MeToo by survivors of sexual victimization, and BLM by people bereaved and otherwise affected by police killings of African Americans.

32. Erica Orden, "Jeffrey Epstein Operated a Vast Sex-Trafficking Network of Underage Girls Who Recruited Other Victims, Prosecutors Say," CNN.com, July 8, 2019, https://www.cnn.com/2019/07/08/us/jeffrey-epstein -monday-court-appearance/index.html.

33. Allie Yang, James Hill, and Ali Dukakis, "How Ghislaine Maxwell Went from High Society to Being Accused of Sex Trafficking," ABC News, June 25, 2021, https://abcnews.go.com/US/ghislaine-maxwell-high-society-accused -sex-trafficking/story?id=78474060.

34. Benjamin Weiser, Rebecca Davis O'Brien, and Colin Moynihan, "Ghislaine Maxwell Receives 20 Years for Aiding Epstein in Sex Trafficking," *New York Times*, June 28, 2022, https://www.nytimes.com/live/2022/06/28 /nyregion/ghislaine-maxwell-news-epstein.

35. Martin E. Comas, "Former Seminole County Tax Collector Facing Sex Trafficking Charges," *Orlando Sentinel*, August 21, 2020, https://www.orlando sentinel.com/news/seminole-county/os-ne-seminole-county-tax-collector -greenberg-fake-ids-minors-20200821-lqt6id6sijbdrj2l7xo6cimz5y-story.html.

36. Jeff Weiner, "Joel Greenberg Cooperating with Feds Since Last Year in Matt Gaetz Sex Trafficking Probe: Report," *Orlando Sentinel*, April 13, 2021, https://www.orlandosentinel.com/politics/joel-greenberg/os-ne-joel-greenberg -cooperating-matt-gaetz-20210413-7chqltr2ujcahax4ewczg5eanm-story.html.

37. Martin E. Comas, "Joel Greenberg Pleads Guilty in Federal Court After Striking Cooperation Deal," *Orlando Sentinel*, May 17, 2021, https://www .orlandosentinel.com/news/seminole-county/os-ne-joel-greenberg-guilty -plea-cooperating-20210517-xpystalvwrfp5dlhoglxwllalu-story.html.

38. Michael Kaplan, "Representative Matt Gaetz's Ex-Girlfriend Granted Immunity in Sex Trafficking Probe," CBS News, January 18, 2022, https:// www.cbsnews.com/news/matt-gaetz-ex-girlfriend-immunity-testimony-sex -trafficking-probe, accessed January 19, 2022; Wesley Alden, "Matt Gaetz's Ex-Girlfriend Testifying Before Grand Jury in Orlando, Reports Say," *Orlando Sentinel*, January 13, 2022, https://www.orlandosentinel.com/1ca1f009-a5cb -4ee3-9298-a16df993df91-132.html.

39. Matt Dixon, "Sentencing for Gaetz 'Wingman' Delayed Until August," *Politico*, May 16, 2022, https://www.politico.com/news/2022/05/16/greenberg -set-to-be-sentenced-in-august-00032764, accessed May 17, 2022.

CHAPTER 14: TWENTY-FIRST-CENTURY EFFORTS
TO COMBAT HUMAN TRAFFICKING

1. Cornell Law School has a good summary of the Wong Wing case at https://www.law.cornell.edu/supremecourt/text/163/228.

2. Hepburn and Simon, *Human Trafficking Around the World*, 13.

3. Ditmore, *The Use of Raids to Fight Trafficking*.

4. Ditmore, *The Use of Raids to Fight Trafficking*.

5. Ditmore, *The Use of Raids to Fight Trafficking*.

6. Ditmore, *The Use of Raids to Fight Trafficking*.

7. "Human Trafficking Intervention Courts," New York State Unified Court System, https://ww2.nycourts.gov/courts/problem_solving/htc/index.shtml, accessed May 17, 2022.

8. Richard Ruelas, "Pimping Charges Tossed Against Backpage Founders," *AZ Central*, August 23, 2017, https://www.azcentral.com/story/news/local/phoenix/2017/08/23/pimping-charges-tossed-against-backpage-founders/596098001, accessed March 22, 2022.

9. This 2018 law is referred to interchangeably as FOSTA-SESTA, FOSTA, and/or SESTA by sex workers, other people affected by the law, and social service providers who work with people affected by this law.

10. The full text of H.R. 1865—Allow States and Victims to Fight Online Sex Trafficking Act of 2017 is available at https://www.congress.gov/bill/115th-congress/house-bill/1865/text. People affected by the law refer to it as FOSTA-SESTA.

11. Charlie Savage and Timothy Williams, "US Seizes Backpage.com, a Site Accused of Enabling Prostitution," *New York Times*, April 7, 2018, https://www.nytimes.com/2018/04/07/us/politics/backpage-prostitution-classified.html.

12. "Pounced.org," WikiFur, https://en.wikifur.com/wiki/Pounced.org, accessed January 15, 2022.

13. Pounced.org posted this statement announcing it was closing on May 3, 2018, at http://pounced.org/why.html; it is archived at https://web.archive.org/web/20180503181331/http://pounced.org/why.html, accessed January 15, 2022.

14. Pounced.org statement.

15. These interviews were conducted using online videocall software on March 23, 2021, during the coronavirus pandemic.

16. Luka is an assumed name. I interviewed Luka on March 13, 2021.

17. Interview with the author March 13, 2021.

18. Shanna K. Kattari et al., "Policing Gender Through Housing and Employment Discrimination: Comparison of Discrimination Experiences of Transgender and Cisgender LGBQ Individuals," *Journal of the Society for Social Work and Research* 7, no. 3 (2016), doi: 10.1086/686920.

19. The text of the bill as of March 22, 2022, is available at https://www.congress.gov/bill/117th-congress/senate-bill/3538.

20. Elliott Harmon, "Congress Must Stop the Graham-Blumenthal Anti-Security Bill," Electronic Frontier Foundation, January 31, 2020, https://www.eff.org/deeplinks/2020/01/congress-must-stop-graham-blumenthal-anti-security-bill, accessed May 22, 2022.

CONCLUSION: WHAT KIND OF HELP IS TRULY HELPFUL?

1. May Jeong, "'You Won't Believe What Happened': The Wild, Disturbing Saga of Robert Kraft's Visit to a Strip Mall Sex Spa," *Vanity Fair*, November 2019, https://www.vanityfair.com/news/2019/10/the-disturbing-saga-of-robert-kraft, accessed May 23, 2022.

2. Information in this paragraph is from Anna Merlan and Tim Marchman, "Operation Underground Railroad's Carefully Crafted Image Is Falling Apart," *Vice World News*, June 10, 2010, https://www.vice.com/en/article/qj8j3v

/operation-underground-railroad-criminal-investigation-human-trafficking
-tim-ballard-jim-caviezel-qanon, accessed May 23, 2022.

3. Zach Sommers, "Missing White Woman Syndrome: An Empirical Analysis of Race and Gender Disparities in Online News Coverage of Missing Persons," *Journal of Criminal Law & Criminology* 106, no. 2 (2016), https://scholarly commons.law.northwestern.edu/jclc/vol106/iss2/4, accessed May 22, 2022.

4. Matt Pearce, "Gabby Petito and One Way to Break Media's 'Missing White Woman Syndrome,'" *Los Angeles Times*, October 4, 2021, https://www.latimes.com/entertainment-arts/story/2021-10-04/gabby-petito-and-breaking-the-white-missing-women-syndrome, accessed May 22, 2022; Carol M. Liebler, Wasim Ahmad, and Gina Gayle, "Not at Risk? News, Gatekeeping, and Missing Teens," *Journalism Practice* 15, no. 10 (2021): 1597–1612, doi:10.1080/17512786.2020.1790407.

5. There are a number of examples from this website post: Mariah Long, "Visual Stereotypes for Human Trafficking," End Slavery Now, https://www.endslaverynow.org/blog/articles/visual-stereotypes-for-human-trafficking, accessed January 21, 2022.

6. Kathy Finn, "Indian Workers Win $14 Million in US Labor Trafficking Case," Reuters, February 18, 2015, https://www.reuters.com/article/us-usa-louisiana-trafficking/indian-workers-win-14-million-in-u-s-labor-trafficking-case-idUSKBN0LN03820150219, accessed January 21, 2022; Sarah Stillman, "The Migrant Workers Who Follow Climate Disasters," *New Yorker*, November 1, 2021, https://www.newyorker.com/magazine/2021/11/08/the-migrant-workers-who-follow-climate-disasters, accessed January 21, 2022.

7. White House, "Fact Sheet: President's Interagency Task Force to Monitor and Combat Trafficking in Persons," January 25, 2022, https://www.whitehouse.gov/briefing-room/statements-releases/2022/01/25/fact-sheet-presidents-interagency-task-force-to-monitor-and-combat-trafficking-in-persons, accessed May 23, 2022.

8. Griffith and Gleeson, "Trump's 'Immployment' Law Agenda Intensifying Employment-Based Enforcement and Un-authorizing the Authorized," 475–501.

9. International Human Rights Clinic, Gould School of Law, USC, *Over-Policing Sex Trafficking: How US Law Enforcement Should Reform Operations*, November 2019, https://humanrightsclinic.usc.edu/2021/11/15/over-policing-sex-trafficking-how-u-s-law-enforcement-should-reform-operations, accessed January 21, 2022.

10. Interview with Jean Bruggeman, March 23, 2022.

11. Ditmore, *The Use of Raids to Fight Trafficking*.

12. Member organizations of Freedom Network USA are listed by state at https://freedomnetworkusa.org/join-us. Scroll down to "Current Members" and "Our Members."

13. The website of the Fair Foods Standards Council is https://www.fairfoodstandards.org; the list of participating buyers is available at https://www.fairfoodstandards.org/resources/participating-buyers. The list of participating growers is at https://www.fairfoodstandards.org/resources/participating-growers.

14. To access the spreadsheet, go to https://worthrises.org/theprison industry2020#block-b153f5e8252bbcf8827a. Scroll down to "Data" to download the spreadsheet. Large companies that contract with private prisons include but are not limited to Victoria's Secret, Dell, and Macy's.

15. Most Freedom Network members offer direct services such as legal support, shelter, and trauma-informed social services.

SELECTED BIBLIOGRAPHY

An Act Concerning Servants and Slaves. Virginia, 1705. Reproduced in "Servants and Slaves in Virginia," available from the National Humanities Center. http://nationalhumanitiescenter.org/pds/amerbegin/power/text8/Beverly ServSlaves.pdf.

Arch City Defenders. *Municipal Courts White Paper*. https://www.archcity defenders.org/wp-content/uploads/2019/03/ArchCity-Defenders -Municipal-Courts-Whitepaper.pdf.

Barroso, Amanda, and Anna Brown. "Gender Pay Gap in U.S. Held Steady in 2020." Pew Research, May 25, 2021. https://www.pewresearch.org/fact -tank/2021/05/25/gender-pay-gap-facts. Accessed December 29, 2021.

Beckman, Marlene. "The White Slave Traffic Act: Historical Impact of a Federal Crime Policy on Women." In *Prostitution*, edited by Nancy F. Cott, 106–22. Munich: De Gruyter Saur, 1993.

Bianchi, Suzanne M., Liana C. Sayer, Melissa A. Milkie, and John P. Robinson. "Housework: Who Did, Does or Will Do It, and How Much Does It Matter?" *Social Forces* 91, no. 1 (2012): 55–63.

Blackmon, Douglas. *Slavery by Another Name: The Re-enslavement of Black People in America from the Civil War to World War II*. New York: Doubleday, 2008.

"Blacks Before the Law in Colonial Maryland." Maryland State Archives. https://msa.maryland.gov/msa/speccol/sc5300/sc5348/html/chap3.html.

Brooks, Jennifer. "'John Chinaman' in Alabama: Immigration, Race, and Empire in the New South, 1870–1920." *Journal of American Ethnic History* 37, no. 2 (2018): 5–36.

Burnham, Linda, and Nik Theodore. *Home Economics: The Invisible and Unregulated World of Domestic Work*. National Domestic Workers Alliance, 2012. https://drive.google.com/file/d/0B1pso2AmSdFoUUxSTopiaHNsU1U /view?resourcekey=0-aFf9nKiEuJkNRTksaFuJfQ.

Cable, George W. "The Convict Lease System in the Southern United States." *The Century* 27, February 1884, 582–99.

Campbell, Sir George. *White and Black: The Outcome of a Visit to the United States*. London: Chatto & Windus, 1879.

Chang, Gordon H. *Ghosts of Gold Mountain: The Epic Story of the Chinese Who Built the Transcontinental Railroad*. Boston: Houghton Mifflin Harcourt, 2019.

Chisolm-Straker, Makini, and Katherine Chon, eds. *The Historical Roots of Human Trafficking: Informing Primary Prevention of Commercialized Violence.* Cham, Switzerland: Springer International Publishing, 2021.

Cloud, Patricia, and David W. Galenson. "Chinese Immigration and Contract Labor in the Late Nineteenth Century." *Explorations in Economic History* 24, no. 1 (1987): 22–42. doi: 10.1016/0014-4983(87)90003-9.

Daluz, Judith. "I Am a Survivor of Human Trafficking: Judith's Story." *The Atlantic,* March 12, 2018. https://www.theatlantic.com/business/archive /2018/03/human-trafficking-judith/553115.

Ditmore, Melissa, *The Use of Raids to Fight Trafficking.* New York: Urban Justice Center Sex Workers Project, 2009. https://swp.urbanjustice.org/news -room/resources.

Ditmore, Melissa, and Juhu Thukral. "Accountability and the Use of Raids to Fight Trafficking." *Anti-Trafficking Review* 1 (2012). doi: 10.14197/atr .201218.

Doe v. Tapia-Ortiz. Case No: 2:14-cv-206-FtM-38MRM (M.D. Fla. Feb. 10, 2017).

Du Bois, W. E. B. *Black Reconstruction in America 1860–1880.* New York: Atheneum, 1971.

Equal Justice Initiative. *Lynching in America: Confronting the Legacy of Racial Terror,* 3rd ed. 2017. https://lynchinginamerica.eji.org/report. Accessed September 18, 2021.

Exploitation of Young Adults in Door-to-Door Sales: Hearing Before the Permanent Subcommittee on Investigations of the Committee on Governmental Affairs, United States Senate, One Hundredth Congress, First Session, April 6, 1987, Volume 1. Washington, DC: US Congress, Senate Committee on Governmental Affairs, 1988.

Fair Labor Standards Act of 1938. https://uscode.house.gov/view.xhtml?path= /prelim@title29/chapter8&edition=prelim.

Fisher, Linford D. "'Why Shall Wee Have Peace to Bee Made Slaves': Indian Surrenderers During and After King Philip's War." *Ethnohistory* 64, no. 1 (January 2017): 91–114. doi.org/10.1215/00141801-3688391.

Foner, Eric. *Reconstruction: America's Unfinished Revolution, 1863–1877.* New York: Harper and Row, 1988.

Galenson, David W. "The Rise and Fall of Indentured Servitude in the Americas: An Economic Analysis." *Journal of Economic History* 44 (March 1984): 1–26.

George Washington's Mount Vernon. https://www.mountvernon.org.

Grieder, William. "These Dark Satanic Mills." In *Sociology: Exploring the Architecture of Everyday Life,* 8th ed., edited by David M. Newman and Jodi O'Brien, 205–6. Thousand Oaks, CA: Pine Forge Press, 2010. First published 1995.

Griffith, Kati L., and Shannon Gleeson. "Trump's 'Immployment' Law Agenda: Intensifying Employment-Based Enforcement and Un-authorizing the Authorized." *Southwestern Law Review* 48 (2019): 475–501.

Grigg, Bob. "Old Newgate Prison." Colebrook Historical Society. http://www .colebrookhistoricalsociety.org/OldNewgatePrison.htm. Accessed July 15, 2022.

Gutman, Herbert G. *The Black Family in Slavery and Freedom, 1750–1925.* New York: Vintage, 1977.

Hadden, Sally E. *Slave Patrols: Law and Violence in Virginia and the Carolinas.* Cambridge, MA: Harvard University Press, 2001.

Haley, Sarah. "'Like I Was a Man': Chain Gangs, Gender, and the Domestic Carceral Sphere in Jim Crow Georgia." *Signs* 39, no. 1, Women, Gender, and Prison: National and Global Perspectives (Autumn 2013): 53–77.

Harris, David A. *Driving While Black: Racial Profiling on Our Nation's Highways.* New York: American Civil Liberties Union, 1999.

Haynes, Dina Francesca. "(Not) Found Chained to a Bed in a Brothel: Conceptual, Legal, and Procedural Failures to Fulfill the Promise of the Trafficking Victims Protection Act." *Georgetown Immigration Law Journal* 21 (2006): 337.

Hepburn, Stephanie, and Rita J. Simon. *Human Trafficking Around the World: Hidden in Plain Sight.* New York: Columbia University Press, 2013.

Hirata, Lucie Cheng. "Free, Indentured, Enslaved: Chinese Prostitutes in Nineteenth-Century America." *Signs* 5, no. 1 (1979): 3–29. http://www.jstor.org/stable/3173531.

Hobson, Barbara Meil. *Uneasy Virtue: The Politics of Prostitution and the American Reform Tradition.* New York, Basic Books, 1987.

Human Rights Watch. *Cultivating Fear: The Vulnerability of Immigrant Farmworkers in the US to Sexual Violence and Sexual Harassment.* New York: Human Rights Watch, 2012. https://www.hrw.org/sites/default/files/reports/us0512ForUpload_1.pdf.

Human Smuggling and Trafficking Center, US Department of State. *Tenancingo Bulletin #9: Traffickers' Recruitment Methods Adapted from Local Customs.* January 24, 2011. http://www.state.gov/documents/organization/155767.pdf.

———. *Tenancingo Bulletin #11: Portrait of a Tlaxcala Trafficker as a Young Man.* January 24, 2011. http://www.state.gov/documents/organization/155769.pdf.

Ichioka, Yuji. "Ameyuki-San: Japanese Prostitutes in Nineteenth-Century America." *Amerasia Journal* 4, no. 1 (1977): 1–21.

Jackson, Gale P. "Rosy, Possum, Morning Star: Work Songs and the Blues." In *Put Your Hands on Your Hips and Act Like a Woman.* Lincoln: University of Nebraska Press, 2020.

Jernegan, Marcus W. *Laboring and Dependent Classes in Colonial America, 1607–1783.* New York: Frederick Ungar, 1960 (reprint of 1931 edition), pp. 162–64. Cited in Murray and Herndon, "Markets for Children in Early America."

Jones, Jacqueline. *American Work: Four Centuries of Black and White Labor.* New York: Norton, 1998, pp. 72–73. Cited in Righi, "The Right of Petition."

Keeler, Clarissa Olds. *American Bastiles.* Washington, DC, 1910. http://data.decalog.net/enap1/Liens/fonds/F9A101.pdf. Accessed August 27, 2014.

Krauthamer, Barbara. *Black Slaves, Indian Masters: Slavery, Emancipation, and Citizenship in the Native American South.* Chapel Hill: University of North Carolina Press, 2013.

Kulikoff, Allan. *Tobacco and Slaves: The Development of Southern Cultures in the Chesapeake, 1680–1800.* Chapel Hill: University of North Carolina Press, 1986.

Kwong, Peter. *Forbidden Workers: Illegal Chinese Immigrants and American Labor*. New York: The New Press, 1997.

Lakwete, Angela. "The Eclectic Industrialism of Antebellum Baldwin County." *Alabama Review* 65, no. 1 (2012): 3–39.

Mangin, Gregg. "Notorious New-Gate Prison." Connecticut Historical Society. http://connecticuthistory.org/notorious-new-gate-prison.

Martin, K. D. "Monetary Myopia: An Examination of Institutional Response to Revenue from Monetary Sanctions for Misdemeanors." *Criminal Justice Policy Review* 29, nos. 6–7 (2018): 630–62. doi: 10.1177/0887403418761099.

McCallum, Leanne. "Reflections from the Field: Disparate Responses to Labour Exploitation in Post-Katrina Louisiana." *Anti-Trafficking Review* 15 (2020): 26, 32. https://doi.org/10.14197/atr.201220152.

McConnell, John Preston. *Negroes and Their Treatment in Virginia from 1865 to 1867*. Pulaski, VA: B. D. Smith & Brothers, 1910. https://archive.org/stream/negroestreatmentoomccorich/negroestreatmentoomccorich_djvu.txt.

Mei, June. "Socioeconomic Origins of Emigration: Guangdong to California, 1850–1882." *Modern China* 5, no. 4 (1979): 463–501.

Miller, Martin B. "At Hard Labor: Rediscovering the 19th Century Prison." *Issues in Criminology* 9, no. 1 (1974): 97, 100. http://www.jstor.org/stable/42909697.

Mittelberger, Gottlieb. "Journey to Pennsylvania." (1750). Historical Society of Pennsylvania. http://www.hsp.org/files/mittelberger.pdf. Accessed September 28, 2022.

Monahan, Thomas P. "Interracial Marriage in a Southern Area: Maryland, Virginia, and the District of Columbia." *Journal of Comparative Family Studies* 8, no. 2 (1977): 217–41. http://www.jstor.org/stable/41601008.

Montiel Torres, Oscar. *Trata de personas: Padrotes, iniciación y modus operandi*. Ciudad de México: Instituto Nacional de las Mujeres, 2009.

Murray, John E., and Ruth Wallis Herndon. "Markets for Children in Early America: A Political Economy of Pauper Apprenticeship." *Journal of Economic History* 62, no. 2 (2002): 356–82. http://www.jstor.org/stable/2698184.

National Labor Relations Act of 1935. 29 U.S.C. §§ 151–169.

O'Brien, John T. *From Bondage to Citizenship: The Richmond Black Community, 1865–1867*. New York: Garland, 1990.

Ojito, Mirta. "For Deaf Mexicans, Freedom After Slavery and Detention." *New York Times*, July 18, 1998. https://www.nytimes.com/1998/07/18/nyregion/for-deaf-mexicans-freedom-after-slavery-and-detention.html?searchResultPosition=4.

Olam, H., and E. Stamper. "The Suspension of the Davis-Bacon Act and the Exploitation of Migrant Workers in the Wake of Hurricane Katrina." *Hofstra Labor and Employment Journal* 24, no. 1 (2006): 145–80.

Pegg, Bruce. *Brown Eyed Handsome Man: The Life and Hard Times of Chuck Berry; an Unauthorized Biography*. New York: Routledge, 2002.

Peláez, Vicki. "The Prison Industry in the United States: Big Business or a New Form of Slavery?" Global Research, March 31, 2014.

Rachleff, Peter. *Black Labor in the South, 1865–1890*. Urbana: University of Illinois Press, 1989.

Raleigh-Adams, Sherry, ed., *Orders, Wills, Etc. 1706–1708*. York County, Virginia, 2005.

Ramchandani, Ariel. "There's a Sexual-Harassment Epidemic on America's Farms." *The Atlantic*, January 29, 2018.

Righi, Brandon Paul. "The Right of Petition: Cases of Indentured Servants and Society in Colonial Virginia, 1698–1746." Master's thesis, College of William and Mary, 2010.

Rönnbäck, Klas. "Were Slaves Cheap Laborers? A Comparative Study of Labor Costs in the Antebellum U.S. South." *Labor History* 62, nos. 5–6 (2021): 721–41.

Ruiz, Nena. "I Am a Survivor of Human Trafficking: Nena's Story." *The Atlantic*, March 12, 2018. https://www.theatlantic.com/business/archive/2018/03/human-trafficking-nena/554846/.

Sheldon, Myrna Perez. "Breeding Mixed-Race Women for Profit and Pleasure." *American Quarterly* 71, no. 3 (2019): 741–65.

Shierholz, Heidi, Lora Engdahl, Julia Wolfe, and Jori Kandra. *Domestic Workers Chartbook*. Economic Policy Institute, May 2020. https://www.epi.org/publication/domestic-workers-chartbook-a-comprehensive-look-at-the-demographics-wages-benefits-and-poverty-rates-of-the-professionals-who-care-for-our-family-members-and-clean-our-homes/.

Smith, Abbot Emerson. *Colonists in Bondage: White Servitude and Convict Labor in America, 1607–1776*. Baltimore: Genealogical Publishing, 2009.

Sweet, Julie Anne. "The Thirteenth Colony in Perspective: Historians' Views on Early Georgia." *Georgia Historical Quarterly* 85, no. 3 (2001): 435–60. http://www.jstor.org/stable/40584446.

Tracy, Natalicia. "I Am a Survivor of Human Trafficking: Natalicia's Story." *The Atlantic*, March 12, 2018. https://www.theatlantic.com/business/archive/2018/03/human-trafficking-natalicia/553100.

"The Triangle Shirtwaist Factory Fire." Washington, DC: US Department of Labor, Occupational Safety and Health Administration. 2011. https://www.osha.gov/aboutosha/40-years/trianglefactoryfire. Accessed September 27, 2021.

US Department of Labor. *Handy Reference Guide to the Fair Labor Standards Act*. https://www.dol.gov/agencies/whd/compliance-assistance/handy-reference-guide-flsa. Accessed July 29, 2022.

Vitale, Alex. *The End of Policing*. London: Verso, 2017.

West, Patsy. "Abiaka, or Sam Jones, in Context: The Mikasuki Ethnogenesis Through the Third Seminole War." *Florida Historical Quarterly* 94, no. 3 (2016): 366–410. http://www.jstor.org/stable/24769276.

Whitehouse, Mary Rose. "Modern Prison Labor: A Reemergence of Convict Leasing Under the Guise of Rehabilitation and Private Enterprises." *Loyola Journal of Public Interest Law* 18, no. 1 (2017): 89–+.

Women's Commission for Refugee Women and Children. *Locking Up Family Values: The Detention of Immigrant Families*. 2007.

INDEX